I0867924

The Sublime South

The Sublime South

Andalusia, Orientalism, and the Making of Modern Spain

✦

José Luis Venegas

NORTHWESTERN UNIVERSITY PRESS
EVANSTON, ILLINOIS

Northwestern University Press
www.nupress.northwestern.edu

Printed in the United States of America

10 9 8 7 6 5 4 3 2 1

ISBN 978-0-8101-3729-5 (paper)
ISBN 978-0-8101-3730-1 (cloth)
ISBN 978-0-8101-3731-8 (ebook)

Cataloging-in-Publication data are available
from the Library of Congress.

For Eva and Lucas, my intended readers

CONTENTS

ILLUSTRATIONS

ACKNOWLEDGMENTS

I would like to thank the National Endowment for the Humanities and Wake Forest University for sponsoring my research for this book. I am grateful to Sally Barbour, Julie Edelson, Candelas Gala, Antonio Gómez López Quiñones, Sol Miguel-Prendes, and Gayle Rogers for their encouragement, support, and insightful comments.

I am thankful for the kind assistance that I received in Seville from the staff of the Centro de Estudios Andaluces, the Archivo General de Andalucía, the Museo de la Autonomía de Andalucía, the Hemeroteca Municipal, and the Biblioteca Blas Infante, in particular Ana Borrego, Paloma Cano Sánchez, Carlos Font Gavira, María Ángeles García Molinera, Vanessa Tellado, and Ana Vicente. In the United States, I have benefited from discussions with friends and colleagues who have enriched my understanding of Spanish cultural history. Thank you to Sebastiaan Faber and José María Rodríguez García, whose exemplary scholarship has helped shape my own thinking and writing. I should also mention the generous advice that I received from Andrew Anderson, Melissa Dinverno, and Jonathan Mayhew at the 2015 American Comparative Literature Association conference in Seattle. Their suggestions made me rethink, and even rewrite, some portions of this book.

My thanks to the editors and staff at Northwestern University Press and in particular to Gianna Mosser for her steady support and outstanding professionalism. This is a better book because of her. My appreciation also goes to the two anonymous reviewers for their thoughtful recommendations and strong endorsement.

The largest debt of gratitude is, as always, owed to my family, without whose support this book would not have been written. Firstly, Jessica, who has patiently seen this project through while tending to our children, Eva and Lucas. My father, José Luis, an exceptional interlocutor for academic and nonacademic matters alike, intervened at a critical moment, allowing me to push the manuscript to completion. *Gracias papá.*

An earlier version of some sections of chapter 4 and the afterword was previously published as a book chapter in *La retórica del sur: Representaciones y discursos sobre Andalucía en el período democrático* (Seville: Alfar, 2015), edited by Antonio Gómez López Quiñones and José Manuel del Pino. All translations are my own unless otherwise noted.

The Sublime South

Introduction

✦

Looping the Loop

On a chilly spring morning in the mid-1990s, the best-selling author Antonio Gala addressed a crowd of restless teens and their patient teachers in the schoolyard of a small-town high school near Cordoba, Spain. The school, which bears the writer's name, was celebrating its twenty-fifth anniversary. At age fifteen, I listened intently to his rousing words. He insisted that we, the Andalusians of the future, are the heirs of a rich cultural tradition stretching back to Spain's medieval Muslim past. What makes us a distinct community within the Iberian Peninsula, he kept repeating, is our strong spiritual link to the lost Islamic world of al-Andalus (711–1492), Andalusia's golden age. Catalans, Basques, and Galicians may have their own languages, but we Andalusians have the Moors, a source of pride, not embarrassment. If we are modern and civilized, it is due, in part, to our Islamic legacy. Gala's remarks reinforced the notion that I was not only Spanish but also—and most importantly—Andalusian.[1] In the heady post-dictatorship period, regionalist patriotism, which had been repressed during the Franco era (1939–75), was running high. We felt more Andalusian than ever, and the feeling was there to stay.

The new feeling thrived on old stories. The myth of Moorish Andalusia that Gala summarized for me and my classmates is a foreign import from the early nineteenth century. Romantic writers from Théophile Gautier to Lord Byron turned Andalusia into Spain's orient, a characterization that Spaniards themselves saw alternatively and contradictorily as a marker of identity and a despised self-image. During the nineteenth century, the country's Afro-Moorish past, which was inextricable from Romantic perceptions, was both an alibi for Spanish colonial intervention in Morocco and a facet of national history that hindered Spain's integration in Europe. Al-Andalus and, by extension, Andalusia sustained an ambivalent Spanish identity where European self and oriental other melded in Möbius strip relations, to use Susan Martin-Márquez's accurate description in her landmark book *Disorientations* (2008), a study of Spanish colonialism in Africa. "Spain," she writes, "is a nation that is at once Orientalized and Orientalizing. The dynamic resembles a Möbius strip, calling into question the possibility of any location 'outside' Orientalist discourse."[2] Whereas Edward Said defines orientalism in terms of colonial opposition, as a "Western style for dominating, restructuring, and having authority over the Orient" (North Africa, East Asia, and South Asia), Martin-Márquez addresses Spain's in-between status, an aspect that Said left largely unexplored.[3]

In this book I examine Spain's shifting engagements with oriental otherness, but instead of looking beyond and across national, ethnic, and racial borders, I focus on a territory that is part of the Spanish nation-state while symbolically caught between inclusion and abjection. To do so, I shift the scale and scope of Said's discourse. Here, orientalism, a transnational phenomenon resulting from European colonialism in Africa and Asia, evolves and manifests intra-nationally, as Spaniards engage in self-orientalism and the orientalization of Andalusians. Through the analysis of verbal, visual, musical, and architectural representations, I trace the twists and turns of this intra-national Möbius strip from the nineteenth century to the early twenty-first century. The loop stretches far and wide. You will find orientalized Andalusia not only in literature and the arts, but also in popular songs, films, television programs, and world fairs. It manifests in the thinker José Ortega y Gasset's erudite writings as well as the performer Lola Flores's songs and movies; in Juan Ramón Jiménez's sophisticated poetry as well as the kitschy Andalusian pavilion at Seville's Expo '92; in art galleries and exhibits as well as prime-time television shows. Amid the mixture of poems and pavilions, philosophers and *folklóricas*, museums and the media, one central concern emerges: how in diverse, often conflicting ways, Andalusia is seen at once as the essence of Spanishness and its exotic other.

In considering this ambivalence, I challenge unitary notions of Spanish culture centered upon the linguistic, cultural, and political hegemony of the central region of Castile. The new academic field of Iberian studies has decisively disrupted, as one critic put it, "Hispanism's cozy monolingualism," which "condemned non-Castilian cultures to outer darkness."[4] But the remedy—placing Castilian "in relation rather than in opposition to other languages" of the Iberian Peninsula[5]—conflates language and culture and still leaves some non-Castilian, yet Castilian-speaking cultures like Andalusia, in the dark. Iberian studies embraces the rhetoric of linguistic and historical difference that has been fostered by Basque, Catalan, and Galician nationalisms since the nineteenth century. My focus on Andalusia moves beyond these opposing, and often mutually negating, essentialisms to probe their internal divisions. Engaging Iberian diversity and plurality from a southern perspective demands reconsidering the terms of the debate. Through the lens of orientalism, the relationship of Spanish national identity to Andalusia defies the logic of center and periphery and the conviction that cultural differences are synonymous with linguistic differences and always play out as self versus other.

This is a study of cultural and intellectual history, but in its motivations and conclusions it is also an exploration of the ideas and beliefs that formed my upbringing. In other words, it establishes my strategic location, which, Said writes, "is the author's position in a text with regard to the Oriental material he writes about." "Strategy," he adds, identifies "the problem every writer on the Orient has faced: how to get hold of it, how to approach it, how not to be defeated or overwhelmed by its sublimity."[6] Unlike the authors Said examines, I do not aim to overcome sublimity from an Olympian perspective; I want to feel its pulse in the repository of cultural images and beliefs that shaped my formative years. Sublimity entails bewilderment. It arouses, Kant says, "enjoyment but with horror"; the kind of awe, wonder, and elation caused by the embrace of contradiction.[7] In tracking down the historical development of the idea of Andalusia, its orientalization, and its contribution to the making of modern Spain, I am piecing together a personal story that, much like a Möbius band, is subsumed by sublimity—by the exhilarating disorientation produced by being at once on both sides of the orientalist divide. "The starting point of critical elaboration," Antonio Gramsci said in a text Said quoted in *Orientalism*, "is the consciousness of what one really is, and is 'knowing thyself' as a product of the historical process to date, which has deposited in you an infinity of traces, without leaving an inventory; therefore it is imperative at the outset to compile such an inventory."[8] *The Sublime South* is a response to this mandate.

Since the late 1970s and early 1980s, coinciding with the proclamation of Andalusia's political autonomy, scores of historians, anthropologists, economists, sociologists, and linguists have produced a massive bibliography devoted to defining and anatomizing Andalusian distinctiveness. The deluge spilled over into pedagogical materials and the mass media.[9] From an early age, I learned to look forward to Andalusia Day, which commemorates the February 28, 1980, referendum that granted the region political autonomy from the central government in Madrid. Every year in school, in anticipation of the holiday, we memorized the Andalusian anthem composed in the 1930s by Blas Infante; used the white and green of the regional flag in arts and crafts projects; and wrote compositions on famous Andalusian artists and writers ranging from Manuel de Falla and Juan Ramón Jiménez to Federico García Lorca and Rafael Alberti. My regionalist pride swelled on these occasions, but it failed to dispel lingering doubts and misgivings: Why were Andalusians living in democratic, European Spain still urged by Infante's anthem to "demand land and freedom"? What land? Freedom? From what or whom? If medieval Muslim Iberia was Andalusia's golden age, as Gala affirmed, why did schoolbooks single out the Christian Reconquest of al-Andalus as the beginning of the Spanish nation's protracted birth? Should we identify with Abd al-Rahman or the Cid; Boabdil or Queen Isabella? Andalusian patriotism heightened blind excitement, not critical sense; as emotions swell, reason abates.

Another episode in my sentimental education as an Andalusian began on February 28, 1989, when Andalusia's first regional television network, Canal

Sur (South Channel), came on the air. Pressing a previously unused button on the TV set filled the family room with an accent, *my* accent, previously unheard in the broadcast media. During the Franco dictatorship, Andalusian Spanish was the idiom of film musicals featuring a benighted folklore realm of bandits, bullfighters, and *bailaoras*, or exotic gypsy dancers in polka-dot dresses. Now the two o'clock news was delivered in Sevillian speech, and the actors and actresses in the jazzy new network shows made no attempt to modify their southern diction.

This sociolinguistic transformation had started with Spain's transition to democracy in the late 1970s. By 1980, the widely read newspaper *ABC* announced that speaking with an Andalusian accent in front of "microphones and cameras" must not be seen as "embarrassing" or "the trait of uneducated people" but a source of pride.[10] The article voiced the collective feeling of the thousands who took to the streets of Seville in December 1977 to demand home rule for Andalusia. Alfonso Guerra, the future deputy prime minister of Spain and a Seville native, addressed the crowd from the balcony of City Hall. Immediately rejecting his fake Castilian pronunciation, the crowd chorused: "Speak Andalusian! Speak Andalusian!" He obliged.[11] During his term in office (1982–91) under the premiership of another *sevillano*, Felipe González, neither politician masked his accent in public. Andalusian Spanish was now the language of national budget laws and social policies, not just flamenco.

The end of Francoism in the mid-1970s saw a concerted institutional effort to free Andalusia from folkloric connotations, not only in Spain, but in Europe and the world. The 1992 Univeral Exposition (Expo '92), a celebration of the 500th anniversary of Columbus's voyage to the Americas, was held in Seville, which for a few months showcased a new Spain eager to cast off its inferiority complex as a European backwater. The exposition's futuristic buildings, laser displays, and avant-garde cultural events attested to Spain's new identity as a modern democratic nation, equal to its northern neighbors. In the Andalusian Pavilion, whose theme was "Andalusia, Tradition and Change," images of local *ferias* (fairs) and religious pilgrimages shared space with sports cars and state-of-the-art ultralight aircraft made in Andalusia. A total of 42,000,000 visitors, including dozens of heads of state and prime ministers, witnessed the staged transformation of Spain and its southernmost region, which seemed to have abandoned for good their symbolic role as exotic flowers on European soil.

The message was reiterated a few years later as I entered, for the first time as a student, the gates of the University of Seville's main building, the mythical tobacco factory of Mérimée's *Carmen*. The three flags gracing the façade—Andalusia, Spain, and the European Union—symbolically connected the building, the institution, and a fully Europeanized (read *modern*) region and nation. Inside, throngs of foreign exchange students testified to the internationalization of a city that had been haunted for decades by

Carmen's oriental and primitive character. Orientation materials informed freshmen, even those opting for a humanities degree, that the university was committed to scientific and technological innovation, participating in a new national mythology in which modernity and Spain/Andalusia were no longer antithetical.

However, representations of an archaic region endured under the glittery official rhetoric of modernization and advancement in local festivals (*ferias, romerías, verbenas*) and the national mass media. Starting in 1995, the state-owned television network, Televisión Española (Spanish Television), began broadcasting *Cine de barrio* (*Neighborhood Cinema*), a popular show that presented and discussed folkloric cinema from the 1950s to the 1970s. Often set in the south and seen as pro-Franco propaganda, the movies I watched with my mother almost every Saturday afternoon took me to a place transitioning from a black-and-white rural paradise populated by gypsy dancers to a technicolor tourist destination where foreign blondes in bikinis fell for local Don Juans. What the sunny atmosphere of these comedies inspired in me was not dread or nostalgia, since I was not reliving past experiences, but befuddlement. I could not accommodate the backward clichés of tourism and traditional folklore on the screen with the persistent messages of modernization and Europeanization that now saturated public spaces.

Adding to the confusion, a book title, Antonio Burgos's *Andalucía, ¿tercer mundo?* (1972; *Andalusia: Third World?*), puzzled me every time I saw it on the blue spine in my grandfather's bookcase. It was lodged (strategically?) between Gabriel García Márquez's novel *Cien años de soledad* and the Spanish translation of Alex Haley's *Roots: The Saga of an American Family*. When I read it during my last year as an undergraduate, I came face to face with the unsettling history and reality of southern underdevelopment that inspired Infante's spirited petition for "land and freedom" in our regional anthem. I answered the question Burgos posed with another: Will the real Andalusia please stand up? Is it a Third-World enclave, a land of rustic rituals, a playground for sun-starved northerners, or is it a progressive community that is fully integrated with Europe? A place that should have rooted an enduring sense of identity and belonging was an unresolved riddle.

I have never been comfortable in my regionalist clothes, especially their patches of Arabism, but not because I hold any kind of animosity toward the Muslim world or want to minimize, as some historians have done, its rich cultural legacy in Andalusia and Spain today.[12] As a teenager, I was astonished to learn from a dusty history book kept on the top shelf of the family library that my own name, Venegas, or "Ibn Egas," was the last name of a Nasrid royal family that became part of the Morisco elite in Christian Granada after 1492.[13] No, I am reluctant to accept the myth that al-Andalus persists in Andalusia not because I repudiate the drops of Arab blood in my veins, but because it smacks of hypocrisy and insincerity. Imputations of cultural intimacy between Andalusians and Arabs ring hollow in view of the violent riots against Moroccan workers in the town of El Ejido in February 2000, a dramatic example of a deeply ingrained hostility toward North African immigration to Spain. In 2004 Muslim prayer in the iconic Mosque-Cathedral of Cordoba was banned. Amid the popular outcry against a hypothetical Arab invasion of Spain, fanned by Osama bin Laden's call to arms to regain al-Andalus for the Muslims, and Islamic extremists' bombing of packed commuter trains in Madrid on March 11, 2004, local and regional governments authorized guards to keep prayer rugs off the Mosque-Cathedral's floor. Still seen as *moros*, the name medieval Christians called their Islamic enemies to the south, Muslim Arabs, whether immigrants, naturalized citizens, or even natural-born citizens, occupy an outsider position in contemporary Andalusian society. This fact undermines the symbolic role of al-Andalus in the creation of regional identity.

The ambivalence of the Moor as both an icon of Andalusian culture and a target of discrimination clarifies my complex investment in regional identity. If any analogy between non-Arab Andalusians and *moros* is not the product of fantasy, it is their shared in-between status, their contradictory sense and experience of acceptance and abjection. This parallel is symbolic, not ethnic. Since the early nineteenth century, following the Napoleonic invasion of 1808, when Spain began defining itself as a nation, Andalusia has occupied a twilight zone in which it is at once the essence of Spanishness and its oriental other. Of course, the region's marginalization also related to purely economic factors, particularly inefficient farming methods, rural poverty and illiteracy, and the glaring class differences caused by the stifling control of absentee landlords over massive estates, a territorial arrangement dating back to the Christian Reconquest. The Andalusian landed oligarchy and bourgeoisie's support of the central government in Madrid during the nineteenth century perpetuated backwardness and stunted the industrialization that made timid inroads in Catalonia and the Basque Country. Development in the north depended on state protectionism, which appeased separatist feelings following the loss of markets in the Americas by stymieing mechanization in Andalusia and turning it into an "interior colonial market" for Catalan and Basque manufactures.[14]

Due to non-inclusive policies, national integration in material and demographic terms eluded the south. The stock exchange and the Bank of Spain, created in 1831 and 1856, respectively, were located in Madrid. From 1848 to 1900, over 6,000 miles of railway and 20,000 miles of road were built, but only a small fraction reached the southern provinces, especially the remote southeast.[15] Urban growth, another important marker of national modernization, lagged in Andalusia from 1860 to 1900, in contrast to Madrid and Catalonia.[16] As the trend continued from 1900 to 1930, the urban population grew from 41.7 to 55.8 percent in Catalonia and from 44.6 to a staggering 71.2 percent in the province of Madrid, while it barely moved from 44.6 to 48.8 percent in Andalusia.[17] Still a peripheral, mostly agrarian and rural region during the second half of the twentieth century, Andalusia, now increasingly depleted by emigration to the industrialized north, continued to supply raw materials and cheap labor to Madrid, Bilbao, and Barcelona but took little, if any, share of the wealth they generated.

Andalusia's peculiar characterization as a backward oriental enclave, though based in history, cannot be detached from the symbolic world conceived by the Romantics who followed Napoleon's troops in search of exotic lands within Europe's borders. Their memoirs, travelogues, and literary works elevated the rusticity that Enlightenment philosophers had reviled. What Voltaire in 1766 deemed "a country of which we know no more than of the most savage parts of Africa, and it is not worth the trouble of being known,"[18] Lord Byron called "Oh, lovely Spain! renown'd romantic land!" in 1812.[19] Either way, whether a bastion of inquisitorial fanaticism or a charming exotic oasis, Spain seemed closer to Baghdad than to Paris. Victor Hugo spent part of his childhood in Spain due to his father's participation in the Napoleonic Wars, and years later he summarized his perception in the poem "Les Orientales" (1828): "Spain is also the Orient; Spain is half African."[20] Stendhal echoed Hugo a year later: "everything in Spain is African. If the Spaniard were a Muslim he would be a complete African."[21] Likewise, Washington Irving's *The Alhambra* (1832) assured visitors to the Iberian Peninsula that they would encounter "the savage and solitary character of Africa."[22] Richard Ford's *Hand-Book for Travellers in Spain* (1845) summed up the message of many travel guides: "Life in the country is a Bedouin Oriental existence."[23] On the pretext that Muslims had lived in the peninsula for over eight centuries (711–1609), foreigners created an enduring and encompassing myth: Spain equals Andalusia equals the orient. This myth raised two interrelated questions about modern nation formation: Can Spain's relationship to northern Europe be conceived beyond mutually exclusive opposites: oriental/occidental, southern/northern, primitive/modern? And do these contrasts attach or detach Andalusia from the idea of Spain as a Western and modern nation?

These debates are far from settled, and they may have to remain so. Either/or categories are too simplistic to analyze how culture works in a country and a region long defined as other by others. My interest, therefore, is in historicizing, not answering, the two questions above. I trace an arch encompassing the late nineteenth, twentieth, and early twenty-first centuries, which have witnessed dramatic transformations of the ideas and representations of Spain and Andalusia in local, national, and international contexts. Underlying these transformations is the paradox that national identity has depended on foreign definitions that conflate Spain with its southernmost region, an oriental enclave in Europe. Even though this idea is mostly the invention of nineteenth-century French, German, and English writers and artists, it was readily internalized by Spaniards.

The anthropologist Julio Caro Baroja stated that the Andalusian Spain of Hugo and Mérimée is also "a national product."[24] *Costumbrismo*, an artistic genre of the nineteenth century that sought to capture the Spanish national essence, is a case in point, since it defined domestic traits in ways that were reassuringly familiar to foreign eyes. The stated goal of *Los españoles pintados por sí mismos* (1843–44; *The Spaniards in a Self-Portrait*), a collection of illustrated sketches of typical national figures, was to correct alien misconceptions about Spain while alerting Spaniards to beware of the invasion of French fashion and ideas following Napoleon's troops. Typical Spain, the volume suggests, is not-France, the cradle of the Enlightenment, which zealous Spanish patriots saw as a threat to their country's deeply rooted traditions and religious beliefs. Paradoxically, the exemplars chosen to represent national authenticity are unnervingly reminiscent of the despised stereotypes created abroad. Unlike similar publications in England and France, *Los españoles* does not portray modern social types—the civil servant, the typesetter, the store clerk—but an archaic world populated mainly by lower-class, often ethnically marked, southern types—the bullfighter, the bandit, the smuggler, the gypsy.[25] Popular periodicals like *Semanario Pintoresco Español* (1836–57; *Spanish Picturesque Weekly*) and well-known nineteenth-century writers from Serafín Estébanez Calderón to Armando Palacio Valdés and José Zorilla continued to place the country's soul in the south.[26]

Beyond the Pyrenees, Spain also donned an Andalusian mask. As if to confirm Romantic stereotypes, the Spanish pavilion at the 1878 Universal Exhibition in Paris was the only building representing a non-Muslim country that had an Islamic façade.[27] Adorned with motifs from the Alhambra and the Mosque-Cathedral of Cordoba, it displayed all the picturesque details an orientalist could desire: patterned stuccos, brick arabesques, and wrought iron. Inside gypsies clad in ruffled polka-dot dresses contorted like eastern dancers to the howling of flamenco singers, or *cantaores*. Throw in a snake charmer, and this dreamy scene could have emanated from distant Araby.

Spain continued to be represented by Islamic-Andalusian monuments at world's fairs into the twentieth century, but the loss of its last colonies in America and Asia in 1898 seeded a change. The equation of *Spanish* with *Andalusian* became anathema for those who wanted to rebuild the nation after the end of empire. Reformers from Miguel de Unamuno and Pío Baroja to José Ortega y Gasset saw the south, its folk culture, and its Moorish character as a despised self-image that was incompatible with national rehabilitation and Europeanization. Ironically, the difference that shores up national identity contradicts assertions of cultural parity with northern Europe. The writer Federico García Lorca was keenly aware of this contradiction and assumed the role of the stock Andalusian in art and life, if only to complicate and ultimately challenge it. His cult of the gypsy, whom he often conflated with the Andalusian Arab, reworks Romantic themes and topics to affirm, not deny, Spain's modernity. In his poems and plays, ancestral traditions and startling metaphors combine to produce the cutting-edge style admired by literary modernists in Paris and London. His avant-garde advanced from, not against, the south.

I use another Romantic commonplace—Andalusia as a sublime site—to examine the making of modern Spain without buying into dead-end binaries—Andalusia versus Spain; Spain versus Europe; south versus north; east versus west. At the end of the eighteenth century, Immanuel Kant described the sublime as the shuddering feeling produced by overwhelming scenes or events in the natural world: a hurricane at sea, a destructive storm brewing on the horizon, a precipice observed from a mountaintop. He also associated the formidable force of the sublime with Spaniards: "In the national character that bears the expression of the sublime, this is either of the terrifying sort, which is a little inclined to the adventurous, or it is a feeling for the noble, or the splendid. I believe I have reasons to be able to ascribe the feeling of the first sort to the Spaniard, the second to the Englishman, and the third to the German." The first group is the only one that cannot temper, shape, and control the impetus of the sublime with the feeling of the beautiful, the origin of the arts and sciences.[28] Kant attributes this deficiency to Spain's racial hybridity. In *Anthropology from a Pragmatic Point of View* (1798), he claims that the Spaniard "arose from the mixture of European with Arabian (Moorish) blood" and remains "centuries behind in the sciences; resists any reform; is proud of not having to work; is of a romantic temperament of spirit, as the bullfight shows . . . and shows in his taste an origin that is partly non-European."[29]

In the next century hordes of travelers, fascinated by what Kant perceived as flaws, crossed the Pyrenees to experience the sublime in Spain, and especially the south, a rugged landscape dotted by awe-inspiring Arabic monuments and populated by dark-skinned, unrefined rustics who inspired both fear and pleasure. Théophile Gautier's travelogue *Voyage en Espagne* (1843–45; *Voyage in Spain*) contains what is probably the most paradigmatic description of orientalized Andalusia as a sublime space:

> Once we had crossed the Sierra Morena, the character of the landscape changed completely. It was as if one had suddenly passed from Europe into Africa. . . . The laurels, the green oaks, the cork trees, the metallic, varnished-leafed fig trees have a freedom, a robustness, a wildness, which mark a climate in which nature is stronger than man and can do without him. At our feet was stretched like a vast panorama the beautiful kingdom of Andalusia. The grandeur of the view recalled the sea. Chains of mountains levelled by distance rolled with undulations of infinite gentleness like long azure billows . . . light poured over that ocean of mountains like liquid gold and silver; every obstacle it met breaking it up in a phosphorescent, spangled foam. . . . The infinite in light is far more sublime and wonderful than the infinite in obscurity.[30]

In 1843, the French writer Edgar Quinet experienced a similar feeling as he observed the "sublimity" of the Mosque-Cathedral of Cordoba, whose innumerable rows of columns and horseshoe arches seemed to extend toward an infinite horizon.[31] Other examples are equally countless, but what I wish to retain of the Romantic notion of the sublime is its slippery, elusive, incomprehensible quality, not its links to the picturesque. A concept dating from the late eighteenth century, the picturesque tries to domesticate the sublime, containing its vast scope as if in a picture.[32] Gautier's description compares the roughness of the Andalusian landscape to "the stuffs one sees in old pictures"; it elicits mild surprise, not the disorienting astonishment that sublime scenes evoke.[33]

As an aesthetic category, the sublime denotes the shock to reason when confronted by the fearsome, infinite power of nature. For Kant, rationality, the preserve of northern Europeans, wins this battle. Encounters with the boundless, chaotic, and dangerous astound but eventually heighten and strengthen reason, which succeeds where the senses fail by organizing these overwhelming sensations under headings like "the infinite," "the absolute," or "God." While for Kant the sublime enlarges the scope of reason, for contemporary philosophers it exposes its limitations. "The sublime," Jean-Luc Nancy announced in 1984, "is in fashion."[34] Jean-François Lyotard, a key contributor to this revival, viewed the Kantian sublime as an anticipation of postmodern challenges to the Enlightenment. The sublime, he wrote, is not a stage in elevating the mind over sensation, but epistemological indeterminacy "which puts forward the unpresentable in presentation itself."[35] Slavoj Žižek explored its ethical and political dimensions in *The Sublime Object of Ideology* (1989). Bringing Kant, Hegel, Marx, and Lacan into the discussion, he perceived the sublime in the beliefs we live by that make us "subjects," including God, the people, and the nation. They are supposed to give meaning to our existence though nobody has seen or fully grasped them. More quicksand than solid rock, they at once provide and cut the ground from under our feet. "The Sublime," Žižek declared, "is the embodiment of Nothing."[36]

These recent approaches invite a revision of Kant's connection between Spain and the sublime. Kant's analysis of national character is basically ethnic stereotyping. To say that Spaniards distinguish themselves in the feeling of the sublime is to underline their harsh character and intellectual backwardness: their inability to attain the order and design of the beautiful, a decisive marker of civilization. Detached from essentialist moral considerations, the sublime stresses not Spain's deficiencies, but its contradictions and ambivalences, which are inextricable from its relation to Andalusia and its Moorish past. The disorienting, paradoxical experience of the sublime captures Spain's indeterminacy as a modern nation, its "split consciousness," which, as Luisa Elena Delgado points out, wavers "between the utopia of modernity and the awareness that this very modernity condemns" Spaniards, "as members of a second-rank nation marked by its Semitic heritage and 'primitivism,' to remain outside its paradigm."[37] The dilemma can be restated as follows: if we ignore the south and what it symbolizes (gypsies, Arabs, the orient), Spain loses its distinctive character, while retaining it prevents Spain from achieving its desired image as a civilized Western country. An "alternating repulsion from and attraction to one and the same object" defines both the Kantian sublime and Spain's contradictory relationship to Andalusia and its Islamic legacy.[38] Unlike Kant, however, I stress Spain's sublimity not in order to reveal defects in temperament, but to underscore its resistance to any fixed form or meaning. If Spanishness is best understood in terms of the sublime, then it is because it is caught up in an unsolvable dilemma—because it poses a riddle that "puts forward the unpresentable in presentation itself," to use Lyotard's words.

The eighteenth-century writer José Cadalso faced this quandary head-on in *Cartas marruecas* (1789; *Moroccan Letters*), an examination of Spanish society in the Age of Enlightenment. His solution was to divide the authorial self into three epistolary correspondents: Gazel, a Moroccan visitor to Spain; Ben-Beley, his teacher; and Nuño Nuñez, Gazel's Spanish friend. The fragmented "I" mirrors national identity, articulated by a born Spaniard and two unbaptized, infidel Moors, who are the mouthpieces of enlightened ideas. Cadalso's shifting narrative positions abolish cultural essentialism and present identity as a process that is always fragmented, always incomplete, always divided between self and other. The real question for Cadalso was not whether to be Spanish or European, oriental or occidental, traditional or modern, but how to be both.

Lately, this ambivalence has been repudiated to assert Spain's normalcy within Europe. The historian Raymond Carr declared in 2000 that "any treatment of Spain as an exceptional case" should be rejected. "It should be studied as one would study the history of any other major European country."[39] Accordingly, recent contributions to the field, including Juan Pablo Fusi and Jordi Palafox's *España 1808–1996: El desafío de la modernidad* (1997; *Spain, 1808–1996: The Challenge of Modernity*) and Javier Tusell's *España, una angustia nacional* (1999; *Spain's National Angst*), either ignore or relegate to the past the cultural elements that "do not fit into the 'modern European' paradigm: gypsies, Arabs, Jews, but above all the 'bastardly' and contaminating mixture of them all," which took place in Andalusia.[40] In contrast, as Cadalso suggests, we can evade marginalization without sacrificing distinctiveness by dispensing with frameworks that make one size fit all. Paraphrasing the historians Mónica Burguera and Christopher Schmidt-Nowara, we may say that Spanish cultural historiography should neither stress nor ignore the disparities between Spain and Europe, but examine how they are inextricable from modernity's "peculiar manifestations" in Spain.[41] Considering national identity through this kaleidoscopic lens may be precarious, even frustrating, but at the very least, we need not ascribe inferiority to difference.

Spanish Orientalism

While Edward Said's *Orientalism* (1978) seems like an appropriate theoretical frame to explore this perspective, it prompts as many questions as it provides answers. How does Spain, Europe's orientalized south and, more important for us, Andalusia, the south within the south, transform, expand, and complicate Said's paradigm? He posits "the Orient" as a cultural category that began to define modern Europe (or the West) as its "contrasting image, idea, personality, experience" after the Napoleonic invasion of Egypt in 1798.[42] Despite its short duration, the campaign had a long-lasting cultural impact. The 23-volume *Description de L'Egypte* (1809–28; *Description of Egypt*), an encyclopedic account of Egyptian history, geography, institutions, and customs, sparked an unprecedented interest in the orient, claiming the attention of scholars, writers, artists, and politicians. During the nineteenth century, the new field of knowledge it created was institutionalized through chairs of oriental studies at European universities and such learned societies as the Société Asiatique and the Royal Asiatic Society. The literary marketplace also responded to the stimulus. Romantic writers satisfied bourgeois curiosity about the far-off territories that metropolitan troops were occupying while helping them to escape increasingly urbanized settings into dreamlands of mystery, passion, and exoticism. Ranging from fiction to travel writing to ethnographic studies and philological treatises, the *Description*'s textual progeny were vast and varied, including Alphonse de Lamartine's *Voyage en Orient* (1835), Edward Lane's *Manners and Customs of the Modern Egyptians* (1836), Ernest Renan's *Historie générale et système compare et des langues sémitiques* (1848), and Gustave Flaubert's *Salammbô* (1862). All these texts described orientals from a position of power: as static objects to be defined and cataloged, "*contained* and *represented* by dominating frameworks," by and for westerners.[43]

The dreamed orient inspired by the *Description* refers almost exclusively to North Africa, East Asia, and South Asia. However, another Napoleonic expedition—the occupation of Spain in 1808—adds layers of complexity that Said left largely unexplored. The Romantic travelers in Napoleon's wake found Spain a suitable backdrop for their oriental fantasies: an ahistorical, mysterious paradise of gypsies and ruins of a glorious Arabic past. Richard Ford encapsulated the shared perception in a witty aphorism: Spain is "a neutral ground between the hat and the turban, and many still contend that Africa begins at the Pyrenees." Its inhabitants, he adds, should be tested "by an Oriental standard," implying that the Spaniard, like the Arab, Bedouin, and Turk, embodied what rational Europeans repressed yet desired: primitive imagination, unbridled emotion, and mindless sensuality.[44] The Romantic orientalization of Spain reversed the so-called Black Legend of Spain's bloodthirsty conquistadors and cruel inquisitors and the negative perceptions spread by philosophes like Voltaire, for whom the Iberian Peninsula was a hopeless den of barbarism and backwardness. Although revalued, stereotypes retained their function as a barrier between Spain and northern Europe. The land that sixteenth-century Protestant reformers and eighteenth-century Enlightenment philosophers had pressed into service to set off northern virtues was celebrated in the early nineteenth century for its premodern charm, unencumbered by industrialization and rampant capitalism. In the Spanish context, therefore, orientalism is not an offshoot of Western imperialism but a fluid paradigm that expresses uneven relations within the West.

Europe's privileged position in the world, Said affirms, was built on difference, exclusion, and bias toward the orient. This marginalization also responded to conceptual divisions between Europe's north and south. Said recognized his oversight in the preface to the 2002 Spanish translation of *Orientalism*. The orient he describes is located "outside" of the dominant culture of French and English colonizers, administrators, scholars, and artists: it represents the "most elevated form of the kind of romanticism that Europeans seek tirelessly." In contrast, "Islam and Spanish culture inhabit each other instead of clashing with belligerence." Spain "is a notable exception in the context of the general European model described in *Orientalism*."[45] He could have added other exceptions, especially Italy. Along with Spain, Italy was pushed to the margins of Europe in the eighteenth century.[46] To the enlightened mind, they were the archaic past to northern Europe's modern future. Their torrid climate and shared Muslim legacy made them oriental. This spatial and temporal partition found expression in Montesquieu's famous theory of climates in *The Spirit of the Laws* (1748): "In northern climates you shall find peoples who have few vices, a sufficient number of virtues, and a lot of frankness and sincerity. Draw near to the southern countries, and you will think you have left morality itself behind: the liveliest passions proliferate crimes."[47] By the nineteenth century, the division between southern and northern Europe had become commonplace. From Kant and Hegel to Max Nordau and Cesare Lombroso, southerners were deemed at once objects of fascination and examples of racial degeneration. The "South," Roberto Dainotto points out, overlapped and interacted with the "Orient" to create a "'state of exception' defining by antithesis the spirit and identity of Europe."[48] Regardless of whether France, Germany, or England is deemed the core of Europe, its "spirit"—shorthand for democracy, prosperity, rationality, and the rule of law—is northern, and is insulated from the deficient, degraded, and exoticized south.

This north-south paradigm deeply affected how orientalism functioned in countries like Spain and Italy. Paradox, Ignacio Tofiño-Quesada points out, "is at the heart of Spanish Orientalism, the narrative of a country that Orientalizes and indeed colonizes the Other (in this particular case, Africa), but which is described as Oriental itself."[49] This ambivalence became particularly apparent after the Spanish-Moroccan War (1859–60). Deflated by colonial collapse overseas and political corruption at home, Spaniards greeted military victory in a border dispute with dispersed nomadic tribes as an opportunity to mend internal rifts and regain international prestige; it was a priceless chance to prove to the world that the racial determinism barring Latins from progress was mistaken. At a time when a nation's level of civilization was measured by the size of its empire, the Spanish presence in northern Africa was a much-needed substitute for the country's lost American colonies. Paradoxically, claims to empire and modernity turned Spain's orientalized image into an asset. The so-called *africanistas*, a diverse group comprised of military officers, scholars, diplomats, and businessmen who believed that the country's regeneration depended on its colonial presence in the Maghreb, contradicted the grotesque caricatures of the bloodthirsty Moor that circulated in the daily press and stressed the similarities, not the differences, between colonizer and colonized. A frequently quoted text by Joaquín Costa is a good example of this rhetoric:

> We will not find a fiber in our bodies, nor a sentiment in our souls, nor an idea in our minds, nor a cell in our brains, nor an air swirl in our atmosphere, nor a furrow in our soil that does not bear the mark of those Berber and Oriental races that made the Peninsula a shining beacon in the dark Middle Ages . . . , and if it is true that Spain, because of its geography and its flora, is linked with Africa and not with Europe, the Spanish people, because of their psychology and culture, must seek out the origin of their civilization and the ancestry of their spirit on the other side of the Strait rather than on the other side of the Pyrenees; it could be said without exaggeration that just as Africa begins in the Pyrenees as far as natural history is concerned, in terms of human history Africa begins for all Spaniards in the soles of their feet and ends in the hairs of their heads.[50]

Appropriately, he delivered these words at the Alhambra Theater in Madrid in 1884 at an event hosted by the recently created Society of Spanish Colonists and Africanists.[51] This and other learned societies lobbied for direct intervention in Morocco, a campaign that eventually resulted in a 1900 agreement with the French to recognize separate areas of influence over Morocco and, in 1912, the creation of the Spanish Protectorate of Morocco. With the permission of the British, who were willing to cede all interest in Morocco as long as the coastline opposite Gibraltar was occupied by a weaker power, the French retained control over the whole country except for a barren northern strip and land in the south around Cape Juby, which were entrusted to Spain. When the French protectorate ended in 1956, Spain ceded the northern zone to the newly independent kingdom of Morocco. The southern area became Moroccan territory two years later, after the short Ifni War.

Like Costa and the *africanistas*, college professors of Arabic also embraced orientalist stereotypes but repurposed their value and function as passports to modernity. Though their work focused on medieval Muslim Iberia, they viewed it as a contribution to national regeneration. In fact, the development of Arabic studies at the universities of Madrid, Zaragoza, and Granada from the mid-nineteenth century on cannot be separated from the impulse to put Spain back on the map of civilized nations. This goal became more urgent after the Spanish defeat by the United States and Cuban secessionists in 1898 known as the "Disaster."[52] Arabists like Francisco Javier Simonet and Julián Ribera y Tarragó used the legacy of al-Andalus to justify colonial intervention in Morocco and to prove that Spain had achieved cultural and scientific distinction long before its northern neighbors. Ribera, who often collaborated with the *africanistas* on educational policies in Spanish Morocco, celebrated the book-loving culture and academic freedom and sophistication of Andalusi society, whose educational system became a model for centers of higher learning across Europe. A hub of artistic innovation, al-Andalus also influenced the development of the courtly love tradition in France and Germany, which was the origin of modern lyric poetry. Andalusi Muslims, Ribera wrote, "knew not only how to preserve their inherited art but also how to transform and renovate it by creating a popular form through which their compositions were broadcast, thus spreading all over Europe."[53] His point from *La enseñanza entre los musulmanes españoles* (1893; *Education among the Spanish Muslims*) to *Historia de la música árabe medieval y su influencia en la española* (1927; *Music in Ancient Arabia and Spain*) is clear: what would later become modern Western civilization first flourished in Spain among the Muslims of al-Andalus.

If the orientalism of Ribera and his disciples was a corrective to historical accounts subordinating Spain as Europe's orient, it did not recognize any debt to Islam. Spanish orientalists believed that the Andalusi golden age happened not because, but in spite of the Muslim occupation. Science, literature, and the arts thrived because the Moorish invaders assimilated to the native population. Simonet flatly denied the Muslim component of Andalusi literature, which he claimed was a local product of "the Hispano-Christian race."[54] Ribera's *La enseñanza entre los musulmanes españoles* contrasted the freedom that teachers enjoyed in what he called "Muslim Spain" with the paralyzing state interventionism in the East. He compared the Arab invaders to a "small amount of red dye"; though "enough to redden the waters of a pond," it did not alter the "chemical composition of either the water or the dye." To these Arabists, the Andalusi enlightenment was only superficially Arab and Muslim. Its essence was Hispanic and Christian.[55]

This ambivalence toward the Afro-Moorish past continued well into the twentieth century, peaking during the early Franco years. The work of Ribera's disciple, the Catholic priest and professor of Arabic Miguel Asín Palacios, laid the ideological groundwork for Franco's brand of *africanismo*, which was a tortured conflation of Spain's Catholic identity and its affinities with the Muslim world. Francoist ideologues distilled Asín's studies, such as *El Islam cristianizado* (1931; *Christianized Islam*), into propaganda justifying the conscription of Moroccan mercenaries in the rebel army during the Civil War (1936–39). Asín Palacios declared in 1940 that the strongest bond between Spaniards and Moroccans was their deep religiosity, which must unite them against the Marxist "dogs without religion" who fought for the Second Republic.[56]

A conservative officer who made his military career in Africa, Franco embodied the unity of Christians and Muslims against godless enemies. After the Civil War, he crafted a public persona as both heroic Christian crusader and friend of the Moors. In public appearances and official ceremonies, he was often escorted by Moroccan bodyguards in white Bedouin robes, the colorful Guardia Mora. Scholarship during the dictatorship further emphasized Spanish-Arab affinities. Due to its conservative bent and its strategic value for Franco's colonial ambitions, Arabism was the only academic field that was not affected by the sweeping purges of research centers and institutions of higher education that took place after 1939. The General Franco Institute of Hispano-Arab Studies and Research and the Institute of African Studies, created in 1938 and 1945 respectively, brought together Arabists and *africanistas* to expand the paradoxical colonialist discourse of brotherhood between metropolis and colony that had justified the Spanish-Moroccan War in 1859.

Scholars who went into exile following the Civil War also debated whether Islam was an integral part of Spanish history and identity. Américo Castro's *España en su historia* (1948; *Spain in Its History*) sparked an intense debate that persists today. Published during Castro's tenure as a professor of Spanish at Princeton University, *España en su historia* conceives of Spain's national identity as the result of the interaction among Jews, Christians, and Muslims during the Middle Ages. *Lo español* or "Spanishness," Castro wrote, is "untraceable before 711."[57] A later formulation of this thesis states that "the Spaniards were—and are—Islamic-Hebraic-Asiatic as much as they were—and are—Christian-European."[58] Reacting against Castro's theory from his exile in Argentina, his friend and political ally Claudio Sánchez Albornoz contended in *España: Un enigma histórico* (1956; *Spain: A Historical Enigma*) that Spain's authentic soul was always Christian-European, despite eight centuries of Muslim presence in the peninsula, a long parenthesis that had devastating effects on the country's national development. Spain's reinsertion into Western civilization came only after the protracted Reconquest against Islam (711–1492), when the country became Europe's shield against barbarous Africa. The polemic continued into the twentieth and twenty-first centuries. Juan Goytisolo's *Disidencias* (1977; *Dissidences*) and *Crónicas sarracinas* (1982; *Saracen Chronicles*) and María Rosa Menocal's *The Ornament of the World* (2002) revived Castro's theories. Serafín Fanjul's *Al-Andalus contra España: La forja del mito* (2000; *Al-Andalus against Spain: The Origin of the Myth*) and *La quimera de al-Andalus* (2004; *The Chimera of al-Andalus*) refute them and support Sánchez Albornoz's views.

This quick historical sketch exposes the limitations of Said's notion of orientalism in the Spanish context. As the Spanish anthropologist José Antonio

González Alcantud wrote, Said's discourse is "insufficient" and should be contemplated not as a "definitive text," but as a malleable paradigm open to paradoxes that disrupt neat dualisms and oppositions.[59] Along these lines, recent studies have refocused images of the orient to assess Spain's development as a nation. In *Exotic Nation* (2009), Barbara Fuchs reveals in rich detail how unifying Spain after 1492 "involved regularizing and regulating Moorishness." She analyzes popular ballads, sartorial practices, and architectural styles in the early modern period to underline the cultural intimacy between Christian Spaniards and their Moorish enemies that complicates "the models of orientalism that critics have developed for northern Europe."[60] Lou Charnon-Deutsch observes a similar process in the uneasy relationship between nation-building and the exoticized Spanish gypsies. With intellectual debts to Said, she stresses the "internal colonization of the Spanish Romany in the construction of Spanish nationalism." Like the Moors, gypsies are at once integral parts of the national self and despised outcasts who must be "if not amputated at least quarantined."[61] In the same vein, Daniela Flesler and Tabea Linhard argue that contemporary Spain is shot through with anxiety at the cultural proximity of neighboring Moroccans, on the one hand, and the historical memory of Sephardic Jews, on the other.[62] Both communities haunt Spain's identity and history, highlighting its in-between status as both European and African.

Orientalism in South within the South

While these scholars focus on the relations between Spaniards and other races and ethnicities throughout history, from medieval Muslims and Jews and iconic gypsies to contemporary African immigrants, I set out to explore Spain's encounters with oriental "otherness" by looking, not beyond ethnic and racial borders, but at Andalusia, a territory of the nation-state that has hovered between belonging and exclusion.

Though nearly synonymous with Spain in the nineteenth century, at the turn of the twentieth century Andalusia, the fabled land of Carmen the gypsy cigar-maker, the Alhambra Palace, and the Muslim civilization of al-Andalus, became a borderland between what the modern nation should and should not be. In 1900, the leading intellectual Miguel de Unamuno wrote that "to save Spain" from cultural decay and political fragmentation after losing Cuba, Puerto Rico, and the Philippines in 1898, northern Spaniards, mainly Basques and Castilians, "must proclaim the inferiority of Andalusians," turn the southern coastal town of Malaga into "a colony," and expunge "all kinds of Bedouinism" from the Iberian Peninsula.[63] Unamuno's hyperbole expressed the conviction, widely held among fin de siècle reformers, that Spaniards must sever ties with Andalusia in order to become a modern nation. Against the Romantic notion that Spain was Andalusia, cultural innovators found the essence of a renewed nationhood in the dry Castilian heartland, which was the antithesis of the colorful south.

The breeding ground for the cult of Castile was the Institución Libre de Enseñanza (ILE; Free Institute of Education), a private school founded in 1876 by a group of dissatisfied professors who opposed the political corruption and inefficiency of the Restoration system, which was controlled by bossism and rigged elections, and Spain's benighted Counter-Reformation Catholicism, which stifled scientific inquiry and liberal-democratic ideas and institutions. ILE liberal nationalism had a distinctly geographical character, pitting the north against the shallow south. Expressing a view shared by many of his colleagues and disciples, the ILE founder Francisco Giner de los Ríos contrasted the austere, almost ascetic Castilian landscape, which intensified the regenerating spirit, to the benumbing beauty of the south, where sensual pleasures drained the willpower and concentration needed to renovate the nation. Now as in the Middle Ages, change would move from north to south, radiating from the center to the periphery.[64]

The writer Antonio Espina captured this view in *La Gaceta Literaria* (*The Literary Gazette*), a journal founded in 1927 and described by its chief editor, Ernesto Giménez Caballero, as the "precursor of the Avant-Garde in Literature, Art, and Politics" in Spain.[65] In issue 7 (April 1927), Espina denied the existence of Andalusian art. The region's soul, he wrote, is rooted in the "orientalism" of medieval Muslim Iberia, which resisted the Christian Reconquest as the manifestation of European civilization. The heir to medieval al-Andalus, Andalusia was essentially a *cultura parada*, or "motionless culture," and was the rearguard, not the avant-garde, of the future Spain.[66]

Two weeks after Espina's note appeared, *La Gaceta* criticized the "Andalusian criterion" of the Spanish Academy for giving a prestigious literary award to Antonio Porras Márquez's *El centro de las almas* (*The Core of the Souls*), a novel infused with cheery southern *costumbrismo*. The *Gaceta* article censured all writers who, despite their unquestionable Europeanist credentials, dealt with Andalusian themes, including the novelist Ramón Pérez de Ayala, who was accused of driving people "crazy talking about Don Juan," the emblem of Andalusian Spain; and the philosopher José Ortega y Gasset, who was mistakenly believed to be preparing a "decisive and *egregio* (egregious or distinguished) hymn" to Andalusia.[67] The latter's "Teoría de Andalucía" ("Theory of Andalusia"), published in the newspaper *El Sol* (*The Sun*) a few days later, proved *egregious* toward the southern region, but in the worst possible sense of the English word. As we shall see in chapter 2, his Andalusia is an oriental enclave frozen in time that must be cut off to rehabilitate the nation.

Like the Madrid intelligentsia, nationalists in Catalonia and the Basque Country condemned Restoration politics, but they targeted Castile, not only because it epitomized political centralism, but also because they believed it was tainted by oriental traits. Catalan patriotism was fueled by the economic interests of prosperous merchants and industrialists but was rooted in the landscape, language, and literature of Catalonia and the belief that it belonged to the European north rather than the Moorish south, which in their view stretched from the Ebro River to the Straits of Gibraltar. The Moors had a negligible impact on Catalonian history. Charlemagne protected the region in the eighth century and created the *Marca hispánica*, comprising Roussillon, Cerdagne, and the area around Barcelona. Nineteenth-century Catalan nationalists used this fact to stress their differences from Spain and Castile, which they felt was still under the spell of Moorish Andalusia and its debased folklore. For example, Enric Prat de la Riba, a pioneering defender of Catalan autonomy, defined Catalan identity against Spain's Semitic heritage and Andalusian *flamenquismo* in *Compendi de la Doctrina Catalanista* (1894; *Summary of the Catalanist Doctrine*), a pamphlet written in the question-and-answer format typical of Catholic catechisms.[68]

Basque nationalism lacked the modernizing spirit of Catalanism. It was a conservative, rural movement that fought to preserve the purity of the Basque race against industrialization and the immigration it prompted. The Catalans waved the nationalist banner in order to promote industrial modernization; the Basques, by contrast, sought to arrest it. However, Basque patriots also saw non-Basque Spaniards, or *maketos*, as Moorish invaders. Sabino Arana, founder of the Basque Nationalist Party, believed that just as the Basque territory in the medieval period had virtually no Muslim presence, contemporary *Euzkadi*, his neologism for the Basque race, must reject contact with the rest of Spain. He adapted the anti-Islamic messages circulating in the press during the Spanish military campaigns in North Africa to his nationalist concerns: "The *maketos*," he wrote in 1893, "are our Moors. With one difference: the Moors hate the Spaniards because they oppress them, and the *maketos* are those who enslave us."[69]

Alternatives to the Restoration articulated the north/south antithesis that separated Spain from Europe within Spain itself. Centralizing and peripheral nationalisms reacting to the old Restoration politics had obvious differences; but they agreed that regenerationist projects, both liberal and conservative, were incompatible with the orientalized south, whether they placed its border at the Ebro River or the Despeñaperros Pass.

This dominant idea did not go unchallenged. The ILE was the heart of Castilian ideology but its residential college, the Residencia de Estudiantes (Students' Residence), became home to distinguished Andalusian writers, notably Juan Ramón Jiménez and Federico García Lorca, who saw cultural reform not as a one-way road connecting Spain with Europe through Castile, but as a process of identification with the orient through Andalusia. Rather than confirming Spain's inferiority, this alternative pathway reconciled the country's southern distinctiveness with its modernizing aspirations. They submitted Andalusian topics to a process of aesthetic "depuration," rendering familiar motifs and images in abstract metaphors. In a 1930 *Gaceta*

Literaria article, the critic and historian Melchor Fernández Almagro stated that the stylization of Andalusian themes shifted the "axis" of literature "from the center to the periphery: from the plateau to the coast."[70] Focusing on a group of young Malaga poets engaged with the journal *Litoral* (*Coast*) (Emilio Prados, José Antonio Muñoz Rojas, and Manuel Altolaguirre, among others), he stressed their debt to Jiménez and García Lorca as well as to "the poets of al-Andalus," who inspired them to see the south as "a purely poetic place"—an interior landscape rather than a cheap folkloric setting. He heralded this new generation of southern writers as the replacement of Unamuno's Castile-loving Generation of 1898, which he described as an outmoded "inland literary phenomenon." Fernández Almagro turned Giner de los Ríos's geography on its head by positing the Andalusian coast, not the Castilian plains, as the landscape stimulating cultural renovation and change in Spain.

Fernández Almagro was not alone in vindicating Andalusia's cultural centrality. The influential Catalonian avant-garde journal *L'Amic de les Arts* (1927–29; *Friend of the Arts*), whose editorial team included the painter Salvador Dalí and the art critic Sebastià Gasch, ran a column celebrating "the young Andalusian poetry." In issue 22 (February 29, 1928), Lluís Montanyà reversed prior Catalan perceptions of Andalusia, arguing that the Andalusian innovators Manuel de Falla, Pablo Picasso, and Juan Ramón Jiménez stimulated "mutual comprehension" among modern art advocates from all corners of the Iberian Peninsula. He praised southern poets like Luis Cernuda, García Lorca, and José Bergamín and periodicals such as Malaga's *Litoral*, Seville's *Mediodía* (*Noon*), and Huelva's *Papel de Aleluyas* (*Hallelujahs Review*), which irradiated the "universal values" of "eternal Andalusia" to "Castile and the world," a phenomenon that the columnist revered rather than reviled.[71] Writing to his friend Fernández Almagro from Barcelona in 1926, García Lorca reported that Catalans had embraced his poetry enthusiastically, recognizing in it the innovating spirit of their nationalism. The feeling was mutual; García Lorca wrote: "I, who am a furious Catalanist, sympathized a great deal with those people, so *constructed* by and fed up with Castile."[72] His trips to Barcelona and the Dalí vacation home in Cadaqués in the 1920s as well as his friendship with Gasch strengthened these literary ties. The avant-garde circles of Catalonia and Andalusia were further united by "the strides these friends took to create the two periodicals preoccupied with the avant-garde spirit," Granada's *Gallo* (*Rooster*), founded by Lorca in 1928, and Dalí's *L'Amic de les Arts*.[73]

Andalusian regionalism also sought to find a place in regenerating Spain. Starting in the early twentieth century as a strictly cultural movement promoted by landowners wishing to emulate the Catalanist bourgeoisie, *andalucismo* soon developed into a liberal political movement that was committed to agrarian reform and land redistribution. The writer and lawyer Blas Infante led the chorus of voices calling for socialist reform in the south and the federalization of politics in Spain. His Andalusia was a dreary reality, not a literary concept; in 1905 José Martínez Ruíz "Azorín" called it *Andalucía trágica*, an underdeveloped land devastated by hunger, unemployment, and destitution.[74] The jurist and sociologist Constancio Bernaldo de Quirós added to the sobering picture in *Bandolerismo y delincuencia subversiva en la Baja Andalucía* (1913; *Banditry and Subversive Crime in Lower Andalusia*) and *El espartaquismo andaluz* (1919; *Andalusian Agrarian Rebellions*). In an effort to dissolve literary stereotypes about the region, he saw the iconic figure of the outlaw, or *bandolero*, who was often glorified as a romantic hero, as a criminal type linked to specific demographic and material conditions, including the accumulation of large landed estates or latifundia in the hands of a few wealthy families; a weak middle class; and the wide chasm between the privileged elite and the extreme poverty of landless laborers.[75] Likewise, Juan Díaz del Moral's *Historia de las agitaciones campesinas andaluzas* (1928; *History of Andalusian Agrarian Rebellions*) invoked the oriental, Arabic roots of Andalusians not to sentimentalize the south, but to explain the agrarian revolts that swept the province of Cordoba in 1918. Scrupulous in his use of archival evidence and documentation, Díaz del Moral ultimately decided that racial traits made southern peasants prone to revolt. Unlike the "Anglo-Saxon worker," they were "enthusiastic, idealistic, inconsistent"; their unbridled passion to change long-standing structures overnight was a consequence of their physiological and spiritual affinities to the Arabs of al-Andalus. He cited Bernaldo de Quirós's *Bandolerismo* on the discovery of ninth- and tenth-century craniums in Cordoba's mosque. After carefully measuring them, Bernaldo de Quirós determined that they were the same size as those of contemporary Cordobans, as measured by the anthropologist Federico Olóriz. "It is unquestionable," Díaz del Moral concludes, "that the heads of Almanzor's contemporaries were very similar to those of present-day men. And there is an even stronger resemblance between their spirits."[76] Drawing on the methods of anthropological criminality popularized by Cesare Lombroso, Bernaldo de Quirós and Díaz del Moral provided a sociological reinterpretation of Andalusia that opposed romantic perceptions but did not dispense with the orientalist marginalization of the region.

Blas Infante sought to do both: to show the real Andalusia behind orientalist abstractions and to invert their negative connotations. Much like his contemporary Arabists, he saw al-Andalus as an asset, not an obstacle, in imagining a modernized region and nation, and an alternative to the corrupt central government. His key work, *Ideal Andaluz* (1915; *Andalusian Ideal*), contended that egalitarianism, tolerance, and prosperity had reigned in Andalusi society under Muslim rule. Rather than civilizing forces, the Christian conquerors were illiterate barbarians who caused southern underdevelopment by expelling Arabs and Jews and dividing their fertile lands among a few noble families, the ancestors of twentieth-century absentee landlords who neglected their latifundia and oppressed the agrarian proletariat. Infante modeled the future Andalusia on its lost splendor. Unlike competing nationalists to the north, he emphasized rather than suppressed Andalusian hybridity, stressing the ethnic and religious tolerance that had thrived in medieval Iberia under Muslim rule.[77] However, like Julián Ribera and others, he gave the credit to an aboriginal Andalusian race that suppressed and finally eliminated the innate intolerance and fanaticism of the Moorish invaders. He thought that scientific progress and artistic activity had burgeoned in Cordoba, Seville, and Granada because the Andalusis were "bad Muslims."[78]

These observations complicate formulations of Spanish orientalism, as does Infante's canonization as the "Father of Andalusia" in 1983 by the post-Franco regional government of Andalusia. Assassinated by fascist gunmen shortly after the outbreak of the Civil War in 1936, Infante fell into oblivion during Francoism. His ideas were revived during the transition to democracy in the 1970s and 1980s, though in modified form. He famously claimed that due to their strong ties with the Mediterranean and the Levant, Andalusians "cannot, and will not ever be Europeans," yet he became the icon of a strongly pro-European Andalusia that claimed its autonomy based precisely on this Afro-Moorish heritage.[79] Taken together, Infante's doctrine and his post-Franco revival contribute to the "disorientation" which, according to Susan Martin-Márquez, arises from Spaniards' "positioning on both sides of Orientalism—as simultaneously 'self' and 'other.' "[80]

In Andalusia, Spanish orientalism loops in twists and turns beyond Said's paradigm and recent revisions by Hispanists. In exploring this aspect, this book joins current debates on the intersection of Europe's north/south division with the formation of national cultures. Nelson Moe and Jane Schneider, among others, have explored "orientalism in one country" by looking at how, starting in the eighteenth century, northern Italians promoted their modern, progressive, and industrious character in opposition to the oriental apathy and provincial backwardness of the so-called *mezzogiorno*, the southern part of Italy, including the islands of Sardinia and Sicily, which was under Islamic rule from the ninth to the late eleventh century.[81] Accounts of Spanish nationalism have neglected this perspective, which also has implications for other orientalized margins (Portugal, Greece, the Balkans). *The Sublime South* attempts to fill this gap.

The first chapter of this book, "The Orient Within: *Andalucismo, Africanismo, Arabismo*," examines the multifaceted texture of Spanish orientalism. It uncovers overlooked intersections between early twentieth-century Andalusian regionalism (*andalucismo*), intellectual justifications for Spanish colonialism in Africa (*africanismo*), and the work of Spanish university scholars of Arabic culture (*arabismo*). All three discourses presented diverse, often contradictory, interpretations of medieval al-Andalus and modern Andalusia as they redefined Spain between the 1898 Disaster and the Civil War (1936–39), a period when the central government deteriorated, separatist nationalisms gained momentum in Catalonia and the Basque Country, and the dark shadow of dictatorship moved across the country. I show that academic studies of Spain's Islamic past not only vindicated colonialism in Morocco, but also provided the arguments, lexicon, and historical sources for the anticolonial, federalist, yet non-separatist *andalucismo* crafted by Blas Infante and publicized in southern journals such as *Bética* (1913–17) and *Andalucía* (1916–20). *Andalucismo* outlived Infante, but not in the form he intended. The leading *africanista* thinker Rodolfo Gil Benumeya kept the term *andalucismo* but replaced its progressive content with the antiliberalism and right-wing Catholicism that grew in strength during the Primo de Rivera dictatorship (1923–30) and went on to monopolize Spanish politics for four decades during the Francoist period. Benumeya's writing often echoes Infante's work, but these affinities hardly stem from direct ideological transmission. Instead, I interpret them as Benumeya's grafting of alien elements onto a preexisting "host" to mutate it. The result: an *andalucismo* where Spanish fascism, Africanist colonialism, and Catholic fundamentalism met the myth of Hispano-Arabic brotherhood.

Chapter 2, "Culture, Modernity, and the South, 1898–1936," shifts from political and intellectual history to literature and the arts in the pre–Civil War period. It reads José Ortega y Gasset's "Teoría de Andalucía" as a key manifestation of the widespread rejection of Spanish stereotypes based upon Andalusia fostered by the Institución Libre de Enseñanza. Published in the leading liberal Madrid daily *El Sol* in April 1927, the article presents Andalusia as an oriental setting incompatible with the values and attitudes (creativity, historical awareness, aesthetic discernment) that would promote Spain's cultural parity with Europe. While sharing Ortega y Gasset's modernizing views, prominent Andalusian artists and writers associated with the ILE challenged their region's marginalization as antimodern. I argue that Juan Ramón Jiménez's critical writings on Spanish literary history, Federico García Lorca's lectures on flamenco, and the composer Manuel de Falla's musical theories, among other texts, can be read as alternative "theories of Andalusia." They reject the picturesque representations that Ortega y Gasset derides while reconciling what he sees as opposites: the region's oriental character and the European, avant-garde outlook needed to regenerate national culture. Here, regional loyalties are invoked neither to condemn nor resolve economic underdevelopment and political corruption, but to craft a stylized, avant-garde image of the south. Andalusia's oriental character was mobilized not to spark ideological or political change, but to rethink the region's symbolic place in the national and global cultures. Both Infante and García Lorca underscored the eastern roots of flamenco; but for Infante, it was the chant of the dispossessed, a cry of pain linking the persecuted medieval Moor and today's poor day laborer. For García Lorca, flamenco represented the sophisticated simplicity of European avant-garde aesthetics, what he called "purity, the Cubist instinct of the sharp line."[82] The south imagined by artistic innovators is neither a real place nor the social, political, and historical entity of regionalist and Africanist versions of *andalucismo*. It is perhaps best understood as a cultural concept that, in the words of a contemporary geographer, is "less a material object, a static geographic category," and much more "a strategic domain."[83]

Chapter 3, "Andalusia and Franco Spain," examines how Franco's regime (1939–75) silenced liberal views on regional and national identity while promoting the old notion that Andalusia is where you can find Spain at its most intense. From the late 1930s to the 1950s, state-sponsored films, including *Carmen la de Triana* (1938; *Carmen of Triana*), *La blanca paloma* (1942; *The White Dove*), and *Morena clara* (1954; *The Light-Skinned Gypsy*), featured romantic stereotypes of dancing gypsies in picturesque Andalusian settings. Coexisting uneasily with the regime's colonial presence in North Africa and its symbolic connections to the Christian Reconquest of al-Andalus, these films perpetuated the orientalist representation of Spain as Andalusia which had been publicized by nineteenth-century European writers. Auto-exoticism had great propagandistic value. Female protagonists, often stock racialized Andalusians, embodied Franco Spain's difference from the liberal European north, and Spain's official depiction as a peaceful land devoid of social unrest. The screen version of the Andalusian countryside is an Arcadia where bosses and peasants live in peace and harmony.

In the 1960s and 1970s, as the dictatorial government entered trade and military agreements with the United States and began to promote tourism, Andalusia shed its archaic flavor to appeal to sun-starved holidaymakers. Musical comedies starring the popular singer Manolo Escobar, and the widely publicized journalism of the conservative ideologue José María Pemán, labored to strike a balance between eternal values and hierarchies and the brave new world of Swedish bombshells in bikinis. At the same time, dissenting voices confronted silver screen fantasies and the falsifications of the official press with the harsh social reality of the south. Juan Goytisolo's brutal realism in *Campos de Níjar* (1960; *Countryside of Níjar*), *La Chanca* (1962), and the essay "Tierras del Sur" (1967; "Lands of the South") inspired the leftist journalists associated with the cultural journal *Triunfo* (*Triumph*) to dismantle the regime's myths and pose questions about the dismal material conditions of the agrarian south. Like Goytisolo, *Triunfo* contributors often emphasized Andalusia's oriental character, though for different reasons. Angry at the social oppression and poverty he witnessed in the sun-baked desert around Almeria, Goytisolo wanted to raise awareness of chronic underdevelopment in the region, which he depicted as a northern African realm, but his orientalizing perspective responded mainly to personal and artistic motivations. His fascination with Andalusians, which anticipated his later attraction to the Muslim world, operated within a self-other dialectic that, as he put it, "retains its irreducible Manichean opposites intact: values turn into anti-values and vice versa."[84] Other ethnicities stand as the antithesis of the despised values of Francoism, as stereotypes in reverse. In contrast, *Triunfo* connected Andalusia with its Mediterranean neighbors to the south and east to stress their shared marginality within global capitalism. Far from being a paradigm to try out in art those beliefs and attitudes that were forbidden in life, orientalism was in the journal's pages a lens to magnify Andalusia's Third World status, the basis of what the frequent contributor Antonio Burgos called the *regionalismo del subdesarrollo* (regionalism of underdevelopment). This formula bound up Marxist concerns about labor and class with the desire to create a distinct regional identity for Andalusia.

Triunfo folded in 1982, seven years after Franco's death. Its revolutionary message was rendered obsolete by a new political order that favored modernization along neoliberal lines. As state power was federalized, each of seventeen autonomous communities had to substantiate its distinctive culture in order to validate self-rule. Asserting particularity while seeking inclusion in a rapidly Europeanizing Spain, Andalusian politicians and intellectuals rapidly crafted a sanitized version of the region's Islamic history and cultural legacy while eliding the rhetoric of underdevelopment and third worldism that gained momentum in the 1960s and 1970s, as well as the messy current reality of African immigration. Neither identical nor antithetical to the Arab world, contemporary Andalusia remains a contentious meeting place between Spain's aspirations and history. In chapter 4, "The Persistence of Myth: Post-Dictatorial Andalusia," I analyze the institutional uses of Andalusia's Muslim legacy by public museums, cultural exhibitions, and the mass media. Focusing on the inaugural telecast of the regional television network Canal Sur, the Andalusian Pavilion at Expo '92, and the Museum of Andalusian Autonomy, I explore the efforts of the regional government to reconcile Andalusia's oriental identity with the demands of consumer society, mass tourism, and economic integration in capitalist Europe.

The afterword, "Breaking the Spell of Identity," discusses the formulations of Andalusia examined in previous chapters as historically conditioned rewritings of the same double exposure: the southern region as the essence of Spanish nationhood on the one hand, and as an internal orient on the other. Taking my cue from theories of the sublime and Walter Benjamin's notion of allegory, I detach this historical inventory from identity paradigms, which cannot be held in good faith once they are perceived as fictions. But how can we "feel Andalusian" if we reject the notion of Andalusian identity? I answer this question through an analysis of Basilio Martín Patino's seven-episode mockumentary *Andalucía: Un siglo de fascinación* (1996; *Andalusia: A Century of Fascination*). Patino's suggestion that a sense of belonging to a community can be found in old symbols, myths, and rituals, and even in the knowledge of their artificiality, allows me to come to terms with my contradictory feelings of attachment and detachment concerning this book's subjects.

Chapter 1

✦

The Orient Within: *Andalucismo, Africanismo, Arabismo*

By the end of the nineteenth century, what had been a world power stretching over continents was a "dying nation," in the words of Lord Salisbury.[1] Spanish national pride was wounded, and internal political problems relentlessly corroded the country's institutional and social stability. The loss of a vast empire in the Americas, decades of abortive governments at home, and fierce civil wars between liberals and conservatives had discredited the monarchy. Unable to reconcile a deeply fractured country, Queen Isabella II supported the ultra-Catholic reactionaries in her court in the 1860s. Excluded from the government, liberals became revolutionaries and drove her into exile in 1868. The 1869 constitution marked a new democratic beginning defined by ideological tolerance and parliamentary representation. It proclaimed universal suffrage and recognized freedom of religion, but theory and practice were at extreme odds in an essentially agrarian and strongly Catholic society which had an illiteracy rate of over 50 percent. The lack of a solid social base doomed the revolutionary experiment. A failed attempt to impose a foreign monarch open to liberal reforms was followed by the First Republic of 1873, which ended in chaos. These resounding political failures prompted the Restoration of the Bourbon monarchy. King Alfonso XII, Isabella's son, returned to Spain as king in 1874 but died at age 27 in 1885. His son, Alfonso XIII, became king upon his birth the following year and went on to rule what on paper was one of the most democratic countries in Europe, as fundamental achievements of the First Republic were restored. The Civil Code was implemented in 1889 to systematize and rationalize the judicial process, and universal male suffrage became law in 1892. But the ignorant electorate was manipulated by a widespread network of political bosses or caciques who orchestrated the peaceful alternation in power of the conservative and liberal parties. This form of institutionalized corruption, which remained in place until 1923, proved long-lasting, but its stability was precarious at best. A raging colonial crisis in Cuba, demands for home rule in Catalonia, antigovernment protests from both the far Right and the far Left, and labor unrest rocked Spain throughout the late nineteenth century and well into the twentieth century. The dissolution of the Restoration system did not end political and social tension, which persisted during the Primo de Rivera dictatorship (1923–30) and the Second Republic (1931–39), coming to a dramatic head with the outbreak of the Spanish Civil War in 1936.

Amid turmoil, ruling elites saw colonial expansion in Africa as a priceless opportunity to foster internal unity and rebuild Spain's international prestige. Antonio Cánovas del Castillo, the architect of the Restoration system and prime minister for six terms between 1874 and 1897, wrote in 1851 that occupying Morocco was "a question of life or death" for Spaniards. Spain's "natural border," he claimed, was not the "narrow channel that links the Mediterranean and the Atlantic" but the Atlas Mountains extending across northern Africa.[2] Cánovas's plan was put into action by General Leopoldo O'Donnell, who sent a Spanish expedition to Morocco in 1859. The result of a petty border dispute near Ceuta, a Spanish enclave in Africa since 1688, the conflict was a long-awaited opportunity to join other European powers in carving up Africa. Spanish troops occupied Tétouan in 1860 but withdrew shortly thereafter due to British intervention.

Colonial endeavors in Africa were reignited by Spain's humiliating defeat at the hands of the United States and Cuban separatists in 1898. The loss of the last remnants of the overseas empire (Cuba, Puerto Rico, and the Philippines) made expansion in Africa a national priority. In November 1912, Spain's colonial aspirations won a small victory when France and Britain granted a protectorate over the barren lands around Ceuta and Melilla. A 7,700-square-mile strip known as the Rif, the Spanish protectorate was inhabited by rebellious Berber tribesmen who stubbornly refused to recognize colonial authority over their territories. Spain's direct military action and attempts to win over local leaders for service in the colonial administration did not prevent violent stirrings. In 1921, the rebel leader Abd-el-Krim and his Riffian allies declared an independent Republic of the Rif and engaged the Spanish army at the Battle of Annual, an utter disaster for the Spaniards in which approximately 9,000 soldiers died. The so-called Moroccan War continued despite growing public discontent with its high material and personal costs. General Miguel Primo de Rivera, who took over the government of Spain with King Alfonso XIII's backing in 1923, organized a joint operation with the French general Henri-Philippe Pétain that eventually forced Abd-el-Krim to surrender in 1926.

On a Sunday afternoon in late winter 1924, with the war still in full swing, the journalist Luis Bello and a professor of Arabic and Hebrew, Mariano Gaspar Remiro, discussed Spain's colonial presence in North Africa at a beer hall in Madrid. Remiro lamented the atmosphere of crisis while underscoring that the occupation of the Maghreb must be seen in light of the Christian Reconquest of al-Andalus. Then, as now, political incompetence hindered and postponed the eventual Spanish triumph over Muslim forces. Bello listened intently. He regretted that Remiro's words, however relevant to contemporary foreign policy, would sound like esoteric trivia to most, if not all, of the other patrons sipping beer at neighboring tables. Remiro was the first director of the Center of Historical Studies of Granada and Its Kingdom. Founded in 1910, it published an academic journal that addressed a wide range of cultural, social, and historical topics while focusing on medieval Muslim Iberia. According to Bello, the work of Remiro's "laboratory" should be placed in the very center of a table gathering "the scholar, the soldier, and the diplomat."[3]

This chapter examines the interaction at this imagined table but makes room for one more participant: the Andalusian regionalist. During the first three decades of the twentieth century, *andalucismo* evolved to become a political movement against the corrupt Restoration system (1874–1923). Although it took inspiration from Catalan calls for autonomy, it did not advocate separatism, nor did it oppose regional identity to Spain's Afro-Moorish past. Instead, it drew on Arabic studies to consolidate its doctrine in journals such as *Bética* and *Andalucía* and, in paradigmatic form, Blas Infante's treatise *Ideal Andaluz* (1915). A close reading of these publications will reveal that the dynamic ties among modern Spain, medieval Muslim Iberia, and colonialism in Africa became more intricate and convoluted from a southern regionalist perspective.

"Spanish Orientalism," Ignacio Tofiño-Quesada writes, "included the Orientalizing of the Other and the assumption of the Self as Other."[4] *Andalucismo*'s links to *africanismo* and *arabismo* in the pre–Civil War period expands and complicates this description, nuancing both the "Orientalizing" mechanism and the meanings of "self" and "other." Spanish Arabists stressed the impact of Andalusi culture on Spain as it progressed toward modernity. *Andalucistas* like Infante concurred but revised what "Spain" and "modernity" might mean from the Iberian south. Opposing separatism, *andalucistas* equated al-Andalus, Andalusia, and Spain, but declared that Andalusia is not Castile and does not want to be Europe, the cradle of imperialism. Meanwhile, prominent scholars of al-Andalus advocated Spanish centralization around Castile and colonialism in North Africa, which Infante and his followers opposed and sought to replace with a pan-Andalusian federation uniting both sides of the Straits of Gibraltar. The differences between *arabismo* and *andalucismo* became dramatically evident when the leading Arabist Miguel Asín Palacios supported the Francoist uprising that claimed Infante's life due to his regionalist ideas. After Infante's death, *andalucismo* was reformulated to support Franco's colonial ambitions in Africa. Rodolfo Gil Benumeya, Asín's disciple, conjured up a contorted version of *africanismo* that conjoined Infante's pan-Andalusian doctrine and authoritarian fascism.

At the center of all these intersections and conflicts were diverse, often contradictory, interpretations of Moorish legacies in modern Spain. Stitched together, they expose interlocking patterns in the fabric of Spanish Orientalism at the substate, state, and suprastate levels. Ignoring them renders partial and incomplete any discussion of Spain's ambivalence as both orientalized and orientalizing, a fundamental aspect of national construction from the nineteenth century on that underwent complex regionalist reformulations in Andalusia in the pre–Civil War period.

Arabism and/as Africanism

Despite Bello's misgivings, Spain's colonial claims in Morocco were deeply intertwined with academic Arabism in the nineteenth and twentieth centuries. Cánovas del Castillo's uncle, the Arabist Serafín Estébanez Calderón, pioneered the type of collaboration that Bello desired. His *Manual del oficial de Marruecos* (1844; *Hand-Book for Officers in Morocco*) is an early manifestation of the active involvement of Spanish scholars of Islam in colonialist endeavors in Africa. Estébanez Calderón put his academic knowledge to practical use, encouraging military leaders to emulate the French invasion of Algeria in 1830. Relying on a wealth of historical texts and documents, he offered a pejorative image of the neighboring country to justify Spain's civilizing mission across the Straits of Gibraltar. Pascual de Gayangos, a professor of Arabic at the University of Madrid from 1843 to 1871, also aligned orientalist scholarship with Spain's colonial ambitions. In 1853, the Ministry of War's Commission for the Investigation of Historic and Military Documents appointed him to find archival proof of Spain's uninterrupted presence in Africa since the medieval period.[5]

Estébanez Calderón's and Gayangos's work reveals the deep ties between Arabic studies and foreign policy in North Africa. But most of the calls for expansion were voiced by so-called *africanistas*, a motley crew of military officers, diplomats, geographers, journalists, commercial agents, and politicians who advocated colonialism as a way to revitalize Spain's economy and patriotic pride. Their collective work crystallized in pro-imperialist organizations such as the Geographic Society in 1876, the Spanish Association for the Exploration of Africa in 1877, and the Spanish Society of Africanists and Colonists in 1883. Geographical, historical, anthropological, and sociological studies about North Africa and such periodical publications as *Europa en África* (1909; *Europe in Africa*), *África Española: Revista de colonización* (1913–17; *Spanish Africa: Colonization Review*), *Revista hispano-africana* (1922–31; *Hispano-African Review*), and *África: Revista de tropas coloniales* (1924–36; *Africa: Colonial Troops Review*) also proliferated. The tide of enthusiasm reached the Royal Palace in Madrid. King Alphonso XIII, nicknamed "the Africanist," became an active supporter of Spain's military intervention and continued presence in Morocco.[6]

Spanish Arabists were mostly concerned with the history of al-Andalus but did not disagree with imperialist policies radiating from Madrid, and they often participated in events hosted by the Africanist societies and served on their advisory boards.[7] Although their scholarly work cannot be reduced to colonial service, their interest in Spain's presence in Morocco remained constant from the late nineteenth century to Moroccan independence in 1956.[8] Francisco Javier Simonet, one of Estébanez Calderón's disciples and chair of Arabic at the University of Granada, is a case in point. The author of an award-winning *Historia de los mozárabes de España* (1897–1903; *History of the Mozarabs of Spain*), he was an outspoken supporter of Spain's declaration of war against Morocco in August 1859. His views reached a wide audience through high-circulation cultural magazines. Writing in Madrid's *La América* in November 1859, Simonet greeted the onset of the war enthusiastically as a "new and beautiful spectacle" that "fills with joy" the eyes and hearts of Spaniards.[9] He saw a small triumph over scattered groups of Moroccan tribesmen as compensation for losing most of the American dominions early in the nineteenth century. It was also seen as the continuation of Queen Isabella's religious war against Muslim infidels by conquering their African territory.[10]

Simonet's articles anticipated what would later become, according to Rodolfo Gil Grimau, the two main trends of Africanist thinking in Spain: the colonial current, which tries to "find a substitute for the lost or almost lost American Empire," and the emotional current, "which sees intervention in Africa—particularly North Africa—as a prolongation of the fights between Christian kingdoms against the Muslims in the so-called Reconquest."[11] The rallying cry "War to Africa!" was also an antidote to the precariousness of the Spanish monarchy, which was on the verge of collapse due to political rivalries, militant labor movements, and the rise of peripheral nationalisms in Catalonia and the Basque Country. Crucial to revitalizing international prestige and attaining unity at home, the success of the Spanish-Moroccan War was guaranteed, according to Simonet, by the strong climatological, affective, and historical affinities between the countries.[12] Invoking geographical proximity and eight centuries of Islamic presence in the Iberian Peninsula, he argued that Spaniards were better suited to occupy North Africa because of their similarities to, not differences with, Moroccans. He broke with the ethnocentrism of French and British orientalism, which opposed a European "we" to an exotic "them." Though more elastic, Simonet's proposal was an equally self-serving view of the interaction between colonizer and colonized.

Other prominent Arabists, including Francisco Codera y Zaidín and his disciples Julián Ribera and Miguel Asín Palacios, known in professional circles as the Beni Codera or "sons of Codera," adopted Simonet's ambivalent approach to Hispano-Arab relations. The Codera school, the backbone of modern Spanish Arabism, saw al-Andalus as a bridge between Islam, Spain, and Europe that was nonetheless independent and culturally superior to the rest of the Arab world.[13] The Beni Codera's underlying assumption was that identification with the orient, a central component of northern European perceptions of Spanish backwardness, could be reinterpreted as a valuable trait that would move Spain from the periphery to Europe's center. The desire to write Spain into the narrative of Western modernity animated studies from Ribera's *La enseñanza de los musulmanes españoles* (1893) to his disciple Asín Palacios's *El Islam cristianizado* (1931). Ribera's wide-ranging explorations of Andalusi legal and educational institutions, poetry, and music expanded the field of Islamic studies while stressing the key role of al-Andalus in the making of European civilization. He argued that the idea of the modern university first entered Europe through "Muslim Spain." He also argued that modern poetry originated with the "exceedingly clever strophic forms" created by the Andalusis during the medieval period. Different from classic Arabic forms, the *zejel* and the *muwashshah* spread throughout Iberia, North Africa, and the orient and were "imitated by the Provençal troubadours, the German Minnesingers, and other European poets."[14] Asín Palacios followed his mentor. A distinguished scholar of Arabic studies and a Roman Catholic priest who became Alfonso XIII's royal chaplain, he focused on the overlap between Islam and Christianity in his investigations of Sufism, Scholasticism, and the work of Dante, which he claimed was inspired by Arabic sources.

With Ribera and Asín at the helm, the field of Arabic studies occupied a prominent position in two institutions that sought to bring Spanish higher education and scientific research closer to European standards: the Junta de Ampliación de Estudios e Investigaciones Científicas (JAE; Board for Advanced Studies and Scientific Research, founded 1907) and its associated Center for Historical Studies (founded 1910; Centro de Estudios Históricos).[15] Ribera and Asín Palacios headed two of the Center's seven sections: History of Hispano-Arabic Philosophy (Asín) and Social Institutions in Muslim Spain (Ribera). Under their supervision, the JAE and the Center published editions and translations of forgotten Hispano-Arabic texts and groundbreaking studies on medieval and contemporary topics, including Pedro Longás's *Vida religiosa de los moriscos* (1915; *Religious Life of the Moriscos*) and Joaquín Vélez Villanueva's *Ensayo sobre la agricultura, el comercio y la industria en Marruecos* (1916; *Essay on the Agriculture, Commerce, and Industry of Morocco*). Ribera's hand was felt in editorial policies and the Center's study-abroad program. Future scholars of Islam were trained among ancient manuscripts in the library and in the field, learning firsthand the language, culture, and customs of their African neighbors to the south.

The Beni Codera also participated actively in colonialist ventures. In 1913, the Board of Education in Morocco asked Ribera and Asín to draft a Spanish-Moroccan glossary, which provided civilians and military personnel in the protectorate with a useful list of "Arabic terms for place names and sociological, religious, legal, economic concepts and the like."[16] Cultural policies in the Protectorate became one of Ribera's main research interests. The two hefty volumes of his *Disertaciones y opúsculos* (1928; *Essays and Tracts*), an anthology of his works, dedicate as many pages to al-Andalus as to Spain's colonialism in Africa. Academic and patriotic interests met in his proposal for a public School of Arabic Studies dedicated to the education of Spanish diplomats, soldiers, explorers, and interpreters serving in the Maghreb. A nursery for future agents of colonialism, the school would be "the instrument to specify and define the projection of the Spanish ideal in Morocco."[17] The curriculum included classical Arabic, the history of the Islamic world and Hispano-Arabic relations, and current commercial, geographic, and political realities in the region. Ribera's school never opened, but he did not give up his ambition to create an Arabism that could address and resolve current national needs.

Under the guidance of Ribera and Asín, Arabism built bridges to connect the nation's past and its desired future, claiming the intellectual accomplishments of medieval Muslim Iberia for modern Spain. It also fostered Bello's desired collaboration between "the scholar, the soldier, and the diplomat," establishing links between academic interests and colonial endeavors in North Africa. The al-Andalus/Spain bond was at once the passport to the Western world of knowledge and science, and a justification for joining neighbors across the Pyrenees in the scramble for Africa. In more than one sense, then, embracing the orient within meant Europeanizing. As Asín explained in 1933 in the inaugural issue of *Al-Andalus*, the official journal of the Schools of Arabic Studies of Madrid and Granada, their "patriotic scholarship" must fulfill the "ineludible duty" of underlining the contributions made to "Europe, and particularly to Spain" by Islamic civilization during "eight centuries of domination and coexistence."[18]

Andalusian Orientalism

Academic perceptions of al-Andalus, integral to Spanish nationalism and colonialism in Africa, also shaped pre-Civil War Andalusian regionalism. Some leading *andalucistas* were scholars of medieval Iberian Islam and Africanist officials. A disciple of Mariano Gaspar Remiro, Isidro de las Cagigas was a trained Arabist who served as a diplomat in Spanish Morocco, Egypt, Libya, and Iran and published several articles and monographs on medieval Hispano-Arabic culture, including *Los mozárabes* (1947–48; *The Mozarabs*) and *Los mudéjares* (1948–49; *The Mudejars*). The Arab world for him was a professional destination, an erudite subject, and essential to the revival of a timeless "Andalusian ideal" that would unshackle the region from material and spiritual stagnation. Other *andalucistas* lacked Cagigas's training but borrowed from the work of Spanish Arabists to advance their regionalist arguments. Blas Infante possessed a sizeable collection of books on Arabic culture, literature, and language, including about a dozen volumes by Julián Ribera and Miguel Asín, which he underlined and annotated frequently. These connections are inextricable from the ideological development of *andalucismo* and its relationship to African colonialism and other Iberian regionalisms, particularly Catalan nationalism.

In the initial stages, during the early twentieth century, *andalucismo* was led by a group of landowning aristocrats and members of the agrarian bourgeoisie who unconditionally supported the monarchy and the Restoration system. Uninterested in Andalusia's chronic underdevelopment and the growing demands of exploited peasants, they promoted a metaphysical conception of identity, represented by the journal *Bética* (1913–17).[19] The epicenter of this gentlemanly *andalucismo* was Seville's Arts Club, the Ateneo, founded in 1887. Its annual festival was an elegant ball that doubled as a public forum for cultural debate. Following the example of the Catalan Regionalist League, a bourgeois political party created in 1901, Seville's *ateneístas* began to promote local art and literature as the essence of a distinct regional identity. Like the League, they saw regeneration mostly as a cultural phenomenon that promoted the interests of the conservative classes and ignored the great poverty and misery of agrarian workers. While the affluent members of the Ateneo were busy building a regional spirit, the destitute peasantry, who made up more than two-thirds of the region's labor force, struggled to make ends meet with below-average wages and unregulated working conditions.

This clubbish regionalism was soon supplemented by a progressive commitment to labor reform, land redistribution, and political independence. Blas Infante became its leading voice. In a 1914 *Bética* article, he claimed that a true Andalusian "ideal" would not flourish unless the region's vast landed estates or latifundia were broken up and returned to the people. After abolishing the oppressive figure of the absentee landlord, city folk must join landless peasants to create a new class of agricultural workers who would cultivate their own land happily and efficiently. This new territorial arrangement would restore a robust collective character, the "soul of the people," that had been lost after the expulsion of the Moors in 1492 and the imposition of the Castilian system of land tenure. To rehabilitate a sense of hope in a dark historical moment, Andalusians must find inspiration in their Muslim ancestors—in their glorious civilization and productive farming practices. It was only by emulating al-Andalus that Andalusia could blast its way into the future.[20]

With Infante's intervention, *andalucismo* began to look back to al-Andalus while veering to the left, becoming a political rather than cultural movement. The journal *Andalucía* (1916–20), *Bética*'s socially oriented successor, describes the movement in 1917 as a socialist and regenerationist "ideal" inspired by Georgism, the economic philosophy developed by the American economist Henry George, which affirms a universal right to land ownership.[21] In 1918 Infante organized the first conference on political *andalucismo* in Ronda, and a year later he signed the *Manifiesto Andalucista de Córdoba*, which took inspiration from the 1883 federalist Antequera Constitution to demand Andalusian autonomy from the corrupt central government and the rule of local caciques, who were appointed by absentee landlords to rig elections. In 1923 the dictator Primo de Rivera banned all regionalist activity in the country and closed down the Andalusian Centers that Infante and his political allies had created to promote his doctrine. *Andalucismo* made a comeback during the Second Republic. In 1931 Infante created the Liberal Juntas of Andalusia, non-electoral political entities dedicated to establishing regional autonomy, and the Republican Revolutionary Federalist Coalition of Andalusia, an unconventional party with members of diverse ideological stripes. His goal was to obtain for Andalusia a statute of autonomy like the one the Catalans had approved by referendum in 1932. A draft of the charter was presented at a regionalist convention in Cordoba in 1933 but was never implemented. Infante's political experiment failed to gain popular and institutional support and was eventually quashed by Franco's victory in 1939, which enforced Spanish unity by eradicating regional nationalisms from the peninsula.

The historian Juan Antonio Lacomba distinguishes the merely idealistic proposals of early *andalucismo*—exemplified by *Bética* and works such as José María Izquierdo's dreamy evocation of Seville, *Divagando por la ciudad de gracia* (1923; *Rambling through the City of Charm*)—from the historically grounded approaches inspired by Infante.[22] Far from being mutually exclusive, these two tendencies, or "paths" as Lacomba calls them, crisscrossed. Neither promoted revolution to foreground regionalist claims. Though devoted to improving the conditions of landless peasants, left-wing *andalucistas*, like their conservative counterparts, felt that a distinct Andalusian personality would not spring from mass mobilization, but would rather come to fruition through the guidance and tutelage of select individuals. Change was understood as a top-down process coordinated by what Infante somewhat pompously called a "legion of priests and apostles," who believed that pedagogy was the prerequisite to ending the "tyrannical regime" that kept the land in the hands of a few while large masses of laborers lived in extreme poverty.[23] Material transformation could not happen without idealistic goals, which both conservatives and progressives defined as a vague spiritual "Andalusian ideal" based on the German notion of *Volksgeist,* or "spirit of the people." Infante maintained that social health always begins with the soul of the nation and then spreads to its body. To revive Andalusia, he wrote, "start with the spirit, then continue with the economy, and finish with the form," by which he meant the federalized state.[24] Deviations from this plan could lead to rudderless anarchy, which was seen as a serious problem by *andalucista* leaders.

Anarchism took hold of the Andalusian countryside in the late 1880s and manifested sporadically thereafter, lasting through the Civil War of 1936–39. Lacking strong organization and discipline, revolutionary groups formed in small villages around the massive latifundia to commit acts of random violence against landowners and their property. In contrast, progressive *andalucismo* was an elitist movement with "attitudes and revolutionary methods that were radically different from those of anarchism and the labor movement."[25] Repeatedly and emphatically, anarchist activism was opposed from the pages of the journal *Andalucía*. In September 1916 the liberal politician and intellectual Alejandro Guichot, the son of Joaquín Guichot, the author of the first *Historia general de Andalucía* (1869–71; *General History of Andalusia*), attributed anarchism to a deficit of "leading class" members who should direct social, economic, and cultural regeneration. A month later, in the article's continuation, he described anarchism as a "problem" caused by the ignorance of landless peasants in need of instruction.[26] In January 1917, Isidro de las Cagigas condemned anarchism as an internationalist movement that erased the patriotic sentiments fostered by *andalucismo*. Feeling Andalusian and embracing anarchist militancy were deemed mutually exclusive.[27]

Closing the gap between regionalist intellectuals and peasant masses hinged on embracing the legacy of al-Andalus as an identity-marker. Cagigas was the first to detach Andalusian regionalism from trivial folklore in *Bética* in 1914. He believed that the "Andalusian ideal" was at once the "collective sentiment of the people" and a spiritual model that "thinkers need to explain to the people," who were not conscious of it and could not unite as a nation.[28] This buried essence had been ruptured by the impositions of alien powers throughout history, and its reconstruction required substantial ethnographic and historiographical artifice. The "Oriental element, the Semitic element," Cagigas wrote, is the most "pure [*castizo*], typical [*propio*], and regional" in Spain's south. This claim is instantly qualified. Oriental traits commingled with "indigenous and Latin elements," barring any "crazy apology for the Orientalism of the Andalusian type."[29]

Also writing in *Bética*, Alejandro Guichot and Rafael Castejón concurred with Cagigas's claims while further qualifying them. Guichot equated the Andalusian ideal with the Arab culture of al-Andalus, particularly the Umayyad Caliphate of Cordoba (929–1031). "Has there been an Andalusian ideal?" he asked and then explained: "In my humble opinion, there was a potent Arab ideal, of vital plenitude: it was not a reform or renovation of a previous lifestyle, but a *replacement* of one life for another that differed completely from the one being replaced."[30] Castejón, a veterinary surgeon, Arabist, and founder of Cordoba's Andalusian Center in 1916, eschewed Guichot's pro-Arabic views to argue that Andalusia's "soul" is a composite, "half Christian, half Moorish." Rather than erasing all traces of the previous culture, the Arabs and Berbers who arrived in the peninsula from 711 on assimilated to the natives. Barely capable of "pitching a tent in the sandy deserts," they acquired their refinement from the peoples they had defeated. Al-Andalus, Castejón wrote, "was neither Arabic nor Spanish. It was exclusively Andalusian. The Arabs just brought in their baggage the rich presents of civilization that shined in the oriental schools at the time. And the Andalusian soul was responsible for immortalizing them."[31] This soul, a purely idealistic construct, was a free-floating category that was somehow above and beyond historical change and ethnic particularities. While Cagigas and Guichot make Moorishness the basis of Andalusian identity, Castejón's Andalusians are culturally, not racially, oriental, heirs of the scientific and philosophical discoveries of the Greeks of Byzantium, the Persians, the Indians, and the Chinese. The warlike, unsophisticated Arabs merely carried a body of knowledge in their saddlebags to Iberia in the eighth century.

Castejón's interpretation became dominant among regionalists after the publication of Blas Infante's *Ideal Andaluz* (*Andalusian Ideal*) in 1915, which originally appeared in installments in *Bética*. Infante's *Ideal*, which is still acknowledged as the definitive formulation of Andalusian identity, is infused by the author's love of the lost golden age of al-Andalus. Muslim culture plays a significant role in his central thesis, which claims that an egalitarian and modern Andalusia should be modeled on the Andalusi enlightenment. Despite his maurophilia, Infante was ambivalent about the place of Islam and Arabic ethnicity in Andalusian history and identity. In orientalizing Andalusia, he followed the strategy of early twentieth-century Spanish Arabists who Hispanicized the Moors. According to James Monroe, Simonet inspired others "to speak of *Spanish* Muslims," suggesting "that Islamic culture in al-Andalus had been primarily a Spanish phenomenon which owed little to Eastern importations."[32] Simonet saw Hispano-Arabic literature as a product of "our soil," made up of homegrown elements, and open to influences from "our nationality and culture" and "the Hispano-Christian race."[33] Ribera also minimized the Arab component of Andalusi civilization. He claimed that a small contingent of Arab invaders could impose their language, religion, and customs on a Hispanic community of non-Semitic racial stock just as a "small amount of red dye is enough to redden the waters of a pond." It did not mean "that the chemical composition of either the water or the dye is sensibly altered in the combination."[34]

In a similar vein, Infante maintains that the Andalusian-ness of the Andalusis was, like their Spanishness, free or almost free of Semitic traces and untouched by Muslim fanaticism and intolerance. His approach to Semitism in *Ideal* is highly ambiguous. On the one hand, he fights off the "stigma of the African origin" by characterizing Africa as the cradle of glorious civilizations, most notably al-Andalus;[35] "Semitic ascendancy," he declares, is Andalusia's "greatest emblem of glory."[36] On the other hand, he connects Semitic races with a degeneracy and decadence opposed to the original pre-711 ethnicity, which he deemed the true origin of al-Andalus. The Berber invasions in 1091 and 1145, respectively, brought a "deluge of Semitic blood,"[37] but Seville, Granada, and Cordoba, the "Athens of the West," remained cultural havens owing to an "Andalusian genius" bereft of "all kinds of relations with the Muslim family" that dissipated the "barbaric rudeness of the tribes recruited beyond the Atlas."[38] Though, strictly speaking, Berbers are not Semitic, Infante argues that in "Spain they were confused with the Arabs, and we should therefore consider them the result of a mixed race" with all the "stigmas" and "virtues" commonly attributed to Semites.[39] In any case, for Infante and for the Spanish Arabists, being an Arab in Spain is one thing; being a Hispano-Arab is quite another.

Infante draws on nineteenth-century orientalists from Germany and France to characterize the Arabs as an admirable ethnic group that is nonetheless inferior to both Europeans *and* a putative "Andalusian race." In the same paragraph he cites Friedrich Ratzel, a professor of geography and ethnography at the University of Leipzig, to assert that Arab civilization constitutes a "historical grandiosity"; Dominique Jean Larrey, chief surgeon of Napoleon's army in Egypt, to point out that Arabs are one of the "most beautiful anthropological types"; and French anthropologist Paul Topinard to celebrate Berber domestic virtues and strong moral sense. However, these positive attributes are the flip side of the "fanatic exclusivism" and "fatalism" that define North Africans as a whole.[40] While acknowledging hospitality, rich imagination, and passion for beauty, the patriot cannot hide his complicity with the ethnocentrism of his sources. In *Anthropo-Geographie* (1882), Ratzel found that all desert people are incapable of the material and cultural progress epitomized in western Europe.[41] Larrey was a distinguished savant who contributed to the *Description de L'Egypte*, a foundational text of French colonialism in the orient.[42] Topinard justified European racial superiority over Arabs and Berbers in such works as *Anthropology* (1890) with pseudoscientific arguments based on arbitrary physiological classifications and measurements.[43]

Infante's discussion of the Andalusian race differs in scale and methods, not intent, from these authors' claims. Al-Andalus was anything but an archetypal Arab society. Its first manifestation was the ancient civilization of Tartessos, believed to have developed around its fabulous capital on the Atlantic coast in southwestern Spain from the ninth to the sixth century B.C., when it was probably destroyed by Carthaginian invaders. An agrarian society that excelled in gold and silversmithing, Tartessos was influenced by explorers from Greece and Phoenicia, which encompassed modern-day Lebanon, Syria, and northern Israel. Hard evidence is scant, but some archeological discoveries suggest the existence of a distinctly Tartessian settlement independent of the Greeks and Phoenicians. The treasure of El Carambolo, a collection of golden diadems, necklaces, and pendants dating from the eighth century B.C. found just outside Seville in 1958, displays both Phoenician motifs and an unusual ornamental style that some archeologists consider indigenously Tartessian.[44] Tartessos is also identified as the mythical island of Atlantis. According to Plato's *Timaeus* and *Critias*, the source of all later versions of the myth, Atlantis was a splendid civilization located beyond the "Pillars of Heracles," which in antiquity designated the promontories that flank the Straits of Gibraltar.[45]

One of Infante's interlocutors, Elena Whishaw, popularized the notion that the original site of this lost world was present-day Andalusia.[46] She was an English archeologist who settled in Niebla (Huelva) in 1915 and published a compilation of her largely unfounded theories in *Atlantis in Andalucía* (1929). She opened the doors of her personal library to Infante, who must have consulted there the works outside his collection that he cites in *Ideal*, including Carlos Cañal's *Sevilla prehistórica* (1894; *Prehistoric Seville*), José Ramón Mélida's *Arquitectura dolménica íbera* (1914; *Iberian Dolmenic Architecture*), and Pelayo Quintero's *Necrópolis ante-romana de Cádiz* (1915; *Cadiz's Pre-Roman Necropolis*).[47] Information selectively culled from these sources led Infante to conclude that the "craniums of Andalusian troglodytes" and such other archeological remains as garments, utensils, weapons, and inscriptions prove the existence of "a completely original civilization that did not originate in Africa, Asia, or Europe, but in Andalusia."[48] He supports this assumption with references to the archeologist Manuel Gómez-Moreno's article "Arquitectura Tartesia" (1905; "Tartessian Architecture"), which maintained that the dolmens found in an ancient necropolis near the southwestern town of Antequera were a Tartessian creation. Since determining the source of these megalithic structures, reminiscent of the Neolithic citadel of Mycenae in Greece, was impossible, Gómez-Moreno speculated that Western civilization originated in Spain rather than Greece, when prehistoric "Oriental invaders" who would later "transform the West" arrived in the Iberian Peninsula."[49] In later publications intended for a general audience, the renowned archeologist mixed history and fantasy to connect these mysterious invaders with the mythical figure of Gargoris, predecessor of Geryon, first king of Tartessos according to legend.[50]

Infante supports this hypothesis in *Ideal*, giving it a regionalist inflection by locating Atlantis-Tartessos in Andalusia: "Andalusia is the fatherland of one of the world's oldest original civilizations and contributed powerfully to the destruction of the prestige of the Ancient Orient."[51] Citing Plato, he speculates that "human civilization" originated in this lost center, now "submerged in the unfathomable abyss of the ocean."[52] Like Gómez-Moreno and Whishaw, Infante blurs the boundaries between fantasy and reality to reverse the Hegelian conviction that "world history travels from east to west; for Europe is the absolute end of history, just as Asia is the beginning."[53] Years after the publication of *Ideal*, Infante was thrilled to see the German historian and archeologist Adolf Schulten propose that Tartessos was either the fabulous lost empire of Atlantis or at least a colony. To prove it, Schulten conducted costly excavations in southwestern Andalusia in 1924. Although his efforts were fruitless, his published research, particularly *Tartessos* (1924), was well received by Infante and his regionalist circle. In a collection of drafts written between 1930 and 1936 and published posthumously in 1984 as *Fundamentos de Andalucía* (*Foundations of Andalusia*), Infante developed the arguments of *Ideal*, conjoining ancient history, archeology, and myth to exalt the primeval Andalusian culture of Atlantis-Tartessos. In expanding his thesis, he "blesses" Schulten, who is "not Andalusian" and therefore provides impartial support for these regionalist postulates.[54]

The Tartessian ethnic and cultural legacy, which was oriental but not Arabic, protected al-Andalus from the vices of the Almohad and Almoravid invaders (1069–1259). Infante's deterministic argument maintains that the cultural splendor of the Kingdom of Granada during the *taifa* period, which began with the breakup of the Caliphate of Cordoba in 1031, proves that the North African tribesmen who entered the peninsula had no "ethnic influence" on the native population.[55] If religious tolerance, scientific progress, and artistic activity thrived before and after the fall of the Umayyad dynasty, it was mainly because the people of al-Andalus were "bad Muslims."[56] Eleventh-century Cordoba remained a haven for "*free thinkers*." The stunning city boasted dozens of academies and institutes of higher learning and numerous libraries, including the caliphal collection at the Merwan Palace, which held some 600,000 books.[57] Echoing Reinhart Dozy's *Histoire des Musulmans d'Espagne* (1861; *History of the Muslims of Spain*) and Ribera's *Bibliófilos y bibliotecas en la España musulmana* (1896; *Libraries and Book Lovers in Muslim Spain*), Infante attributed the Andalusi intellectual splendor and love of books to their non-Arabic roots and their lack of religious fanaticism.

Infante saw al-Andalus and, by extension, Andalusia as an in-between space that was neither eastern nor fully western. Wearing a Moorish mask became necessary both to demonstrate Spain's contributions to European civilization and to justify Andalusia's cultural and historical distinctiveness. Orientalizing Andalusia and Hispanicizing the Moors were twin strategies to incorporate Spain into mainstream European history through al-Andalus. The result is epistemologically rich: the Arabists altered the negative view of Spain's Afro-Moorish character by showing Europe's indebtedness to al-Andalus while simultaneously differentiating medieval Muslim "Spaniards" from Muslims elsewhere. In a similar fashion, Infante elevated Andalusia from a regressive backwater to the birthplace of world civilization. In both cases, the Semitic component of medieval Muslim Iberia is downplayed to stress the continuities between Greco-Roman, Islamic, and Western cultures in the Iberian Peninsula. In proposing the continuous presence of an orient in the Spanish and Andalusian selves, Infante and the Arabists constructed collective identities that challenged the east-west logic of orientalism but did not undermine its racism.

Flamenco Politics

Infante's mythical al-Andalus was the blueprint for his proposed social, economic, and political reforms. The region's past plenitude was embraced as a model to improve its dreary, socially fragmented present. This model also bridged the class gap between progressive bourgeois regionalists and peasants with anarchist sympathies. Infante was convinced that in embracing the Andalusi legacy, intellectual leaders and landless peasants would jointly reawaken a lost sense of collective pride. Since 1916, he had taught Andalusian history at the Andalusian Center in Seville. Free and open to the public, his lectures were hailed in the journal *Andalucía* as "the best medium to affirm our personality and stimulate our rebirth through the memory of our glorious past."[58] But this was a losing fight to gain the support of the working classes, who were either stranded in the remote countryside, without the means or time to attend history classes, or more exposed to bars than books in the capital. In turn-of-the-century Seville there were 160 taverns and only 8 bookstores, and 60 percent of the population was illiterate. No substantial changes in this dismal reality were experienced within the next twenty years.[59]

Despite poor immediate outcomes, Infante created a regionalist message that outlived him, reaching our days as the standard narrative of Andalusian history and identity. Based on *Ideal Andaluz*, the patriot's pedagogy focused on the Christian Reconquest as a cataclysmic event in Andalusian history. If early twentieth-century Andalusia was riddled with poverty, illiteracy, and political fraud, it was mainly because four centuries earlier rapacious Christians had chased the Muslims from their fertile lands. The end of al-Andalus was not merely a cultural disaster. In seizing enormous estates or latifundia, which remained largely uncultivated, the victorious invaders marginalized the Morisco population, who accepted Christian baptism to avoid exile. Deprived of property, they became landless peons or *jornaleros* at the mercy of their new masters. Ethnic conflicts prompted their forced expulsion from Spain between 1609 and 1614. Some remained by assimilating with marginal groups of outlaws, particularly the gypsies.[60] Their situation did not improve with the disentailment of the church's property in the nineteenth century; a few wealthy families, unwilling to partition their massive plots, retained control of the land.[61]

The Reconquest had eradicated not only al-Andalus, but also the "peasant middle class," which was considered to be the "collective conscience" that would "purify and strengthen the regional genius, the basis of a robust sentimental regionalism."[62] This belief was the foundation of regionalist politics in Andalusia during the Second Republic. *Andalucismo* had suffered a major setback with Primo de Rivera's shutdown of the Andalusian Centers in 1923, but they revived in 1931 under the aegis of the Liberalist Juntas of Andalusia and the Republican Revolutionary Federalist Coalition of Andalusia. Owing to the Coalition's radical proposals for land reform, distrust of the newly established republican system, and rumored involvement in a peasant uprising against the government at the Tablada military base in Seville, the party's candidacy to the Cortes in 1931 was discredited and failed. Infante was disheartened by the charges against his party, but he was convinced that his dream of Andalusian autonomy had never been closer to becoming reality. Fueled by anger and hope, he took only a few weeks to dash off *La verdad sobre el complot de Tablada y el Estado Libre de Andalucía* (1931; *The Truth about the Tablada Plot and the Free State of Andalusia*). This book refuted the accusations against the Coalition while nuancing Infante's ideas about Andalusia. In it he still sees al-Andalus as a beacon illuminating the dark ages and as a "model or archetype" for modern Andalusia. But now Andalusia's oriental roots set it apart from Europe as well as other Spanish communities, especially the Catalans.

Since its first stirrings in the Seville Arts Club and the journal *Bética* in the early twentieth century, *andalucismo* had kept a watchful eye on the Catalan Regionalist League, an autonomist conservative party founded in 1901. The interest was mutual. In spring 1913, the Catalanist leader Francesc Cambó, who was almost an idol for the *Bética* group, was invited to Seville to preside over the floral games, a festivity that mimicked the Catalan *jocs florals*, a medieval poetry competition reinstated in 1859 to reawaken patriotic feelings and restore Catalan as a literary language. In his inaugural address, Cambó repressed the anti-Andalusian feelings of his fellow Catalanists, including Pompeyo Gener and Joan Maragall (see chapter 2 below), and declared that the future of a unified Spain lay in the hands of a Catalan-Andalusian alliance.[63] According to a *Bética* contributor, his words were heard as a "spell" that magically "awakened the Andalusian regionalist ideal."[64]

However, by 1931 Infante felt that Catalanism was too "European," which was an understated way of saying too elitist and ethnocentric.[65] He was voicing a general sentiment that had been brewing at the Andalusian Centers before Primo de Rivera shut them down in 1923. Writing in the Centers' official venue, *Andalucía*, in October 1916, Vicente Galiana still felt that the incantatory "lesson of Catalonia" was a much-needed "incentive to shock [Spanish] regions out of lethargy,"[66] but a few months later the pseudonymous "Juan Sin Tierra," a frequent contributor, underlined important differences in "goals and procedures." While *andalucistas* were committed to freeing the "masses from economic slavery," the conservative Catalanists of the League seemed unmoved by the heartrending conditions of peasants and proletariat. "New organizations" in Catalonia, notably the *Mancomunitat* set up in 1914 as a confederation of the region's four provincial councils, merely replicated "old procedures" and defended the rights of the industrial bourgeoisie.[67]

Infante's *Verdad* picked up where Juan Sin Tierra left off, offering additional differences. If Enric Prat de la Riba, the *Mancomunitat*'s first president, declared that "Catalonia was for the Catalans," Infante embraced an "*antinationalist nationalism*," believing that "in Andalusia there are no foreigners."[68] While Prat de la Riba opposed a Europeanized Catalan identity to Spain's Semitic heritage and Andalusian *flamenquismo*, Infante saw in flamenco singing not a debased spectacle, but a pure "feeling" that captured Andalusia's rich mixture of eastern and western influences, which was superior, he thought, to European culture.[69]

Popular flamenco songs of love, death, and suffering constituted both a defining regional marker and a link between the post-Reconquest Muslim diaspora and the exploited Andalusian peasantry. For Infante, the grief-stricken protests of the landless *jornalero* echoed the doleful cries of exiled Moors and oppressed Moriscos, and were the origin of *cante jondo* or "deep song." He believed that flamenco's cadences and intonations, which had reverberated in Andalusia for centuries, would be "more accurate than any electoral law in finding the true representatives of the Andalusian people."[70] This Romantic notion is the central argument of *Orígenes de lo flamenco y secreto del cante jondo* (*The Origins of Flamenco and the Secret about Deep Song*), an unfinished manuscript he composed between the late 1920s and early 1930s, which was edited and published by Manuel Barrios in 1980.

The origin and meaning of flamenco were the source of heated debate in the early twentieth century. Theories were formulated by musicians and musicologists as well as social reformers, poets, and even anarchists.[71] As a flamenco enthusiast, Infante was well aware of them. He owned an impressive collection of flamenco records and a good number of studies, including Francisco Rodríguez Marín's *La copla: Bosquejo de un estudio folklórico* (1910; *Flamenco Song: An Outline of a Folkloric Study*), Manuel de Falla's *El cante jondo: Cante primitivo andaluz* (1922; *Deep Song: Primitive Andalusian Song*), and Eduardo Martínez del Portillo's *Cante Jondo* (1929; *Deep Song*). His sources on flamenco extended beyond these titles, and were hidden in unlikely places. His library contained a sizeable collection of Arabist scholarship, including studies by Simonet, González Palencia, and Cagigas, some issues of the journal *Al-Andalus*, and about a dozen books by Asín Palacios and Julián Ribera, including *Historia de la música árabe medieval y su influencia en la española* (1927; *Music in Ancient Arabia and Spain*), *Dante y el Islam* (1927; *Dante and Islam*), and *El Islam cristianizado* (1931; *Christianized Islam*).[72] Infante was particularly drawn to Ribera's work, which constitutes a fundamental yet ignored source for his interpretation of flamenco.[73]

At the Museum of Andalusian Autonomy in Coria del Río, which houses Infante's archive, I had the chance to confirm that Ribera's works, particularly those dealing with Arabic music, are underlined and annotated. Infante's marginalia on them show that he took particular note of the Arabist's efforts to link classical tradition, Arabic culture, and Spanish civilization. In Asín Palacios's introduction to Ribera's *Disertaciones y opúsculos* (1928), Infante underlined a sentence that summarizes Ribera's contributions to Arabic studies and Spanish historiography:

> Ribera, in restoring medieval music in all the artistic perfection found in modern music (tonality, harmony, expression), re-establishes historical continuity in this cultural aspect, demonstrating that in music, and in the other fine arts and philosophical and exact sciences, the Arabs, especially the Spanish Arabs, were the heirs of the classical culture that they transmitted to medieval Europe. There are no

> breaks in this historical trajectory: Byzantium and Persia inherited their culture from Greece; then Islam fused classical culture with the cultures of the Far East, enriched it, and transmitted it to Spanish Islam, which impregnated it with indigenous elements and handed it over to medieval Europe, which owes our brilliant artistic culture more than is commonly thought.[74]

Asín Palacios reiterates this point by citing an article by the Yale professor of Arabic D. B. MacDonald in the October 1927 *American Historical Review*:

> It is an outstanding characteristic of the modern Spanish historical school that it frankly recognizes the importance of Arabic studies for the understanding of the Spanish civilization in its widest aspects—social, literary, theological, legal—and does not regard the Moslem dominance in Spain, with its influences, as a period to be ignored or to be got rid of as quickly as possible. It thus accepts the fact that the Spanish peninsula was one of the bridges between Islam and Christendom and sees the whole of medieval Europe as affected by the multifarious influences which passed over that bridge.[75]

Three intense pink pencil strokes beside this passage in Infante's copy denote his deep enthusiasm and wholehearted agreement with this statement. It is not hard to imagine the mixture of recognition and validation he must have felt when reading this and other sections of Ribera's anthology. His underlining, scribbling, and scrawling draw a road map of affinities. Take Ribera's contention that the "fanatic" rule of the Almoravids, "unintelligent" and "rude" "African barbarians," could not extinguish a native population of "clever Europeans who were daringly speculative, highly enlightened, and knowledgeable about all the arts of the most refined civilization."[76] Or his belief that none of the Umayyad rulers were born to "aristocratic Arab women," since their Arabic ancestors preferred to marry "blonde women," often slaves from Galicia and the Basque Country. In the margin, Infante added: "there are no references to Andalusian slaves" in Ribera's source (Ibn Hazm's *The Ring of the Dove*), implying that the arrival of the Moors in 711 was not an invasion but a process of peaceful assimilation with the native "Andalusian" population, a thesis he outlined in *Ideal Andaluz* and developed in *La verdad sobre el complot de Tablada*.

What Infante must have found most compelling in Ribera's work is his glorification of the artistic accomplishments of those he consistently designates "Andalusian Moslems" or simply "Andalusians." Ribera insisted that the Andalusis did not only preserve Arabic musical and literary traditions, inherited from Persia and Byzantium; they also transformed and renovated them in new strophic and melodic forms that spread all over the Iberian Peninsula, Europe, and North Africa. He built on the Arabist theory of the Jesuit scholar Juan de Andrés (1740–1817), who claimed that the roots of European literature were found in the princely courts of Islamic Spain. Following Andrés, Ribera tracked the influence of medieval Andalusian art, epitomized by the courtly poet Ibn Quzman (d. 1160), through Christian Spanish songbooks or *cancioneros*, the rhymes of Provençal and German minstrels, and African and oriental songs composed as far away as Baghdad.[77] Ribera's musical theory cut two ways: if Europe owed a "debt of gratitude to the Andalusian Moors," so did present-day Spaniards. A full understanding of twentieth-century Spain was impossible without realizing that regional folk-music traditions and the collective identities they express "all came from a common origin, created in a truly Spanish system, the product of Andalusian genius."[78]

Nonetheless, according to Infante, Ribera's work needed further refinement. "It is regrettable," he wrote in *Orígenes de lo flamenco*, "that Mr. Ribera, who along with his disciples and other European Orientalists has done so much for the revival of what they call the *marvelous* culture of al-Andalus, has not applied his exceptional skills to carefully considering the origins or causes [of flamenco] instead of paying very limited attention to this issue."[79] Ribera dedicated no more than a few passing comments to the connections between medieval Andalusi melodies and deep song. He was convinced that Christian invaders did not silence Moorish musicians, and that the Moriscos continued to play Muslim zithers and flutes, infusing their traditional music with doleful tones "obviously suited to their new situation as a subject race."[80] Their "melancholy and loneliness and bitterness" permeated "many medieval Spanish songs in the *Cancionero de Palacio* and also many sad modern Andalusian songs, especially the *soleares*," a basic form of flamenco from which other types, or *palos*, derived.[81] Infante extended Ribera's Morisco hypothesis in a new direction, conceiving a bond between runaway medieval Moors and twentieth-century *jornaleros*.

For Infante, flamenco was both a musical form and an ethnographic and sociological category. *Lo flamenco* or "flamenco-ness"—rather than simply "flamenco"—connects an eternal cultural essence (the "Andalusian genius") to historical conditions widely separated in time but very close in substance: the predicament of the Morisco population under Christian rule from the sixteenth century on and the dreadful conditions of the dispossessed peasantry in Andalusia during the early twentieth century. Beyond Ribera's scant references to flamenco, Infante found little support for his thesis. Antonio Machado y Álvarez, a pioneering voice on the subject, classified a substantial corpus of songs and melodies by theme in *Folklore Andaluz* (1881) but did not clarify what Infante calls their "objective determining factors." Some, like Francisco Rodríguez Marín, were misguided by fanciful flights; in *El alma de Andalucía en sus mejores coplas amorosas* (1929; *The Soul of Andalusia in Its Best Love Songs*), he claimed that the word *flamenco* originated from the resemblance between flamingos (*flamenco* in Spanish) and the attire and poses of the aristocratic patrons and gypsy performers at drunken dancing and singing parties or *juergas*.[82] Influenced by the work of his teacher Felipe Pedrell, the Andalusian composer Manuel de Falla did stress flamenco's oriental nature and its debts to the gypsies, Arabs, and Moriscos. Likewise, Estébanez Calderón noticed the kinship between flamenco songs or *coplas* and North African songs in *Escenas Andaluzas* (1846; *Andalusian Scenes*). But none of them fully answered Infante's questions: "When was flamenco's first manifestation? Why did it come into existence? How did it reveal itself?"[83]

Infante encapsulated the "when," "why," and "how" in an elegant yet suspicious etymological interpretation. Finding historical truths in philological change, he posited the term *fellah mencus* (which he spells "felah-mengu")—"expelled or runaway farmer" in Arabic—as the lexical origin of the Spanish word *flamenco*.[84] This etymology has subsequently been discredited since the word *mencus* does not exist in classical Arabic. "Exiled" is *manfi* or *mankus*; and a word that is close phonetically, *manqus*, means "relapsing patient or ill person."[85] In any case, Infante's solution to the etymological riddle raises a greater mystery: the origin and development of a timeless Andalusian identity. Rooted in Tartessos and the Andalusi golden age, Andalusian identity became inextricable from flamenco after 1609, when the persecuted Moriscos, or *fellah mencus*, who decided to remain in the peninsula were forced to hide from authorities by mixing with the Spanish underclass, notably the gypsies. As new members of *gitano* bands, these runaway peasants expressed their longing and loss in a variation of the Andalusian choral folk songs studied by Ribera. It indicated, Infante wrote, "a social commotion that was both dislocating and atomizing, disruptive of the social group whose mode of expression it was."[86] This creative process had to remain clandestine for fear of expulsion during what Infante called elsewhere the "*felahmenca* era" spanning the sixteenth to eighteenth centuries.[87] Toward the end of the eighteenth century, flamenco became increasingly visible thanks to the Spanish nobility's interest in gypsy music, dance, and mannerisms. As deep song emerged from anonymity, its true essence degenerated in the music hall, tavern, and brothel. Infante's goal was to restore it to its original role, expressing the tragic fate of an eternally Andalusian Moorish farmer.

This interpretation places the archetypal Andalusian in the indistinct zone between ethnicity and class-consciousness. According to Timothy Mitchell, Infante's "basic procedure" in outlining his thesis was "to project egalitarian sentiments onto old ethnic and pseudoethnic lyrics." His rereading of "ethnicity as class struggle" allowed him to "enlist deep song in the service of social revolution," a path followed by other flamencologists such as Rafael Cansinos Assens and the Caba brothers.[88] Mitchell's interpretation is accurate, but it tells only half the story. Flamenco undergirded *andalucismo*'s egalitarian social program and identity politics, but it also stratified the working masses and the intellectual elite. Flamenco, the idiom of the outcast, is a lingua franca available to all Andalusians, though its interpretation requires a gifted singer, or *cantaó*. Like the poet, legislator, and, priest, the *cantaó* shapes, in Infante's words, "formless sensibility" into articulate expression, conveying the feelings of "many silent voices."[89] Popular rather than plebeian, flamenco singing demands selection and refinement; like soccer and bullfighting, it is for the people but not by the people. While many can appreciate a stirring *copla*, an adroit *faena*, or a well-coordinated *jugada*, only a select few possess "the skills and conditions" necessary to become a flamenco composer, a bullfighter, or a professional soccer player.[90]

Infante and his fellow *andalucistas* rendered flamenco as a paradigm of the social order they sponsored: an egalitarian community in which the artistic or intellectual leader retains interpretative mastery over a vastly varied social and historical reality. Like the *cantaó*, the political representative is both curator of the community's past and creator of class consciousness. Through flamenco's putative Moorish roots, Infante conflates Andalusia and al-Andalus in an ahistorical establishment of the region's defining difference. Centuries of complex encounters, internal dissent, and historical change are tidily subsumed into a common identity by which politicians can speak for laborers. This transformation of history and class into aspects of a totalizing identity brings *andalucismo* and *arabismo* ideologically close to each other. Infante's political writings and the erudite investigations of Ribera and Asín significantly differ on Iberian Moorishness, but a basic ambivalence toward the "orient within" remains constant. Wavering between inclusion and rejection, they all adduce the figures of the "Spanish" and "Andalusian" Muslim, the Morisco, and the *fellah mencus* to establish a social, cultural, and symbolic continuity between al-Andalus, Andalusia, and Spain that disavows or at the very least minimizes Islamic influences. This messy play of identification with, and difference from, the Moor cuts across southern politics, national cultural reform programs, and historiographical revisions of Spain's past. It also framed *andalucismo*'s engagement with colonialism in Africa.

Andalusia beyond Andalusia: Pan-Andalusianism and the Question of Morocco

In pre–Civil War Spain the term *andalucismo* designated not only a regionalist movement. Early definitions looked toward expansion into Africa. From its initial formulation in Cagigas's *Bética* articles, *andalucismo* was intertwined with *africanismo*. Cagigas's contribution to colonialist discourse during the 1910s cannot be separated from his key role in the configuration of Andalusian regionalism. In 1914, he stated that the "Semitic element" which defined the "Andalusian type" was also the nexus between Andalusians and Moroccans.[91] Rather than simply positing blood brotherhood, he developed a biological conception of geography. The true border of Andalusia, he wrote, is in the north of Africa, since shared topographical features spark strong moral and cultural similarities. In practical terms, this kinship vindicates Andalusia's leadership of Spain's colonial involvement in the Maghreb: "Andalusia and its Andalusians are called upon by historical reasons, geographical reasons, and racial affinities to honor Queen Isabella's testament."[92] Cagigas's words recall Simonet's invocation of the Catholic queen in 1859 and Joaquín Costa's conviction that Spain and Morocco are two halves of the same geographical entity and the home of the "Ibero-Berber" race.[93] Originally delivered at an event organized by the Spanish Society of Africanists and Colonialists in Madrid in March 1884, Costa's remarks would shape and influence Africanist discourse well into the twentieth century.[94] Cagigas's text certainly reverberates with Costa's ideas, but his goal was not so much to support Spain's colonialist policies as to enlarge an Andalusian imagined community.

In later publications, Cagigas expanded his theories on geography and race, further connecting them to the mission and goals of *andalucismo*. In 1916, he claimed that Andalusia and Morocco originally formed an island separated from the Iberian Peninsula and Africa by two straits connecting the Atlantic and the Mediterranean.[95] He cited the noted German geographer Theobald Fisher (1846–1910) but did not mean to "demarcate the materiality of a chunk of land, but the natural community that it animates under the same ideal."[96] A year later, he found support for his pseudoscientific arguments from the anthropologist Federico Olóriz, who used skull measurements to posit a hybrid Spanish race while defending its European, rather than African, origin. Olóriz noted "geographic and historical reasons to believe that there is affinity between the African and European populations gathered around the Strait and that they share a similar cephalic index," but his findings revealed that this index differs greatly between Andalusians, on the one hand, and Arabs and Berbers, on the other. He concluded that the population of southern Spain came "from the interior" and was not "imported from the African coast."[97] Reading Olóriz selectively, Cagigas emphasized ethnic hybridity and defined Andalusians as a "border people, a 'bridge people,'" a special trait that made them the answer to the Moroccan question. Their hybridity meant concatenation, not contamination. Spanish intervention in Moroccan territory was an embrace of distant cousins, not an alien invasion. Where others saw a colonial problem, Cagigas saw "a prolongation of our region." In keeping with Infante's class-oriented reading of ethnicity, he singled out the Andalusian day laborer as the perfect candidate to colonize Spanish Morocco.[98] Unwittingly perhaps, he does not consider the inverse trajectory, African immigration to Spain, a detail that subtly belies his convivial message.

Against Cagigas's class-oriented interpretation, conservative writers counterposed a hierarchical understanding of Hispano-Arabic relations that did not always harmonize with calls for fraternal unity across the Mediterranean.

Left-wing and right-wing *andalucistas* shared the idea that Andalusia and Morocco constituted a historical, cultural, and even racial unit, but they assessed it differently. José Zurita y Calafat's "El problema de las alianzas" ("The Problem of the Alliances"), published in *Bética* in March and April 1915, was the first sustained attempt to write *andalucismo* into traditionalist accounts of Spanish history that equate Catholic faith with national identity. Zurita y Calafat, a staunch defender of landowning interests in the rural south, invokes Hispano-Moroccan ties to discourage Spaniards from forming international alliances with the rival colonial powers France and Britain. Readers are reminded that historically, the French and British seriously damaged Spain's international reputation and hindered its expansion in Africa. Zurita draws heavily on the writings of the Jesuit priest Jaime Balmes, a nineteenth-century Catholic crusader against secularism, anarchism, and socialism, to suggest that Spain's destiny as an imperial power will be best served by severing ties with nations driven by materialistic rather than spiritual goals. Spanish colonialism marks the rebirth of a spiritual brotherhood between Africa and Spain: "Moroccan life and Spanish life, in history and geography, are two parallel lives" bound by common religious ideals. However contradictory, Spain's divine mission to maintain the "integrity of faith" abroad relates to the Reconquest, a "noble enterprise" shared by Portugal, Spain's only genuine ally.[99] Zurita's international policy was a clumsy attempt to reconcile the myth of pan-Andalusian brotherhood with conservative views that saw the Christian fight against Islam during the Middle Ages as the forge of the nation.

Subsequent conservative definitions of *andalucismo* labored to provide more convincing resolutions to the conflict between fraternal kinship and religious difference. Unexpectedly, some came from Cagigas. During the Primo de Rivera dictatorship (1923–30), Infante suspended his political activity and retreated to the southwestern fishing village of Isla Cristina to work as the local notary. Cagigas remained in touch with him, but permanently abandoned his regionalist fervor and devoted himself to colonial diplomacy. By 1923 he was a highly ranked official in Spanish Morocco and went on to reconstruct the small northwestern town of El-Ksar el Kebir (Alcazarquivir in Spanish), a project that brought him institutional recognition and a coveted post as consul in Tétouan in 1929. With professional success came a noticeable change in his writing. He began publishing on urban projects and other Africanist matters in *Unión Patriótica* (*Patriotic Union*), the official magazine of the eponymous right-wing, ultra-Catholic organization that supported the Primo dictatorship. Whenever Cagigas dealt with Muslim Iberia, he omitted nationalist and socialist references to political *andalucismo*, focusing instead on strictly philological and historical topics such as the etymological origin of the term "al-Andalus," Hispano-Arabic coins, and the survival of Christianity after 711 in Mozarabic communities across the peninsula, "stretching the evidence as far as it would go in an attempt to prove that the Christians of al-Andalus continued to oppose the idea of peaceful co-existence with Islam."[100]

Cagigas's new scholarly focus perfectly suited Primo de Rivera's promotion of Catholicism as the essential basis of national identity, which later was continued by Franco's regime.[101] Some *africanistas* took it as a call to cut the fraternal bonds that seemed to connect Spain and the Muslim world through al-Andalus and Morocco. In 1928, Humberto Cortacero Henares, who would join the Francisco Franco Institute for Hispano-Arabic Research after the Civil War, firmly declared in the journal *África* that the "Andalusian soul is not Arabic." Andalusia's personality emerged "under Roman rule, seven centuries before the Arabs arrived in our peninsula." The word "our" here means not-Muslim. Al-Andalus is described as a brilliant civilization during the Dark Ages, but also as an "exotic flower" on Spanish soil.[102] Supporting the traditionalist equation of Spanishness with Catholicism, Cortacero attributed the "persistence of the national spirit" from 711 to 1492 to the Christian Mozarabs. Persistence was rewarded with the discovery and colonization of the New World, but only when Castile fully absorbed Andalusia in 1492 and cast out "that alien element that hindered peninsular unity for eight centuries." Therefore, to speak of "Arabic *andalucismo*" in the context of present-day Africanism has no meaning for Cortacero. Spain's presence in Morocco is not a revival of al-Andalus, which was neither primarily Arabic nor exclusively Andalusian. Now, as then, Christian Spaniards must "incorporate Muslim people into the rhythm of culture and progress," a euphemism for colonization, exploitation, and discrimination against Islam.[103]

Cortacero's analysis was a direct response to Rodolfo Gil Benumeya's reappraisal of *andalucismo*. A prominent Africanist intellectual during the Primo de Rivera and Franco dictatorships, Gil Benumeya (born Rodolfo Gil Torres) considered Andalusia's Arabic past to be an asset rather than a threat to national values and goals. From the mid-1920s, he articulated his views in countless articles published in magazines such as *África*, *Revista Hispano-Africana*, and *Revista de la Raza* (*Review of the Race*) and in a long list of books, including *Mediodía: Introducción a la historia andaluza* (1929; *Noon: Introduction to Andalusian History*), *Ni Oriente, ni Occidente: El universo visto desde el Albayzín* (1930?; *Neither Orient nor Occident: The Universe as Seen from the Albayzín*), *Relaciones y nexos de la Iglesia Católica con el mundo árabe* (1947; *Relations and Ties between the Catholic Church and the Arab World*), *Hispanidad y arabidad* (1952; *Hispanicity and Arabicity*), *Andalucismo africano* (1953; *African Andalucismo*), and *España dentro de lo árabe* (1964; *Spain within the Arab World*).[104] Despite his long and productive career, his *andalucista* ideas attained final form early on, in the numerous articles he published in *África* during the 1920s.[105] He combined Infante's analysis of Andalusian history and identity with his mentor Asín Palacios's scholarly investigations into the Christian roots of Islam. Rejecting the regionalist and socialist connotations of *andalucismo*, he aligned it with traditionalist views of national identity.

At face value, Gil Benumeya's thought bears striking resemblances to Infante's. They both put the Andalusi legacy at the heart of Spain and believed that present-day Andalusia acquired its "true personality" during the Islamic period.[106] They also extended Andalusia's border into the Maghreb. During a 1924 trip to the tomb of an exiled Andalusi king in the village of Aghmat in southern Morocco, Infante was struck by numerous cultural and ethnic affinities between Moroccans and Andalusians. Feeling at home in a foreign land, he became convinced that traces of the lost world of al-Andalus were to be found in the music, architecture, and character of the inhabitants of the neighboring country. Although he echoed the *africanista* rhetoric of brotherhood, his goal was not to repair Spain's bruised international image, but to reunite peninsular Andalusians with the descendants of exiled Andalusis who were settled from Tangiers to Damascus.[107] Like Infante, Gil Benumeya imagined a transnational community covering Spain, the Maghreb, and the Mediterranean Levant, and united by the legacy of al-Andalus. Andalusia and Morocco, the core of what he calls the lands of Mediodía (Noon), converge in a

> geographic and spiritual modality that partakes in the particular tendencies of both territories [Andalusia and Morocco] and possesses a very singular Asian character that distinguishes it from what is purely Castilian and Kabylian [Berber]. The Andalusian soul . . . created in the past a brilliant culture that was destroyed by competing fanaticisms (a Gothic one to the north and a typically African one to the south) and whose scattered remains on the shores of the Straits of Gibraltar urgently demand concentration on a few chosen sites to prepare the way for the vast cultural renaissance of the Semitic western civilization that was produced in Andalusia.[108]

Finally, both Infante and Gil Benumeya considered Andalusian civilization superior to Eastern cultures. While the Andalusian race resisted the influence of the barbaric Almoravids and Almohads, Mediodía is perched between a decaying West and the orient, defined as the "past, the remote reverie of races lost in a time out of history."[109]

Gil Benumeya's debt to Infante persisted after August 2, 1936, when Francoist troops assassinated the latter near the town of Carmona, about twenty-five miles outside of Seville. Gil Benumeya was careful not to mention the regionalist martyr by name in works such as *Marruecos andaluz* (1942; *Andalusian Morocco*) and *Andalucismo africano* (1953).[110] This nominal omission is emblematic of the deeper ideological silencing of Infante's *andalucismo*, which was incompatible with Francoist authoritarianism. In an act of ideological contortion, *Marruecos andaluz* drew an analogy between Andalusian regionalists and the Moroccan troops Franco led during the Civil

War: both groups did the "same thing"; that is, they pulled Spain away from Europe's hegemonic grip by "bringing the Moors to defend the name of God and the continuity of the Spanish race."[111] Eventually, Gil Benumeya failed to defend the indefensible and declared with relief that Infante's *andalucismo* "disappeared at last due to the general march of Spain, which followed other paths and solutions."[112]

Gil Benumeya contributed in no small measure to this disappearance. Rather than planting the seeds of Infante's thought, he carefully separated the grain of Hispano-Arab unity from the chaff of liberal politics. He retained the old name, *andalucismo*, while grafting new, often antithetical, meanings onto it.[113] He emptied the al-Andalus myth of its political connotations and turned it into a spiritual realm that he defined against "false regionalist, nationalist, or communist predications."[114] Gil Benumeya proclaimed with open hostility that "*andalucismo* is not and must not be an infamous regionalism that is bad for Spain and al-Andalus. No! *Andalucismo* is a culture."[115] This culture justified Spain's colonial presence in Morocco but opposed Infante's proposals for political decentralization.

Infante translated the cultural affinities he experienced during his 1924 trip to Aghmat into the language of federalism. In *La verdad sobre el complot de Tablada* (1931) he requested that the Spanish government delegate political control of the Moroccan Protectorate to Andalusia; if it were to be truly protected, it would have to join Andalusia as an "autonomous federal state."[116] In contrast, Gil Benumeya, writing in *África* in 1928, stated: "All true Protectorates are moral Protectorates. Knowing the Muslim soul is the foundation of our protection."[117] Knowledge becomes assimilation, for "the eternal ideal of Semitism," the key to the Muslim soul, is, according to Gil Benumeya, essentially identical to the Christian faith. This Semitic ideal is a vague concept often used interchangeably with Islamic *baraka*, the God-given power to attain mystical insights about the world, and it is the meeting point of "Christian Semites, Muslims, and Sephardic Jews" hailing from Andalusia and "Tangiers to the Holy Land of Palestine, from Catholic Mount Lebanon to Muslim Mecca."[118] This spiritual community opposes not only "the communist threat" of Berber rebels in Spanish Morocco but also the working-class orientation of Infante's *andalucismo*.[119] What united Andalusians and the Andalusi diaspora in Morocco for Gil Benumeya was a strong anti-materialist tendency, not cultural ties that, in Infante's mind, translated too easily as leftist ideology.

Infante underlined the similarities between flamenco and the Moroccan popular music he heard during his 1924 sojourn. When he listened to the musical suites known as *nubat* in a courtyard in Rabat, he immediately recognized the nostalgic longing for the homeland of the displaced Andalusian *fellah mencus*, the predecessors of twentieth-century *jornaleros*.[120] Where Infante hears the eternal cry of the dispossessed, Gil Benumeya hears a vague "Andalusian sadness." To Gil Benumeya, flamenco is a mystical outpouring, not a lament for material loss.[121] "There is a special Andalusian sadness," he wrote in 1929, "a scorched sadness of Bedouin nostalgia; it is the sadness of 'cante hondo'; of love . . . of the tragic optimism that is the will to want to believe. This is the 'deep' and authentic Andalusia, the land where Semitism has yielded its most complete and magnificent expression."[122]

This expression often reads like fascist apology. [123] For Gil Benumeya, the orient stands for the "masses" and "unruly crowds" prone to communist insurrection, and the occident, the cradle of parliamentary democracy, is dismissed as a "bunch of wills that come and go." In contrast, Semitism is "hierarchy, internal discipline," and the trait of "a charismatic conqueror."[124] Wedged between the oriental red threat and Western degeneration, this emphasis on faith over intellect and body resonates with the anti-materialist authoritarianism of Primo de Rivera's and Franco's reactionary regimes. Not coincidentally, the ideal denizen of Mediodía resembles a devout legionnaire rather than a rebellious peasant: a "monotheistic, disciplined man of ardent passion contained by the rigid barriers of moral law." More suited to the cassock and the combat helmet than the hammer and sickle, this figure mirrors the male gender model in the Primo military dictatorship and anticipates that of the post–Civil War years: the warrior-monk who embodies both military values and strong religiosity.

Tomás García Figueras, a decorated officer of the Riffian War (1921–26) and Franco's right hand in Morocco after 1936, concurred. In a prosaic tone more fitting to his field experience than Gil Benumeya's lofty rhetoric, he finds strong proof of Benumeya's pan-Andalusianism not in *baraka*, but in two eggs. In the midst of a difficult pacification process in barren, remote lands among unfriendly natives, he is pleasantly surprised when rebel leaders refer to his telegraphist, "a Christian who is an Andalusian," as a "brother" to whom "a pair of eggs," a precious gift amid the food shortage on the battlefield, are due. Almost bathetically, the eggs betoken the author's faith in Morocco's future "under the tutelage of Spain, mother of nations."[125]

In making Andalusian identity and Hispano-Arab fraternity compatible with antiliberal ideology and right-wing Catholicism, Gil Benumeya followed his teacher, Miguel Asín Palacios. Asín Palacios's scholarship on the crossover between Islam and Christianity was essentially a contribution to conservative patriotism. Significantly, Marcelino Menéndez Pelayo—a champion of militant Catholicism who stated that Spain achieved true splendor only when it acted as "evangelizer of half of the world" and "the hammer of heresies"[126]—fervently encouraged young Asín's doctoral work on the Persian theologian al-Ghazali. Menéndez Pelayo wrote the prologue to the published dissertation, and in a 1901 letter, Asín asked him to highlight its relevance for "the history of Spanish philosophy."[127] Menéndez Pelayo complied, stating that the book's value resided in its successful treatment of "the capital issue of [al-Ghazali's] influence on the philosophy of the Spanish Arabs, who revered this Persian doctor as a master, as well as his influence on medieval

Christian philosophy, to which his thought arrived through Spain."[128] Asín's subsequent studies further illuminated what he saw as an unbroken continuity: Greek philosophy, Christian mysticism, and Islam in medieval Spain, which, he claimed, was a real yet illegitimate son of Christian civilization.[129] As James Monroe points out, Asín's thesis that Islam is a passive recipient of influences coming mainly from Christianity "is dangerous insofar as it creates a one-sided picture and denies the possibility of there being a Muslim spirituality independent of that of other religions."[130] This was also a shrewd move on Asín's part to turn an ancestral enemy into a valuable ally.

Establishing links between *arabismo*, *africanismo*, and *andalucismo*, Gil Benumeya hitched Asín's ahistorical understanding of Islamic-Christian connections to his colonialist doctrine. To fulfill their civilizing mission in Morocco, he contended, Spaniards must always keep in mind a number of interrelated maxims: first, Islam is not an "exotic religion hostile to Christianity"; second, jihad, or holy war, is only launched against irreligious men, that is, "the pagan, the atheist, the communist, the Confucian, etc.," not fellow Christians;[131] and third, until the late nineteenth century, "nobody said 'Spaniards and Moors,' but *Moors and Christians*. Different opinions within the same family." No longer the antithesis of Catholic Spain, "Islam is," in Gil Benumeya's words, "a valuable testimony to our past that deserves respect and scholarly attention, following the example of the erudite academic and priest Mr. Miguel Asín, an indefatigable researcher and friend of Hispano-Arabic science."[132] Asín remained a reference of choice in Gil Benumeya's later publications, including *Hispanidad y Arabidad* and *España y el mundo árabe* (*Spain and the Arab World*).

If Gil Benumeya's perception of Islam was shaped by Asín's investigations, Asín took a page out of his disciple's book to justify Moorish support for the 1936 Nationalist uprising. His article "¿Por qué lucharon a nuestro lado los musulmanes marroquíes?" (1940; "Why Did the Moroccan Muslims Fought on Our Side?") reinforced the bonds between the antiliberal, anti-leftist Franco regime and the idea of pan-Andalusian fraternity. Friends rather than foes, Muslims and Christians are godly people who should join forces to defeat "dogs without religion." In Asín's opinion, which sharply contradicts Infante's, the legacy of al-Andalus left a "subconscious sediment" that predisposes Spaniards and Moroccans not to long for the halcyon days before the Christian Reconquest but to continue that crusade in the present by fighting atheist Marxism.[133] Patriotic responsibility shifted from defending Christianity against Islam to suppressing the anti-Spanish red scare. "What had been the external Other," historian Sebastian Balfour explains, "was mobilized against the internal other," the leftist rebel.[134]

This formula summarized nationalist uses of religion in Morocco during the Civil War. Al-Andalus stood for both a shared historical past and a spiritual model that confirmed Spain's superior status in the Hispano Moroccan broth erhood. Colonial administrators, following the Arabists, saw contemporary

Islam as a degradation of Spanish Islam, which Asín characterized as a Christianized Islam. To be good Muslims, Moroccans must embrace the Andalusi legacy and greet Spanish leadership with enthusiasm. This message justified and promoted military collaboration against the Second Republic, which was portrayed as a godless, anti-Islamic regime. Religious propaganda was supplemented with boatloads of complimentary Spanish lambs for Ramadan, promises of material wealth for conscripts, state-sponsored pilgrimages to Mecca from 1937 to 1939, speculations on the possible return of Islam to Andalusia, and even the Islamization of Franco; rumored to have converted to Islam, he was idealized as a hero who was protected against bullets by divine *baraka*.[135]

Besides wartime concerns and practices, Asín Palacios and Gil Benumeya set the tone for the development of Arabic studies and Africanist thought during the Franco dictatorship. After 1939 "the decision to start from scratch or from the purest right" guaranteed the survival of Arabist conservatism.[136] Although Asín and his teacher Julián Ribera had joined the Junta de Ampliación de Estudios and the Center of Historical Studies, their presence at these liberal institutions was short-lived. Quite suddenly, in 1916, Asín and Ribera withdrew from their posts. While the apparent cause of their resignation was a personal conflict between Asín and José Castillejo Duarte, the JAE's secretary, the truth is that both were out of their ideological element at the Center. Their sympathies for Catholicism and conservative politics did not mesh with the liberal, anti-Catholic project to reform the Spanish educational system along liberal and secular lines.[137] Years later, Asín's disciple Ángel González Palencia denounced the Center's "sectarian partiality" and its animosity toward "rightist" intellectuals Ribera and Asín.[138] The right-wing tendency of Arabist scholarship obliterated regionalist interpretations of Spain's presence in Africa after Franco's victory. The official decree that created the Board for Research and High Culture in Morocco in 1941 stated that the foundation of a "glorious revival of Hispano-Arabic culture" would not be an independent Andalusia within a federalized nation-state, as Infante had wished, but a monolithic, centralized Spain, "the true Spain ruled by its chieftain, Franco, the friend of the Muslims."[139]

Broadly understood as a historiographical, political, and cultural field of inquiry into the place of Muslim Iberia in modern Spain, Spanish orientalism reshaped regional and national identities, redefined collective ideas about the past, and shaped a complex set of colonial and class relations during the early twentieth century. As such, it was the meeting point of *arabismo*, *andalucismo*, and *africanismo*. Often studied in isolation, these enmeshed discourses share a common terminology and approach as well as the conviction that modern Spain cannot be explained without identifying an orient within the national self, a phenomenon that disrupts the Eurocentric paradigm pitting the western "I" against the eastern or African "them."

Resistance to dominant interpretations of "otherness" did not mean abandoning hierarchical thinking or even recognizing the Arabic character of Spanish and Andalusian history and culture. Multivalent and internally fragmented, the domestic orient was far from a monolithic category. The object of diverse and often contradictory interpretations, it was used to highlight Spanish and Andalusian contributions to Western civilization; to bolster Andalusian claims to political autonomy; to close the gap between labor and politics in the rural south; and to justify Spanish colonialism in North Africa and even the participation of Muslim soldiers in Franco's army during the Civil War. In all these variations, Spanish orientalism built mythical al-Andalus as a mirror and a pillar for the regenerating nation, but the pillar could not support the colliding ideas the mirror reflected. Writings and rewritings of the Andalusi legacy testify to the deep contradictions that plagued identity formation in Spain and Andalusia in the pre–Civil War period. They made strange bedfellows: Blas Infante, a reformist victim of fascist violence; Isidro de las Cagigas, a close collaborator of Infante who became a distinguished diplomat under Franco; Miguel Asín Palacios, a Roman Catholic priest who celebrated the rebel uprising against the Second Republic; and Rodolfo Gil Benumeya, Asín's disciple, who simultaneously developed and debunked Infante's *andalucismo* as he articulated and justified authoritarian *africanismo*. Although national identity came to be understood in the singular rather than the plural after 1939, Spanishness continued to be shaped and defined by its interaction with Andalusia and its Moorish past. Franco Spain was, to a large degree, Andalusian Spain.

Chapter 2

✦

Culture, Modernity, and the South, 1898–1936

Andalucismo, *arabismo*, and *africanismo* ran parallel to attempts at cultural modernization and Europeanization after the colonial losses of Cuba, Puerto Rico, and the Philippines in 1898. For those involved, ranging from philosophers and linguists to poets and painters, Andalusia was less real than imagined, less place than commonplace, less history than cliché. Nonetheless, they asked the same basic question as their contemporary regionalists, Arabists, and colonists: what is the south's significance for the reinvention of Spain as a modern nation? José Ortega y Gasset, a leading *Europeizante*, or "Europeanizer," felt that the subject had not received the critical attention it deserved. On March 5, 1927, he published his book proposal in the liberal Madrid daily *El Sol*. He never wrote the book, but its rationale summarizes how many early twentieth-century Spanish writers and artists assessed Andalusia.

The region's mysteries, Ortega y Gasset proposes, could be unlocked by considering oriental peoples, to whom Andalusians are closer in character than to Europeans. As a people with millennial roots but no history, southerners are akin to the stock Persians, Indians, and Egyptians imagined by Europeans from Montesquieu to Hegel. They inhabit a lush environment, reminiscent of distant Araby, which requires minimal physical and intellectual effort. Art, literature, science, and religion, essential building blocks of Western civilization, are not their concern, in Ortega y Gasset's view.[1] The message is understated yet clear for those familiar with his Europeanizing endeavors: to find a place among its northern neighbors, Spain should look away from its south.

Just a few weeks after this short piece, *El Sol* published Ortega y Gasset's "Teoría de Andalucía" ("Theory of Andalusia"). Here, he opens with sweeping hyperbole: nineteenth-century Spain was Andalusian. Andalusian politicians, historical events, and stereotypes shaped Spain's image at home and abroad until 1900, when the cultural manifestations of the industrializing north gained momentum, shifting the country's center of gravity.[2] This is a welcome change. Ortega y Gasset insists that southern stereotypes, seen as a deplorable bric-a-brac of wayward bandits, flamenco singers, and carefree merrymakers, must be discarded if Spaniards wish to attain cultural parity with Europe. To reach this goal, they must also fight off the oriental indolence of the Andalusian peasants, who are imagined as lazy hedonists ruled by a "vegetative ideal," in stark contrast to the actual living conditions of the landless poor in the region.[3] Unlike vigorous and creative Castilians, who have been the vanguard of historical change in Spain since the Middle Ages, Andalusians are seen as plantlike organisms who indulge in pleasures that are neither "spiritual nor founded on historical principles."[4]

These views were far from idiosyncratic. Along with the desire to Europeanize the country and the cult of Castile as the locus of national essence, determining the place of Andalusia in the modern nation was a persistent preoccupation of Madrid's pre–Civil War intelligentsia. In the minds of liberal reformers like Ortega y Gasset, Andalusian Spain, a land more exposed to oriental traditions than enlightened ideas, was the iconic image of a country that fell to pieces after 1898.

This chapter contextualizes Ortega y Gasset's theory of Andalusia by exploring its ties not only to other contemporary expressions of anti-Andalusian nationalism (whether centralizing or peripheral), but also to critical voices who opposed the region's marginalization as antimodern. Artists and intellectuals who shared Ortega y Gasset's modernizing spirit, from the poet Juan Ramón Jiménez to the composer Manuel de Falla, highlighted the importance of their region's oriental heritage to progressive cultural nationalism. Surprisingly, they did so by revising rather than rejecting Ortega y Gasset's views. Their feat was to redraw established hierarchies, transforming the perceived degenerative effects of southern culture into a way for Spain to claim a place among civilized nations. Taken together, their alternative theories of Andalusia saw the region neither as an exotic icon nor as a backwater, but as an imagined space that reconciled Spain's orientalism with its modernizing aspirations.

Against Andalusia

Nineteenth-century Spain had an Andalusian accent. Painting and literature were infused with stock images of the south, from colorful flowerpots under blue skies to brave bullfighters to traditional rituals and festivities. Popular novels by Juan Valera, Fernán Caballero, and Pedro Antonio de Alarcón and *costumbrista* paintings by Valeriano Domínguez Bécquer and Manuel Rodríguez de Guzmán featured a picturesque Andalusia that embodied a timeless national character. Commercial advertising and the popular press brought this image to the pantry, the dinner table, and the family room. Liquor bottles, matchbox covers, and illustrated magazines promoted an orientalized self-image through Moorish-looking, dark-skinned women in typical flamenco poses. For example, Carbonell olive oil containers have featured the same scene since the company's foundation in 1866: in the center, against the undulating Andalusian landscape, "a girl posed before an olive tree, a fringed shawl over her simple white dress, with a high comb, and a carnation behind one ear, her arms raised to gather olives, but in a gesture taken from flamenco."[5] Carbonell cans marketed both a kitchen staple and a specific notion of collective identity. Corporate and national brands mirrored each other.

Southern exotic types created a "common idiom of Spanishness,"[6] but also a repertoire that cast Andalusia as "the female to an increasingly industrialized northern Spain, much as, as Said argues, the Orient was the female to a male Europe."[7] Colonial disaster and internal political fragmentation exacerbated this view. Catalan nationalists demanded independence not only from a corrupt and benighted Spanish state, but also from Castile's Andalusianized, regressive culture. Liberal reformers in Madrid defended Castile's centrality, but sought to regenerate the nation by symbolically detaching it from Andalusia.

Alfonso del Mar, a correspondent at the 1900 Paris world's fair, exemplified this attitude in his chronicle of the Spanish pavilion. The "strange wailings" and exaggerated wiggling of the Andalusian gypsy dancers who greeted visitors represented the "Spanishness that we should hide like an ulcer instead of exhibiting it with grace."[8] Writing in 1903 for the Madrid newspaper *El Globo* (*The Globe*) from Tangier, Pío Baroja echoed del Mar's misgivings, stating that Andalusia belonged in Africa rather than Spain. Unlike contemporary *africanistas*, he did not mean anything positive by this remark. The colonialist magazine *África Española* (*Spanish Africa*) declared in 1915 that Tangier "should be a Spanish city. Life in it is the same as it is in our own country, in an Andalusian town."[9] Baroja reversed the argument: Tangier was exactly like Andalusia, which is why it should not be part of a Europeanizing nation: it is picturesque yet depraved, ruled by apathy and drunkenness; the difference between Andalusians and Tangier natives would hardly be noticeable were it not for language and clothing.[10] Again, Baroja spells out the incompatibility of modern Spain and Andalusia in *Divagaciones sobre la cultura* (1920; *Digressions on Culture*), where he complains that national progress has been hindered by the nineteenth-century enthusiasm for ethnically branded southern folklore.[11]

Perhaps the most vociferous critic who railed against the identification of Andalusia with modern Spain was the notorious writer Eugenio Noel, the pseudonym of Eugenio Muñoz Díaz. A self-appointed apostle against *flamenquismo*, or degrading Andalusian folklore, he toured Spain and Latin America in the 1910s lecturing against bullfighting and flamenco music and dance. Reviled by bullfighting enthusiasts across the country—he barely escaped mob lynching in Seville after one of his incendiary public lectures—Noel obtained the support of Ortega y Gasset, who gave him a journalistic platform in his weekly magazine, *España*.[12] The success of Noel's column won him a book contract for *Señoritos, chulos, fenómenos, gitanos y flamencos* (1916; *Dandies, Pimps, Freaks, Gypsies, and Flamencos*), a volume that summarizes his controversial campaign.[13] Here he states that Andalusia is graced with "African hospitality" but is torn asunder by class inequality, a chronic problem aggravated by popular culture, including bullfighting, which Noel sees not as an artistic manifestation, but merely as an opportunity for peasants to join the ranks of their oppressors.[14] Rather than love of courage, elegance, and skill, the root of taurophilia is the pauper's dream of emulating his bosses, "marrying their daughters, driving their cars," and "buying their estates."[15] Whereas bullfighting inhibits class equality, flamenco deep song celebrates the pessimism and apathy that hopelessly hinder social and economic modernization in the region.[16]

This depreciation of Andalusia persisted undiminished among Catalan nationalists, who dispensed with the idea of Spain altogether. Catalanism was closely connected to economic growth and industrialization in Barcelona in the late nineteenth century, and it channeled the bourgeois disaffection with the central government in Madrid. Increasing demands for self-rule by Catalan industrial leaders concurred with *modernisme*—a cultural movement that relinquished unitary images of the Spanish nation revolving around the exotic south.[17] In trying to create a national, non-Spanish, modern, and European cultural identity for Catalonia, they opposed *flamenquismo* as the face of an increasingly decrepit Spain. In 1887, the painter Santiago Rusiñol published "Una 'juerga' trista" ("A Sad Juerga") in the inaugural issue of the Catalan arts magazine *Luz* (*Light*). Despite his interest in Andalusia—some of his garden paintings immortalized Granada's Generalife quarter—he offers a demystifying snapshot of a *juerga*, a riotous, drunken celebration that hypostasizes the region: going to Andalusia and not seeing a *juerga*, he wrote, "is like going to Egypt and not seeing the pyramids."[18] The poet Joan Maragall opposed this debased form of entertainment to Catalonia's aspirations to become an independent European nation. In "La indepèndencia de Catalunya" ("The Independence of Catalonia") of 1895, he declared that in order to be a part of Europe, Catalans must reject and even boycott flamenco festivals and bullfights, which he compared to the jokes and bizarre pantomimes of an African tribe.[19]

Rusiñol and Maragall's anti-flamenco diatribes echoed Pompeyo Gener's *Heregías* (1887; *Heresies*), a foundational text of Catalan nationalism. Steeped in the doctrines of scientific racism popularized by Arthur de Gobineau, Gener, an influential voice among *modernistes*, combined anti-Semitic and orientalist arguments in an attempt to explain the causes of Spain's decadence: "We have been doubting for a while whether most of Spain would be capable of progress and modernity. Only in the northern and northeastern provinces have we observed true racial and organizational elements that will allow the development of a culture like that of Indo-Germanic nations."[20] Disregard for these provinces, particularly industrialized and forward-looking Catalonia, and identification with the south are the main reasons for Spain's dreadful condition. According to Gener's sweeping historical and ethnographic generalizations, Spain is a second-rate nation because it looks "down," a term that denotes both a geographical location and a moral condition. He argues that in the south, what prospers

> are the degenerations of inferior elements imported from Asia and Africa . . . . It can be said that as the Moors were expelled, the Asturs and Old Castilians were overcome by the African spirit. The Saracens gained in influence what they lost in territorial possessions. Thus, New Castile conquered Old Castile, Andalusia conquered Castile, the Gypsified element conquered Andalusia, and this element conquered Spain as a whole. As Indo-Germanics by origin and temperament, we cannot tolerate the dominance of inferior elements or their tendencies and we therefore feel proud to oppose them, to differ from such majorities, to be heresiarchs against such orthodoxy.[21]

Like Baroja and Noel, Gener is determined to bring this downward spiral to a halt, although his indeterminate "we" will come to mean Catalonia, not Spain. By 1900, Gener separates Catalonia, not the diffuse "northern and northeastern provinces," from the rest of the country. In the first issue of *Joventut: Periódich Catalanista* (*Youth: Catalanist Review*), a weekly arts journal closely connected with *modernisme*, he states:

> We [Catalans] believe that our race is superior to that of the majority of Spaniards. Science tells us that we are Aryan . . . we want to be worthy descendants of such a noble race, and march along with the other free European nations at the forefront of civilization. . . . We are also committed to expel everything the Semites from yonder the Ebro River brought to us: the customs of fatalist Moors, lazy habits, blind obedience, cruelty, recklessness, apathy, *Gypsification* [*agitanament*], banditry, and stupid arrogance.[22]

Thus, turn-of-the-century nationalisms, both Catalan and Spanish ones, rejected Andalusia in the name of national regeneration. If views on the identity of Spain and the relations of the different Iberian communities had conflicted since the late 1880s, there was, however, considerable consensus about the banishment of the orientalized south from the modern nation.

Don Quixote vs. Don Juan

The vilification of Andalusia in intellectual circles in Madrid and Barcelona coincided with the increasing emphasis that centralizing nationalism placed on Castile as the spiritual heart of the nation. Fin-de-siècle intellectuals who engaged in national soul-searching found in Castile an alternative to the Andalusian Spanishness despised by many. Heavily influenced by the Romantic idea that each nation has an unchanging *Volksgeist* or "spirit of the people," liberal historiographers believed that Spain's character was unmistakably Castilian.[23] Rafael Altamira, the most distinguished Spanish historian writing in the early twentieth century, observed in his monumental *Historia de España y de la civilización española* (1899–1911; *History of Spain and Spanish Civilization*) that the central plateau constitutes a "primordial element" in the Iberian Peninsula.[24] Geographical centrality betokens historical significance. During the sixteenth and seventeenth centuries the plateau witnessed the consolidation of a superior Castilian civilization to which the kingdoms of Leon and Navarre as well as the coastal territories submitted. In Altamira's historiographical scheme, Andalusia was the cradle of Muslim influences, a foreign element assimilated into national culture as defined by Castile.[25] In addition to Castile's geological, political, and cultural prominence from the Middle Ages on, its language is singled out as the spiritual origin of the Spanish nation. Rather than a mere system of communication, Altamira argued in 1911, Castilian is the expression of "a whole mentality, a way of seeing life."[26]

These essential traits were ascribed to the iconic figure of Don Quixote. In 1905, the 300th anniversary of Cervantes's novel inspired a cult of the mad hero as the emblem of a defeated yet regenerating nation. Leading intellectuals interpreted the book and its main character in light of the post-1898 cultural situation. Unamuno's *Vida de Don Quijote y Sancho* (1903; *Life of Don Quixote and Sancho*) embraced Quixotic madness as morally superior to material growth and progress; Ortega y Gasset's *Meditaciones del Quijote* (1914; *Meditations on Quixote*) rejected Unamuno's celebration of irrationality and proposed looking at reality in a Cervantean fashion, discovering all its richness, depth, and meaning; and Ramiro de Maeztu's *Don Quijote, don Juan y la Celestina* (1926; *Don Quixote, Don Juan, and the Celestina*) advocated chivalric honor to keep Spain from moral and political decadence.

Quixotism was not solely the subject of highbrow intellectual debate. In 1912 the liberal minister Santiago Alba decreed that all students at public elementary schools must read a daily passage from *Don Quixote*. The conservative Natalio Rivas ratified the ruling in 1920, noting that the novel is "the most immortal and distinguished book of all centuries, a profane Bible of the modern age."[27]

Claimed by liberals and conservatives alike, Don Quixote remained an icon of Castilian Spanishness. In 1905 Azorín expressed an idea shared by many, including Unamuno, Ortega y Gasset, and Maeztu, conflating Don Quixote's heroic values with the people and landscape of Castile. Following in the footsteps of the errant knight, Azorín finds in Spain's central tableland and its inhabitants the foundation to regenerate Spain and regain its former imperial glory. Don Quixote's spirit manifests itself not in the biographies of great generals and statesmen, but among the dwellers of small Castilian villages in tune with their surroundings: "Isn't this the environment in which great, strong, powerful, tremendous but solitary, anarchic wills of adventurers, seafarers and conquistadors were born?"[28]

Azorín's words are paradigmatic of the Myth of Castile, which viewed the land of Don Quixote as the soul of Spain and the overseas empire that Spaniards, under the leadership of admirers of the hero's self-sacrificing restraint, were to conquer and colonize again, albeit in spiritual rather than material terms. Christopher Britt Arredondo calls these pro-Castilian intellectuals Quixotists. The Quixotists (Unamuno, Azorín, and Maeztu, among others) blamed Spain's decline in the world on the encounter, in 1898, between Don Quixote and Robinson Crusoe—between the waning Spanish empire and the waxing North American superpower. For the Quixotists, national regeneration meant defending the nation's cultural values, found in Castile, "against the threat of spiritual decadence posed by the increasing dominion of Robinson Crusoe's utilitarian and materialist values."[29]

In this transatlantic battlefield Don Quixote's nemesis was Robinson Crusoe, the incarnation of the Anglo-American empire, but within Spain his foil was Don Juan, the hedonistic lover from Seville. In 1908 the literary critic Víctor Said Armesto published *La leyenda de Don Juan* (*The Legend of Don Juan*), in which he contrasts Andalusian Spain with Castilian Spain, symbolized by Don Juan and Don Quixote respectively. "On the one hand," he writes,

> the romantic knight, the heroic idealist, self-sacrificing and earnest in his madness. On the other hand, the adventurous lad, the happy womanizer, the overwhelming sensualist, frivolous and shameless. The force that informs our collective national soul is refracted in these two figures. *Don Quixote* inhabits Castilian Spain, the central one, with its infinite horizon and its immense heaths; tenacious and brave Spain, constant in adversity, ascetic and accommodating. *Don Juan*'s cradle is Andalusian Spain, the southern one, bathed by the ardent, stirring sun, the Spain of lavishness and pomp, of boisterous happiness and unbridled love, the Spain that is improvident, reckless, and unruly, yet always chivalrous and lavishly generous.[30]

Intended as a rebuttal of the Italian scholar Arturo Farinelli's denial of Don Juan's Spanishness, Said Armesto's book sparked considerable debate on the symbolic relationship of Andalusia and philo-Castilian Quixotism.

In a review of Said Armesto's study, Unamuno expressed his preference for the Castilian knight. Said Armesto's defense of Don Juan's Spanish identity inspires shame in Unamuno rather than pride. "As a Spaniard," Unamuno confesses, "I am not in the least flattered, since Don Juan never was my cup of tea."[31] The Andalusian libertine, living only for the here and now, with complete disregard for spiritual matters, is a pernicious influence upon the Spanish people, who are in dire need of strong collective ideals. "Don Juan is alive and kicking while Don Quixote sleeps and dreams, and that is the source of our predicament," Unamuno declares.[32] In 1923, at the outset of the Primo de Rivera dictatorship, he elaborated on this opposition to ridicule the Andalusian dictator, a flamboyant aristocrat and high-ranking military officer whom he styled as Don Juan.[33] Unamuno contends that now more than ever, the primacy of intelligence over unruly appetites must be proclaimed, placing the sober and chaste Don Quixote over the "idiot Don Juan, the rake, the show-off," and the inspiration for all negative stereotypes of Spaniards.[34]

Ramón Pérez de Ayala, who parodied the myth of Don Juan in two novels, *Tigre Juan* (*Tiger John*) and *El curandero de su honra* (1926; *The Healer of His Honor*), contributed to this debate in his essay *Las máscaras* (1919).[35] Revising Said Armesto's thesis, he argued that what makes Don Juan the perfect personification of the Andalusian character is not his unruliness and rowdiness, but rather his Semitic understanding of love. Inherited from the Spanish Moors, this understanding is at odds with Christian spirituality.[36] While Christianity is founded on Mary's feminine purity, Islam embodies "sensual, lustful, and materialist" tendencies.[37] Lodged between these two extremes is the womanizer from Seville. A hybrid of sorts, "half Christian, half Muslim," he is Spanish, though not fully Western or European.[38]

Ortega y Gasset's "Introducción a Don Juan" ("Introduction to Don Juan"), published in *El Sol* in June 1921, also places that character in a liminal position. Contrary to Unamuno, Ortega y Gasset sees Don Juan as a hero who lives as he pleases without fearing death. Instead of condemning his philandering, Ortega y Gasset takes it as an archetype of life, as an eternal search for answers that are always as "enchanting" as they are "insufficient."[39] He stresses that Don Juan and Seville, the myth and its setting, cannot be understood without each other. Seville infuses the legend with inebriating oriental exoticism and the "bright colors of a masquerade."[40] But this mask hides the hero's universal significance, turning what could have been a lofty metaphysical search into banal amorous pursuits.[41] Things would have been different had the story taken place in what Ortega y Gasset calls "our Castile," which would have enhanced, not hidden, the myth's true meaning.[42] The jagged hills around Toledo near Madrid inspire an almost martial awareness of one's surroundings that clash with southern hedonism. In a land that incites military concerns rather than sensual pleasures, Don Juan would have been more Quixotic, more inclined to fight than flirt. Quite significantly, a warlike attitude is the remedy Ortega y Gasset prescribes for a deteriorating nation in *España invertebrada* (1921; *Invertebrate Spain*): "The same genius that invents a suggestive program for collective life knows how to muster an exemplary army, the vital symbol and unparalleled expression of that program."[43] Don Juan could have been such an exemplary figure had he abandoned his native Andalusia and joined Cervantes's knight errant across the Castilian tableland.

Despite their diverse approaches, Said Armesto, Unamuno, Pérez de Ayala, and Ortega y Gasset coincide in the conviction that true, essential Spain is

Quixotic and Castilian, and Don Juan's Andalusia is a deviation or defect to be ignored or corrected. Ortega y Gasset summarized this belief with characteristic incisiveness: "Spain was made by Castile, and there is reason to believe that, in general, only Castilian heads possess the right organs to perceive the great problem of integral Spain."[44]

Castilian Spain and Its Institutions

Castile's centrality to intellectual projects of national regeneration owes much to Spanish Krausism. A liberal humanist doctrine inspired by the writings of the nineteenth-century German philosopher Karl Christian Friedrich Krause, Krausism combined idealism and rationalism with an active social and educational agenda.[45] One of Krause's most prominent adherents, the Andalusian Francisco Giner de los Ríos, founded the Institución Libre de Enseñanza (ILE; Free Institute of Education) in 1876. In 1910 the Residencia de Estudiantes (Students' Residence), a selective residential college modeled on Oxford and Cambridge, was created to further the ILE's mission: training a select minority of well-rounded intellectuals through scientific inquiry and a keen appreciation for literature, architecture, and the arts. Upon finishing their formal education, this elite group would lead the masses toward social and political harmony, an ideal state sorely lacking in a country divided by political corruption and civil strife.

The *how* of this change was as important as the *where*. For the poets, painters, critics, and historians associated with the ILE, intellectual reform could not happen in a vacuum; it was a geographically bound process. Echoing the Don Quixote-Don Juan contrast, most of them opposed orientalist notions of Spain as Andalusia, embracing instead a mythical Castile, imagined as the source of an unchanging national character that could harmonize with European civilization and culture. The path to Europe did not pass through the south for many *institucionistas*.

In "Paisaje" (1885; "Landscape"), Giner de los Ríos programmatically singled out the Castilian plateau and its environs as the main source of inspiration for the regeneration of national culture. He uses the term "landscape" to designate the moral attitude that specific geological, botanical, and geographical attributes inspire in the observer. Giner argues that just as "the desert, the palm tree, the camel, the tent, and the Bedouin form an indivisible whole," so Iberia's craggy central plateau cannot be separated from the sobriety of its inhabitants. When Giner refers to Castile as "the backbone of Spain," he is not only talking about natural features, but also establishing a moral hierarchy that subordinates the Atlantic seaboard and the shores of the Mediterranean, particularly Andalusia, to the virile culture of the center.[46] Clothing clues us in to the center-periphery differences, which are most evident along the north-south axis. As we move south, the simple black attire of austere *toledanos* turns into the gaudy dresses of cheery Andalusian women.[47] Sartorial taste correlates with geography and character. The masculine temperance of Castile contrasts with the "feminine beauty" of Galicia and Asturias, let alone the effeminate flamboyance of Andalusia, pointedly represented only by women (*las andaluzas*) in the text.

Giner's moral reading of the Iberian landscape influenced the painters, writers, and intellectuals who gravitated toward the ILE.[48] Aureliano de Beruete, an art professor at the ILE and one of Giner's closest friends, helped to cement the Castilianization of Spain. Oil paintings such as *Vista del Guadarrama* (1901; *View of Guadarrama*), *El Tajo* (c. 1904; *Tagus*), and *Afueras de Madrid* (1906; *Outskirts of Madrid*) capture the stark simplicity of the Castilian plains. (See figure 2.1.) Their brown, yellow, and grey tonalities reflect the reduced chromatic scale of the Castilian terrain and clothing that Giner linked to sobriety and restraint. Beruete's son, the art historian and Prado Museum director Aureliano Beruete y Moret, stressed the simplicity, veracity, and depth of his father's painting: "He prefers the plain colors of the arid Castilian flatlands and the city of Toledo to rich and exuberant nature. For this reason, his works lack effect, but the truth he instills in them allows him to interpret the sad poetry of dusty and ruined Castile."[49] Other prominent landscape artists such as Darío de Regoyos and Ignacio Zuloaga also re-created the nation through depictions of the Castilian plateau, equating country and countryside, *país* and *paisaje*, even when they stressed the decay and sadness of its inhabitants, once an imperial race and now a defeated people in need of spiritual regeneration.

In forfeiting commemorative and picturesque themes, landscape painters reacted against previous national styles such as historical painting and, most pointedly, *costumbrismo*. In the nineteenth century, *costumbrismo* was popular with the Spanish middle classes as well as European tourists, who were attracted to orientalizing depictions of stereotypical figures such as the gypsy, the bullfighter, and the flamenco guitar player.[50] A commercial success, *costumbrista* scenes and types competed with historical painting as the repository of official national images. Beginning in the late eighteenth century, Spanish monarchs often commissioned series of paintings that promoted national unity and collective image-building. The chosen subjects for transmitting this message, José Álvarez Junco writes, were "predictable," ranging from Saguntum, Numantia, and Viriathus to the Catholic kings, Columbus, and Emperor Charles V.[51] Queen Isabella II (reigned 1833–1868) continued this tradition but favored artistic initiatives centered upon picturesque scenes and popular customs. In 1853 she commissioned a gallery of the customs of all forty-nine Spanish provinces. The Sevillian Manuel Rodríguez de Guzmán, the artist in charge of the project, was selected due to his widely acknowledged status as the best *costumbrista* painter of the time. Although he completed only four canvases, these colorful depictions of traditional scenes such as the *feria* of Seville and the *Romería del Rocío*, the annual religious pilgrimage to the

Figure 2.1. Aureliano de Beruete, *Vista del Guadarrama desde El Plantío* (1901). Copyright © Carmen Thyssen-Bornemisza. Collection on loan to the Museum Carmen Thyssen Malaga (Spain).

Rocío Chapel in southwestern Spain, replaced the representation of the country based on historical events and promoted a folkloric, markedly Andalusian interpretation of national identity.[52]

As a genre, *costumbrismo* is characterized by brilliant tonalities and cheerful hues. Manuel Wssel de Guimbarda's *Escena costumbrista en el Alcázar de Sevilla* (1872; *Costumbrista Scene in the Alcázar of Seville*) features the most common motifs: flamenco dancing, a matador attired in the traditional glittery dress or *traje de luces*, and an orientalist setting; here, a *mudéjar* courtyard in the Alcázar of Seville (figure 2.2). Framed by lavish ornamentations and intricate plasterwork, the scene bursts with bright colors, from the enamel-like tints of the backdrop tiles to the dresses and shawls worn by the dancers. Wssel's painting catered to the foreign taste for Andalusian exoticism, but it also exhibits images, motifs, and techniques that were commonly infused with patriotic meaning in the mid- to late nineteenth century.[53]

Impressionist landscape painters who took their cue from Giner de los Ríos expunged all anecdotal, picturesque, and folkloric elements from their pictures. In their work, *costumbrismo*'s strident tones and saturated colors are replaced by unembellished flatlands and dull tonalities reminiscent of Castilian clothing. As Darío de Regoyos wrote in *España Negra* (1899; *Black Spain*), his elemental, often somber and depressing depictions of Castile are intended as a corrective to the "blue skies and the joyfulness of the bullring"

Figure 2.2. Manuel Wssel de Guimbarda, *Escena costumbrista en el Alcázar de Sevilla* (1872). Copyright © Carmen Thyssen-Bornemisza. Collection on loan to the Museum Carmen Thyssen Malaga (Spain).

that shaped stock representations of the nation.[54] Regoyos's Castile was desolate, austere, and impoverished, but it contained the Quixotic seeds of future renewal.

Articulations of Castile-centric national identity on canvas often influenced those in print. Azorín dedicated his essay *Castilla* (1912; *Castile*) to Beruete, who inspired his prose.[55] With concise sentences, short and simple like impressionistic brushstrokes, Azorín depicts a Castilian countryside that mirrors the nuanced blue, grey, and brown tones of the painter's landscapes. Like Azorín, Antonio Machado, an ILE alumnus, employed a blend of dull tints in his poetic *Campos de Castilla* (1912; *Countryside of Castile*): "Silver hills / gray heights, opalescent rocks / through which the Duero bends / round Soria like a crossbow."[56] Echoing Giner's theory of landscape, Ortega y Gasset perceived in Machado's Castile a harmonious combination of moral, geographical, and sensory elements. According to Ortega y Gasset, Machado's inner self melds with "the purple hills over the grayish-brown land," transmuting them into "a warrior with a helmet, a shield, a harness, and a crossbow standing in the barbican," and exteriorizing the glorious past of a land of conquerors. Ortega's reading of Machado suggests that national history does not reside in lifeless archives and medieval chronicles but emanates directly from the warrior-like Castilian land.[57]

Machado's sober sensibility and poetic style, which reflected both a specific geographical setting and an essential form of Spanishness, proved largely incompatible with his native Andalusia. In 1912, devastated by his wife's death, he left the northern highlands around Soria for the rural southern city of Baeza, where he spent seven years teaching high school French and Spanish. During this period, he started using metrical forms inspired by Andalusian popular songs but kept singing about Soria, its mountains, lands, and inhabitants. Writing on April 4, 1913, from Lora del Río, a town on the Guadalquivir River between Cordoba and Seville, he feels disconnected from the place he had known since childhood:

> Back in the landscape of my native land,
> feeling like a foreigner in these native scenes—
> I had a homeland [*patria*] where the Duero flows
> between grey cliffs
> and ghosts of ancient oak woods
> up in Castile, mystic and warlike land
> . . . .
> here in these Andalusian lands of mine,
> the place where I was born, I long to sing.
> My childhood memories are here,
> images of palm trees and of light,
> and in the midst of golden glory,
> of distant bell towers with their storks,
> of cities with streets bereft of women,
> under their indigo skies, deserted squares
> lined with orange trees aglow
> bearing round vermilion fruit;
> and a shady garden where the dusty limbs
> of a lemon tree
> hold pale yellow lemons,
> reflected on the clear mirror of a fountain
> . . . .
> but the thread that binds the memory to the heart
> is missing, the anchor on its brink,
> or else these memories are soulless things.[58]

The grey cliffs around Soria stand in marked contrast to the vermilions, yellows, and indigos of the fertile Andalusian lowlands, which inspire memories that are blindingly radiant yet "soulless" and creatively unstimulating. Chromatic and atmospheric differences manifest deeper stylistic and ideological contrasts that diminish Andalusia as a poetic setting and image.

Jorge Luis Borges once said that Machado "was an Andalusian who made himself into a Castilian."[59] Pedro Salinas supported this appraisal in a 1933 review of Machado's *Poesías completas* (*Complete Poems*). Salinas is amazed that an Andalusian poet, from a land that is commonly associated with "picturesque joviality and riotous partying, can pronounce the most grave, serious, and melancholic words uttered in his time." He quickly explains the apparent paradox: proximity with Castile, a land of mystics and heroes, gave Machado's poetry its solemnity and sobriety. He simply had to outgrow Andalusia to become a "poeta de lo interior," which for Salinas amounts to being a *poeta del interior*, an inland poet.[60]

Salinas's assessment is representative of the veneration of Castile and the vituperation of Andalusia fostered by the linguists, literary scholars, and historians associated with the Center of Historical Studies, with which Salinas was associated. The Center was founded in 1910 to carry out Giner's plan to train an intellectual elite capable of steering Spanish society and politics away from stagnancy. The Philology Section, perhaps the most influential one, was headed by Ramón Menéndez Pidal from 1910 to the outbreak of the Civil War. He defined the limits and orientation of Spain's intellectual and literary field by supervising the scholarly, editorial, and pedagogical work of a select group of advanced graduate students. It is no exaggeration to say that his idea of Spain acquired paradigmatic status among early twentieth-century liberal reformers.[61]

Menéndez Pidal stressed Andalusia's marginality within Spain. In *La España del Cid* (1929; *Spain of the Cid*), he posited the south as an eternal, metaphysical entity whose unchanging character has held for more than a thousand years, since the times of al-Andalus. Combining philological criticism and patriotic concerns, Ménendez Pidal's book seeks to strengthen communal ties in the present through "great historical memories."[62] In his historical schema, the Cid, the quintessential Castilian, embodies national unity while the south stands as a regressive force impeding his "more evolutionary, more vital" spirit. During the Reconquest, "change was one-directional: Northern men, like the Cid, invaded and transformed al-Andalus. Later, Southern and Northern men invaded New Castile: they changed it and changed in it. But the South has prevailed many times." And this is something that must change if Spain wishes to regenerate: "The North should perhaps intervene now to solve the modern deficit of reconstructive longing."[63]

A similar distinction between Castile and Andalusia is found in the work of Tomás Navarro Tomás, a distinguished phonetician who studied under Menéndez Pidal and was appointed to the Center of Historical Studies in 1914. In "El acento castellano" ("The Castilian Accent"), a speech he read upon becoming a member of the Spanish Academy in 1935, he argued that accent, not just language, is at the very root of Spanish *Volksgeist*. Haphazardly mixing phonology, psychology, and history, he affirms that an "accent manifests the collective continuity of a given psycho-physiological attitude."[64]

Virility, austerity, and harmony are the defining features of both the Castilian accent and the Spanish character. Accents from other regions and countries manifest other characters that are best understood as deviations from a linguistic and spiritual norm. Prominent among these is the Andalusian accent. He had studied it in detail in "La frontera del andaluz" (1933; "The Frontier of Andalusian Spanish"), an article first published in the Center's flagship journal, *Revista de Filología Española* (*Review of Spanish Philology*). In his less technical Academy speech, he describes the accent in a way that strongly recalls Giner de los Ríos's characterization of *las andaluzas*. Whereas Castilian prosody is "strong" and "manly," Andalusian speech is "soft," "weak," and "particularly suited to be uttered by elegant feminine mouths."[65]

For Giner, Salinas, Menéndez Pidal, and Navarro Tomás, Andalusia is at the edge of the nation. Their academic views reproduced and projected within the Iberian territory the cultural frontiers that traditionally separated Spain from its neighbors to the north. In imagining modern Spain, these scholars transferred orientalist stereotypes not to Spain, as nineteenth-century Romantics did, but to its southern region. If, as Edward Said wrote, the orient was figured as female by Europeans in the age of empire, so Andalusia was considered the woman of a rehabilitating Spain, which was associated with the masculine and military character of Castile.[66] Andalusia, a land thought to breed languid sensuality and emotionalism, became a scapegoat that both epitomized and exorcised Spain's idiosyncrasies.

The Ortega y Gasset Paradigm

José Ortega y Gasset brought the ILE-inspired project to build a new nation to new levels of sophistication and complexity, placing it in dialogue with pre–Civil War politics. He reinforced the idea that cultural transformation would arise not only from a struggle between old and new, tradition and change, but also between north and south. In "Teoría de Andalucía" (1927; "Theory of Andalusia") and other related texts, he cast national identity in terms of a double contrast: against a monolithic view of Europe and against a debased perception of the peninsular south. Whereas he rejected the center-periphery paradigm that placed Spain below northern European nations, he reproduced it intra-nationally, by projecting onto Andalusia Spain's perceived oriental character, which he deemed a non-European, antimodern deficiency.

Hardly an original analysis, Ortega y Gasset's "Teoría de Andalucía" resonates with other contemporary views. For instance, like Eugenio Noel, he sees Andalusians as apathetic and lazy, uninterested in cultivating their fertile land. His characterization of "frivolous, almost feminine" Andalusians recalls Giner's description of the flamboyant *andaluzas* dressed in gaudy colors; and again following Giner, he contrasts Andalusian superficial sensuality with Castilian deep sobriety. Andalusia, an agrarian culture indifferent to spiritual concerns and idealistic goals, stands in stark contrast to bellicose Castile, the cradle of warriors and heroes who despise the peasant as "an inferior being."[67] Whereas Castilian culture belongs in the West, where "the Emperor's sword was the State's supreme symbol," Andalusia is like China, whose values are symbolized by "the Emperor's fan."[68]

An important contribution to the debate about Andalusia's place in modern Spain, Ortega y Gasset's "Teoría" is also a veiled challenge to the type of patriotism promoted by the Primo de Rivera dictatorship (1923–30). With the support of King Alfonso XIII, on September 13, 1923, General Miguel Primo de Rivera announced the formation of a military government to end political turmoil, the colonial crisis in Morocco, and class warfare. Ideologically, Primo's regime sponsored an extreme-right nationalism that sought to replace the liberal Spanish identity promulgated by the ILE. Equating Catholicism with Spanishness, *primorriverista* discourse favored a traditionalist brand of patriotism, which guided sweeping reforms of the educational system and informed governmental propaganda campaigns.[69]

One way in which official propaganda contradicted liberal views on national identity was by "Andalusianizing" the nation.[70] José María Salavería, a supporter of the dictatorship, offered a paradigmatic formulation of this view: Andalusia is "the synthesis and glory of Spanishness. Just as Spanishness exists only fragmentarily in the rest of Spain, it manifests itself wholly in Andalusia."[71] Seville's 1929 Ibero-American Exhibition was the culmination of this interpretation. In preparation since early in the century, the exhibition was meant to contribute to national regeneration and a renewed sense of transatlantic brotherhood in the wake of the colonial disaster of 1898. After 1925, when Primo de Rivera's provisional military government became a permanent civilian directory, the exhibition was also an opportunity to rally mass support for an increasingly unstable regime. Taking control from the local organizing committee, the dictator sped up the project while enthusiastically endorsing the regionalist/orientalist conception of its main architect, Aníbal González Álvarez.[72] The Plaza de España, the exhibition's centerpiece, consisted of an enormous semi-elliptical building, later to become a film set for *Lawrence of Arabia* (1962). It was designed in the Arabic revival style known as *neo-mudejarismo*. Around the edge of the building, forty-eight alcoves adorned with ceramic tiles represented characteristic historical events from each of the Spanish provinces. Set against the Islamic-inspired gardens of the María Luisa Park and at the end of the Avenida de la Raza, the plaza was a perfect symbol of Primo de Rivera's Andalusianized Spain. So was the exhibition's publicity poster, a bright and colorful scene depicting the nation as a joyful and young Andalusian lady, precisely the figure that Giner had opposed to the sober restraint of Castilians.

Ortega y Gasset was silent about Primo's 1923 military takeover, perhaps greeting the dictator's grandiose promises to regenerate a decrepit political system and modernize a chronically underdeveloped nation with a certain degree of enthusiasm. By the time the Ibero-American Exhibition opened its gates to the public, he had become an outspoken critic, relinquishing his university chair on March 18, 1929, and joining other intellectual leaders in protesting the government's repression of student demonstrations.[73] We might trace this change of heart back to Ortega y Gasset's 1927 Easter vacation in Seville and Andalusia, when he wrote "Teoría de Andalucía."[74] As he was drafting his manuscript, he had the chance to stroll around the exhibition site, observing how iconic monuments, such as the Plaza de España, were taking shape. The resulting text can be read as an inversion of the swelling national pride that grew apace with each new building around the plaza.

If Aníbal González's decorative architecture, with its *mudéjar* bricks and enameled ceramics, exemplified the Andalusization of Spain, Ortega y Gasset maintains that any correlation between the nation and its southernmost region is unlikely to crystallize in the future if Spaniards choose modernization over regressive traditions and rituals. Without any direct reference to the Primo regime, which had imposed a strict system of censorship, he condemns the "multi-color farce" promoted by *primorriverista* propaganda as the essence of Spanishness. For Ortega y Gasset, it is a mask that hides the region's true identity: Andalusia is "the oldest civilization in the Mediterranean—older than Greece and Rome." Referring to ancient Tartessos and the myth of Atlantis, he asserts that "growing evidence indicates that before the winds of history blew from Egypt and, in general, from the Oriental to the Occidental Mediterranean, there were gusts blowing in the opposite direction. A cultural current, the oldest one on record, departed from our coasts and, gliding over Lybia, splattered the Orient's bosom."[75] This ancestral culture still persists since, according to Ortega, life in twentieth-century Seville is not essentially different from that in Tartessos, and it is likely to remain the same for another thousand years.[76]

Andalusia's ancient origin is not, however, an entirely negative attribute. Ortega y Gasset was fascinated with the "growing evidence" that inverted Eurocentric paradigms, espoused by Hegel and others, where history moved from east to west, reaching plenitude in modern France, Germany, and England. In this international context, Spain was a secondary player that failed to keep up with the progressive north. Ortega y Gasset found a way out of this subordinate position through the work of the German historian and archeologist Adolf Schulten, which he publicized in Spain in the 1920s.[77] Schulten insisted yet could never prove that the fabled island of Atlantis flourished in the lower Guadalquivir region around Cadiz, the hypothetical site of Tartessos. Ortega y Gasset welcomed Schulten's hypothesis as a sign of a new cultural pluralism in Europe. The early twentieth-century search for long-forgotten cities like Tartessos, Troy, Crete, and Atlantis disturbed the twin notions that universal history is exclusively northern European and non-European societies are, as Ortega y Gasset put it, "marginal forms of humanity, accidents of secondary value whose only significance is to underline the substantive, central character of European progress."[78] Marginalized Spain could only benefit from this polycentric history, particularly because one of the most important lost civilizations seemed to still linger in its southern territory. Partly thanks to Andalusia and its connection to Tartessos/Atlantis, Ortega y Gasset can haul Spain from the periphery of the modern world. No longer a stagnant backwater, Spain becomes the cradle of an ancient world that achieved cultural refinement and material welfare long before Greece and Rome.

But this is only half the story. Acting according to a "have one's cake and eat it too" principle, Ortega y Gasset played on the dual characterization of Andalusia as Atlantis/Tartessos and as a land of benighted folklore to restore within the nation the hierarchies he challenged in an international context. What separates Andalusia from modernizing Spain is not just the merry "bric-a-brac" the *primorriveristas* loved, but also the traits that link contemporary *sevillanos* to ancient Tartessians. In "Las Atlántidas" (1924; "Atlantises"), Ortega y Gasset wrote that Tartessians, like Andalusians, were peaceful to a fault, "surrendering to invaders with deplorable ease." Their "soft, polished, delightful" life resembled the indolent, effete Andalusian "vegetative ideal." They also shared the sentimental disposition of decadent civilizations. Everything about Tartessos, from its religious cults to its daily routines, emanates a "romantic softness" that recalls the frivolous and effeminate gestures attributed to Andalusians in "Teoría de Andalucía."[79]

Indolence and an unthinking, ahistorical existence are both commonalities between Andalusia and Tartessos and the vices that Spain must shake off to become a modern country. Andalusia's placid nature, commendable at first blush, is anathema to someone who values the warrior-like capacity to conquer and transform one's environment. In *España invertebrada*, Ortega y Gasset attributes Spain's post-imperial decline to its rural temperament, which distanced it from great historical fights, smothering it in a "vegetative destiny."[80] This vegetative attitude, typical of Andalusians, recalls what Hegel termed in *The Philosophy of History* (1837) the charming "flower-life" of India, which despite its intoxicating allure is unworthy in every respect in the light of "Human Dignity and Freedom."[81] Subject as they are to irrationality, despotism, cruelty, and sensual vagaries, Indians, like other orientals, are unable to intervene decisively in world history, the domain of western Europe.

Although Ortega y Gasset openly opposed Hegel's determinism,[82] he turns his east-west dichotomy on a north-south axis that cuts across Spanish geography. In "Teoría," Ortega y Gasset repeatedly identifies himself as a man from the north, who perceives Andalusian life as "too simple, primitive, vegetative, and poor."[83] The vegetative ideal, his rendition of Hegel's Indian flower-life, consigns Andalusians to a pre-rational, oriental state that clashes with the desired values of a modernized Spain. This becomes clear in *España invertebrada*, where he urges Spaniards not to become a nation of *fellahs*.[84]

As in Blas Infante's false etymology of "flamenco" (*fellah mencus*) discussed in chapter 1, this Arabic term, which means "peasant" or "farmer," becomes an intricate metaphor collapsing class, ethnicity, and geography. Whereas Infante saw the Moorish *fellah* as the avatar of a superior Andalusian culture that Spaniards should respect and emulate, Ortega y Gasset subordinates Spain's Arabic roots and the rural south to the modernizing aspirations of Madrid's intellectual elite. Alternatively mythified as Tartessos/Atlantis and despised as a land of idle *fellahs*, Ortega y Gasset's Andalusia is a prism that supports his critique of Eurocentrism while refracting undesired moral, social, and cultural values.

The South Writes Back

Surprisingly, Ortega y Gasset's provocative remarks about Andalusia did not elicit any significant public response. Open dissent against Ortega y Gasset's portrayal of the region came from voices outside of his immediate intellectual circle. On May 6, 1927, the Madrid newspaper *La Voz* (*The Voice*) published a rebuttal to his characterization of Andalusian cuisine as unsophisticated and primitive,[85] "similar in its simplicity to the diet of Chinese people."[86] Two months later, Rogelio Buendía Abreu published a more comprehensive "Vindicación de Andalucía" ("Vindication of Andalusia") in the Huelva daily *Las Noticias* (*The News*), assaulting Ortega's views as fundamentally "wrong."[87] Andalusians, Buendía wrote, were the first to defeat Napoleon at Bailén and could hardly be called non-bellicose, nor lazy, since they comprised most of the crew on Columbus's first expedition to the New World. Their oriental character is equally discredited: a putative Andalusian community fought hard to repel the Arab invasion of 711, and only a small portion of present-day Andalusia was ever under the influence of proto-oriental Tartessians.[88]

Those who crossed paths with Ortega y Gasset in Madrid challenged the philosopher's anti-Andalusian sentiments in more subdued yet systematic ways. Juan Ramón Jiménez, a strong advocate of the ILE, along with younger Andalusian poets such as Federico García Lorca and Rafael Alberti, who cut their literary teeth in the halls of the Residencia de Estudiantes, embraced Ortega y Gasset's modernizing spirit but shifted its geography, proposing that creativity, historical awareness, and aesthetic discernment are not necessarily at odds with Andalusia. They proposed an alternative path to modernity, taking Ortega y Gasset's suggestion to abandon the center-periphery paradigm decisively further. To do so, they overcame the dead-end binaries Ortega y Gasset opposed when considering Spain's relation to Europe but reproduced when defining Andalusia. If Ortega y Gasset shifted Spain's place in Europe, they shifted Andalusia's place in modern Spain. This meant fighting inherited stereotypes without losing a sense of place. Rafael Alberti highlighted in his memoirs the commitment to strip away "a frivolous, effortless and even vulgar *Andalucismo*" that he shared with the other Generation of 1927 poets, most of whom hailed from the south.[89] The common strategy used to detach the southern from the shallow was either to refine or to abandon the local color of nineteenth-century *costumbrismo*.

The editors of *Mediodía* (*Noon*), a poetry magazine founded in Seville in 1926, proposed a pithy maxim that the poets of 1927 made theirs: "depuration."[90] This artistic method privileged form over content, creating complex metaphorical worlds inspired yet ultimately detached from external reality. Depuration was essentially a stylistic operation. Poetic innovators saw the south through the lens of artistic sophistication, in line with European avant-garde trends, not through solidarity with the oppressed working classes. Their fight was not against social injustice, but against worn clichés to be eradicated from the printed page. García Lorca acknowledged the popular roots of his work—he once wondered what would become of rich children were it not for the maids that connect them with popular wisdom—but he also claimed, voicing the shared opinion of other members of the Generation of 1927, that his poetry was a far cry from the voice of the people. If not aristocratic, he observed, it is certainly "depurated" since it displays a "vision and technique that contradict the simple spontaneity of popular art."[91] This ambiguous relationship with the masses was criticized by Juan Chabás, a disaffected member of the 1927 group who fled to exile following the Civil War due to his affiliation with the Communist Party. Chabás characterized his fellow poets as a "dehumanized generation" whose absorbing commitment to poetic purity made them blind to social conflicts and material concerns.[92] Though seemingly withdrawn from daily existence, however, this artistic stance was partly a response to the degraded image of Andalusian Spain that many saw as an obstacle to the rehabilitation of national culture.

The Universal Andalusian

Remapping modern peninsular culture from an Andalusian vantage point became a lifelong concern for Juan Ramón Jiménez, who was widely acknowledged as the mentor of the Generation of 1927. When in exile in Puerto Rico, he recalled that his intellectual relationship with Ortega y Gasset at the Residencia de Estudiantes forty years earlier, from 1913 to 1916, grew stronger by the day. But contrary to what the philosopher wished, he refused to "sing to Castile like Unamuno or Antonio Machado, or like a combination of both."[93] "Octubre" ("October"), a sonnet he published in 1917, garnered the enthusiastic praise of Francisco Giner, Manuel Bartolomé Cossío, and other friends of the Institución Libre de Enseñanza, mainly because it was a perfect synthesis of Castile-centric Krausism. In it, the poet considers ripping his heart out and tossing it in the "infinite Castilian landscape" to see if it grows into "the pure tree of eternal love."[94] The applause did not keep

Jiménez from planting his heart somewhere else: "I had the conviction that I was Andalusian, not Castilian." While he deeply identified with the Krausist ethos, its leaders, and institutions, he refused to embrace the central flatlands as the spiritual heart of a renewed Spain. Instead, he fashioned himself as the "Universal Andalusian," charged with elevating southern culture from local color "to the abstract universal."[95]

The phrase "Universal Andalusian" may date from 1923, but the impulse was older. In a letter to the Malaga-born poet José Sánchez Rodríguez, Jiménez praised his effort to rediscover Andalusia in his poetry collection *Alma andaluza* (1900; *Andalusian Soul*). Like Giner de los Ríos, Jiménez alludes to Andalusia as a flamboyant woman, but only to discard the image as a crude falsification. Sánchez Rodríguez, the "true singer of Andalusia," does not disfigure the region with gaudy colors and exotic motifs. Instead, his verse evokes a melancholy "Andalusian virgin."[96] Sánchez Rodríguez swept out local color from his female Andalusian types but still held on to orientalist exoticism. As Francisco Villaespesa wrote in the prologue to *Alma andaluza*, the book destroys the "Andalusian myth of French travelers and novelists, of German postcards and English tambourines," but it remains haunted by "Semitic dark virgins," the rhythmic swinging of "African palm trees," and the bright white houses reminiscent of "Oriental sepulchers."[97] Jiménez's letter to Rodríguez, an epistolary review of the book, echoed Villaespesa's prologue almost verbatim, while pointedly omitting all orientalist references. In so doing, he anticipates his later aversion to *alhambrismo*, or the nostalgic evocation of Andalusia's Arabic past.[98] In a 1936 article published in *El Sol*, Jiménez finds *alhambrismo*, like all kinds of exoticism, incompatible with the ideal of artistic purity that defined his mature poetry.[99]

A decade after he sent his letter to Sánchez Rodríguez, Jiménez was still committed to de-orientalizing the region. In 1911 he could barely conceal his irritation when Ramón Gómez de la Serna depicted Moguer, Jiménez's hometown, as a poetic world populated by the "Shulamites" that Jiménez evoked in his verse.[100] The biblical reference to the Song of Songs and Solomon's mysterious lover, the Shulamite, placed Moguer and its poet in a legendary orient. Recoiling from the association, Jiménez wrote a letter in response: "as far as my residence is concerned, I don't live in Moguer or anywhere else . . . I live in the universe."[101]

Nonetheless, the creative work Jiménez was producing at this time nuances and even contradicts his huffy repudiation of local attachments and orientalist associations. In "El poeta en Moguer" ("The Poet in Moguer"), written while living in his hometown from 1906 to 1912, he makes a telling distinction between Salvador Rueda's fake literary evocations of classical Greece and his own Andalusian elegies (e.g., *Platero y yo*, 1917), whose focal point is Moguer, a place with what he believed were real ties to Greek mythology. A palimpsest of actual and imagined geographies, Jiménez's Moguer is simultaneously a small coastal town in southwestern Andalusia and a mythical oriental territory: "Tartessos, Monsorium, right next to the infernal lake of Palos."[102] This reference collapses the legend of Tartessos and the Homeric myth that situates in today's Huelva, near Moguer, the Styx River and the lake that it forms around Hades, the Greek land of the dead. These fanciful associations were the object of serious scientific research in the early twentieth century in Spain. Contemporary geographers cited ancient sources, including the voyage of the fifth-century B.C. Carthaginian seaman Himilco, to situate both Hades and Tartessos in southwestern Spain, between the Tinto and Guadalquivir river deltas.[103] Jiménez's interest in this fabled cartography is literary rather than geographical. His later evocations of Tartessos will support his revisionary and rather self-serving genealogy of modern Hispanic poetry, built around himself and his native land. Though determining to what extent Jiménez's references to Tartessos were motivated by Ortega y Gasset's characterization of Andalusia is impossible, they were certainly instrumental to the poet's revision of Castile-centric cultural maps.

A number of events and circumstances pushed Jiménez to further define his personal image of the south, its universal projection, and its orientalist dimension. On July 19, 1924, back in Madrid after a two-week stay in Granada and the Alhambra, Jiménez wrote to Isabel García Lorca, Federico's sister, about the trip and the reflections it evoked: "My future, like my past, is in Andalusia and only in Andalusia," he declared. Andalusians, he added, must escape narrow regionalist attachments and "Andalusianize" the world, a thought he asks Isabel to share with her brother.[104] Despite the beckoning gesture to Federico, Jiménez's grandiloquent aspiration was nothing if not deeply personal. Transforming long-standing perceptions of Andalusia was part and parcel of his untiring self-promotion, an attitude that explains his controversial relations with the younger poets of the Generation of 1927; he had run-ins with Guillén, Salinas, Bergamín, and Cernuda and he snubbed García Lorca's poetry more than once. Although he was widely acknowledged as the mentor of this poetic group, a series of petty disputes ended up souring his friendships with them and boiling over into full-blown controversies.

"El Andaluz Universal" ("The Universal Andalusian"), a short text written in 1923, expresses Jiménez's almost pathological urge to assert and publicize his unrivaled position at the pinnacle of modern Spanish poetry. Half condensed autobiography, half poetic manifesto, the text is a brazenly self-congratulatory description of his artistic motivations and goals. In the midst of exalted expressions of commitment to aesthetic purity and resounding claims to unparalleled genius, Jiménez adds a few brushstrokes to his personal interpretation of Andalusia: "My Oriental Fate brought me flying to the western south," which is both the setting and the creation of the bard's supreme poetic activity.[105] Andalusia, Jiménez implies, *c'est moi*.

The universalization of Andalusia lies at the core of Jiménez's writings on literary history, which are characterized, as Gayle Rogers aptly suggests, by the "movement from a semi-periphery to a center, whether within a country or in a global context."[106] His criticism intertwines the poetry of North American modernists who declared their literary independence from Europe (Whitman, Poe, Dickinson, Frost, Lowell, Pound) with the verse of Spanish American *modernistas* who rejected Spain's artistic supremacy.[107] This transnational perspective remains incomplete if we ignore its intra-national dimension. Andalusia was peripheral to many of Jiménez's contemporaries, but he knew it was the cornerstone of his poetic world and, by extension, of modern Spanish poetry. His voice was universal, but with a distinct Andalusian accent.

This perspective is forcefully articulated in "El 'colorista' nacional" ("The National 'Colorist' ") and "Recuerdo al primer Villaespesa" ("Memory of the First Villaespesa"), both published in *El Sol* in 1936. Jiménez's goal in these short pieces is twofold: to distance his mature work from the aesthetics of *modernismo* and to claim authority over the latest generation of poets, who have deviated from his exacting standard of purity. He marks a sharp contrast between the simplicity of his mature poetry and the garish exoticism of *modernista* verse, which, he admits, captivated him in his youth. Embracing an evolutionary framework, he sees his abstract style and austere diction as the result of quarantining and eliminating his early *modernista* excesses. In his opinion, few, if any, of his contemporaries succeeded in this purgative process. The latest literary movements, including "*ultraísmo*," "*creacionismo*," "*jitanismo*," and "*marinerismo*" (the last two terms coined by Jiménez to take a jab at García Lorca and Alberti), are judged a poor combination of spiritual superficiality and linguistic dazzle. An island amid a cacophony of shallow voices, Jiménez's poetry is, by his own account, synonymous with "control, serenity, unity," and so is his Andalusia, which stands in opposition to the ubiquitous "tambourine Andalusia" and its reincarnations in the work of younger poets, including García Lorca, Alberti, and José Moreno Villa.[108]

Jiménez's revisionist historiography attained final shape and scope during his exile period in Puerto Rico and the United States, from 1936 to his death in 1955. As the literary critic Francisco Javier Blasco explains, the exiled poet was "more interested in revising historically and aesthetically the origins and evolution of twentieth-century Spanish and universal poetry than in intervening directly in the different debates around post-Civil War Spanish poetry."[109] This revision fleshes out the central arguments of the *El Sol* articles published in 1936. Jiménez's understanding of Spanish literary history is best appreciated in "Poesía abierta y poesía cerrada" ("Open Poetry and Closed Poetry"), published in *La Torre* (*The Tower*) in Puerto Rico in 1953. Dispensing with traditional periodization—Renaissance, Baroque, Romanticism, Neoclassicism, Symbolism—he argues that all poetry fits two broad categories: open and closed. Open poems are unadorned lyrical expression and constitute "the most national and universal" form available to contemporary Spanish writers; closed poems favor superficial stylistic features over spiritual intensity and are "international and foreign."[110] Jiménez finds the basic attributes of open poetry in the *duende* and *ánjel* of his homeland. Broadly defined as half-earthly, half-divine entities, *duende* and *ánjel* constitute a sort of southern *Volksgeist*. Andalusians often use *duende* to refer to the heightened, magnetizing emotion that gifted bullfighters and flamenco singers and dancers elicit in their audiences, but Jiménez detaches the mysterious figure from southern stereotypes to designate poetic authenticity, which he associates with individual talent rather than folk culture: "*Duende* and *ánjel*," sometimes hard to tell apart, "are the inner hosts of the authentic poet."[111] Drained of their specious connotations, the impish spirit and its angelic counterpart become avatars of a genuine and thoroughly purified Andalusia, a place where regional experiences can acquire universal poetic meaning.

The sea is the constant backdrop of this idealized landscape. With no small measure of self-promotion, Jiménez claims that "*duende* and *ánjel* need the sea more than other human entities," an affinity he shared.[112] His most influential work, *Diario de un poeta reciencasado* (1916; *Diary of Newlywed Poet*), later retitled *Diario de poeta y mar* (*Diary of a Poet and the Sea*), stages the poet's ever-shifting engagement with the Atlantic Ocean as he journeys to the United States to meet his bride, Zenobia Camprubí. The sea is not represented as external nature, but as the poet's inner creation, almost indistinguishable from his soul:

> I do not know if today the sea is
> —its blue color adorned with countless
> foams—,
> my heart; if my heart today
> —its crimson adorned with countless
> foams—,
> is the sea.
> One from the other,
> they enter and depart, replete and infinite,
> like two singular entities.
> Sometimes the sea drowns my heart,
> up to the very heavens.
> My heart drowns the sea sometimes,
> up to the very heavens.[113]

In Jiménez's poetic universe, the seascape emblematizes his own creative plenitude while challenging the centralizing patriotism he encountered at the ILE and the Residencia de Estudiantes. In his discussion of *duende* and elsewhere, he opposes the sea and what it represents—Andalusia, "open" lyric expression, and of course his own work—to landlocked Castile. In his estimation, "Castilian poetic writing," which is typically associated with the arid Spanish plateau and lacks *ánjel* and *duende*, is "closed."[114]

If the locus of open poetry is the coast, its historical origin is found among the "Andalusian Arabs of Cordoba, Seville, Granada," the true precursors of poetic "openness."[115] Jiménez claimed that the Moorish poets of al-Andalus influenced the development of modern European literature by creating new themes and forms. Digging deeper, he finds that the oriental character of modern Spanish poetry harkens back past the Spanish Moors to King Argantonius and the legendary world of Tartessos, which Jiménez frequently mapped onto his native Moguer and environs. He embraced the argument of Spanish Arabists and Andalusian regionalists, who claimed that the inhabitants of al-Andalus were Spaniards descended mainly from the Tartessians, not from Arabic invaders. In "El romance, río de la lengua española" (1959; "The Ballad: The River of the Spanish Language") he describes Moguer as "the flatland of the Tartessians, where ancient geographers . . . situated Atlantis."[116] With this remark, he seems to overcome his disgust with Gómez de la Serna's appreciation of his hometown, which he now equates with Tarshish, often identified by biblical historians with the city of Tartessos and mentioned in the Old Testament as a mysterious place that had trading relations with King Solomon (1 King 10:22).[117]

This Tartessos-Tarshish connection allows Jiménez to reiterate Andalusia's cultural ascendancy over Castile. In a very convoluted argument, he claims that the beauty of the Shulamite, Solomon's lover, is compared to the "lilies of Tarshish" in the Song of Songs. Fray Luis de León, an iconic sixteenth-century Castilian poet who translated this biblical book into Spanish, would have been a lesser poet without Tarshish-inspired Solomon as his model. According to this bizarre logic, the Castilian literary tradition owes one of its classics to Solomon's love of Tarshish. Therefore, Jiménez concludes, a millenary rock from Moguer-Tartessos-Tarshish should be more valuable to a "true Spaniard" than a mere Renaissance brick from Salamanca, the Castilian town where Fray Luis de León occupied a university chair in theology.[118]

Still, Jiménez's references to Tartessos and the Andalusian Arabs should not be understood as a wholehearted vindication of the oriental character of Spanish culture. Despite the importance accorded the medieval poetry of al-Andalus in his idiosyncratic literary chronology, no names are mentioned, no sources are cited, no lines are quoted, and no critical comments are made. Jiménez's interest is not philological but geopolitical. He seems to have no special sympathy for Andalusi literature and culture beyond its value as an argumentative crutch in reevaluating the place of his poetry on Spain's cultural map.

Exoticism as Modernity

Federico García Lorca and, to a lesser extent, Luis Cernuda contributed to Jiménez's mission to link modern Spanish culture to Andalusia. Like Jiménez, they sought to turn regional idiosyncrasies, which were often seen as primitive deviations from modernity, into nationally and globally accepted cultural standards. Unlike Jiménez, however, they understood that the content never goes beyond the phrase; that Andalusia is a relational concept, not an essence waiting to be unearthed from layers of falsifications and misrepresentations. Jiménez somewhat unjustifiably censured García Lorca's work, even though it heeded his advice to "Andalusianize" Spain and the world. He once confessed to his friend Juan Guerrero Ruiz that García Lorca was just one more *alhambrista* and that his best work, *Romancero Gitano* (*Gypsy Ballads*), indulged in shallow exoticism incompatible with his notion of Universal Andalusia.[119] But if García Lorca embraced all the trappings of orientalist exoticism that Jiménez dismissed as cheap *alhambrismo*, he did so to highlight, not deny, the region's affinities with cultural modernity, which he also detached from the myth of Castile.

In summer 1922, García Lorca summed up this sentiment in a letter to Melchor Fernández Almagro. He shared his excitement about a work in progress, "a popular and very Andalusian" poetry collection that would be published years later in Ortega y Gasset's *Revista de Occidente* (*Review of the West*) as *Romancero Gitano* (1928). Using the *romance*, a quintessentially national metrical form, to demystify the cult of Castile was one of his motivations. García Lorca's Andalusian ballads evoked people, landscapes, and places that "seemed to have never existed for poets," a neglect that made him cry out: "Enough of Castile already!!"[120] This artistic interest in Andalusia persisted from *Poema del cante jondo* (*Poem of the Deep Song*), written in 1921 and published ten years later, to his famous lectures on *duende* in Buenos Aires in 1933, to his poetry collection *Diván del Tamarit* (*The Tamarit Diwan*), which was published posthumously in 1940. Throughout, García Lorca opposed what he called a "false Andalusian vision" to the poetic purity and sophistication of his work.[121]

Fernández Almagro elucidated this contrast in a 1928 review of *Romancero Gitano*, published in *Revista de Occidente*. García Lorca, he wrote, "escapes from the commonplace through a silver bridge. On the other side, the reality that he was forced to abandon persists, but is now transfigured." *Romancero Gitano* recharged worn myths with new vitality, cleansing the figure of the gypsy of "the grease of the dirtiest *costumbrista* literature."[122] Similarly, García Lorca cited the "slobber" of those who insist on seeing in *Romancero* debased folklore while ignoring the "purity" of its construction. *Romancero Gitano*, an "anti-picturesque, anti-folkloric, and anti-flamenco" collection, reveals an authentic Andalusia.[123] What bespeaks authenticity is not objective facts, but innovative style.

Take "Canción del jinete" ("Song of the Horseman"), a haunting poem from *Romancero*. In one of his public lectures, García Lorca characterized its protagonist, a mysterious gypsy riding a black steed to Cordoba, as "the prodigious Andalusian Umar ibn Hafsun, exiled forever from his homeland." He was referring to the Andalusi Christian rebel who fought the Cordoba-based Umayyad Caliphate in the ninth century. In an unexpected twist that must have shocked his original audience, García Lorca presented this gypsified Christian Arab, an emblem of Spain's culturally and racially hybrid past, as the most "profound," "elevated," and "aristocratic" representative of "Andalusian and universal truth."[124] The nomadic outcast is the face of the region, and the octosyllabic *romance*, a stanza form strongly associated with Castile and the Reconquest of al-Andalus, is the chosen medium. Here, form and content break boundaries to create identity. A seeming contradiction, "Canción" celebrates a sense of place and belonging, while insisting that self-questioning, not self-assertion, is the way to achieve it.

García Lorca's imagined south, an idealized, preindustrial setting devoid of social tensions, should not be judged for its ethnographic, sociological, and historical accuracy, but rather understood as a revision of the liberal-humanist project initiated by the Krausists and promoted by Ortega y Gasset, the ILE, and the Residencia de Estudiantes, which García Lorca attended from 1919 to 1928. He shared the Krausist belief that a visionary elite identifies the unchanging soul or essence of the nation and produces art in harmony with it, thus creating a pathway to national revitalization; but he also thought that the country would become more universal not (or perhaps not only) by closely identifying with northern Europe and Castile, but by restoring Spain's profound association with eastern culture through Andalusia. "In response to degenerate *flamenquismo* on the one hand and *castellanismo* on the other," García Lorca produced his own *teoría de Andalucía*.[125]

The poet began to formulate this theory when he was barely in his twenties. On February 19, 1922, about a month before the celebration of the Cante Jondo contest that he organized with the composer Manuel de Falla in Granada, García Lorca delivered a lecture, "Cante Jondo: Primitivo Cante Andaluz" ("Deep Song: Primitive Andalusian Song"), at the local Arts Club. Intended as a promotion for the event, the lecture is also an artistic manifesto. In a letter sent to Antonio García Solalinde a day after the talk, García Lorca justifies its publication in a local newspaper with the tongue-in-cheek remark: "in Granada, I am a sort of Ortega y Gasset."[126] Beyond its jocular tone, this punchline, perhaps a mockery of Ortega y Gasset's exclusive claim to cultural authority, shows a desire to participate in ongoing debates about national culture. All mockery acknowledges authority, if only to debunk or ridicule it.[127]

The young poet felt sure that in organizing the music contest, he and Falla were performing a patriotic act. He urged his Granada audience to guard the "limpid beauty" of deep song, an eminently rural phenomenon, against the debauchery, alcoholism, and immorality of "the tavern, the late-night orgy," and "the dance floors of flamenco cafés."[128] In his opinion, the degradation of deep song only happens in cities; it preserves its Arcadian purity among "sailors who sing at sea, women who rock their children to sleep in the shade of grapevines, and rustic shepherds on mountain paths."[129] Timothy Mitchell sees García Lorca's contrast between an idealized preindustrial community

Figure 2.3. Manuel Ángeles Ortiz, promotional poster for Concurso de Cante Jondo, Granada, Spain (1922). Copyright © 2018 Artists Rights Society (ARS), New York / VEGAP, Madrid.

and an incipient entertainment industry in urban areas as the manifestation of a "phobiclike reaction to mass culture in general and particularly to popular commercial song as it was developing during the first decades of the twentieth century." "Popular music," Mitchell adds, "was the intelligentsia's foil, something to unite against."[130] True. But García Lorca's words also meant to dispel the negative connotations attributed to Andalusian song and dance by proponents of a regenerated, Europeanized Spain.

For many of García Lorca's classmates and professors at the ILE, flamenco dancing and singing, along with gypsy culture, formed a despised self-image, and they were reluctant to support the festival. Manuel Ángeles Ortiz, who painted the publicity poster for the event, wrote that the organizers actively sought ILE approval by expunging all elements that might connect deep song with boisterous *juergas*. Ortiz's failure to do so provoked harsh censure. For instance, Francisco Giner's nephew, Fernando de los Ríos, a former ILE student and professor and the chair of political theory at the University of Granada, criticized the artist for including a glass and a bottle of wine in his Cubist poster (figure 2.3).[131]

García Lorca's lecture, which drew liberally from three promotional articles on *cante jondo* that Falla published in a Granada newspaper, is a sustained contribution to this purgative process.[132] Purging *cante jondo* aimed to reconcile Andalusian folk culture with the ILE's modernizing project, while restoring deep song's link to "the impenetrable Orient," a distant, mysterious locale whose blurry geographical coordinates encompass India, Persia,

Egypt, Byzantium, and Arabia. García Lorca's knowledge of this territory was entirely literary.[133] He saw analogies between deep song and the Asian poems he found in Gaspar María de Nava Álvarez's *Poesías asiáticas* (1883; *Asiatic Poetry*), an anthology of Persian, Turkish, and Arabic verse translated into Spanish from English versions of the originals. A precursor of Romanticism in Spain, de Nava praised oriental poetry for its "picturesque images" and "enthusiasm," features that he urged Spanish poets to assimilate and imitate.[134] These features also defined Andalusian songs for García Lorca: "When our songs reach the very heights of pain and love they become the expressive sisters of the magnificent verses of Arabian and Persian poets."[135]

Despite these similarities, García Lorca argued that deep song is not a mere transplant from the orient to the West but a "purely Andalusian chant" that "possesses its own intimate, unmistakable national character." Historical events such as "the Spanish Church's adoption of Byzantine liturgical chant; the Saracen invasion; and the arrival in Spain of numerous bands of Gypsies" infused Andalusian folk music with distinctly eastern qualities, but an Andalusian spirit predated them.[136] This distinctive character is tightly linked to the guitar, a musical instrument that

> worked upon the dark, oriental, Jewish, and Arabic substance of the song, which babbles in its old age like a child. The guitar has made deep song into something Western. It has created unequaled beauty out of the Andalusian drama—the struggle of the Orient and the West—which has made Baetica an island of true culture.[137]

Halfway between east and west, García Lorca's Andalusia also straddles the boundary between the archaic and the modern. While he agrees that flamenco cafés are a loathsome spectacle that should be expunged from modern society, he believes that the ancestral, eastern roots of *cante jondo* should not be written off. In Madrid, he established contacts with avant-garde artists such as Guillermo de Torre, who published the Ultraísta manifesto in 1920; Ramón Gómez de la Serna, an advocate of Futurism in Spain; and the future vanguard filmmaker Luis Buñuel.[138] García Lorca did not fully buy into these new artistic trends, but they had a visible impact on his views of deep song. In his 1922 *cante jondo* lecture, he stated that the concise form of the *coplas* epitomizes the expressive precision sought by his friends in Madrid: "All of us poets who to some degree are concerned with pruning and caring for the overluxuriant lyric tree left to us by the Romantics and post-Romantics are astonished by these poems." If the lyrics evoke Romantic feelings of "sorrow" and "pain," it is only "in the service of the purest, most exact expression."[139] Andalusian song exemplifies the avant-garde repudiation of realistic mimesis while sharing its auto-referential qualities, or, to use Ortega y Gasset's words, the capacity of a work of art to be "nothing else but art."[140] Deep song, García Lorca affirms, "is song without landscape, withdrawn into itself."[141]

This aesthetic effect, akin to the de-realization of the world that Ortega sees as a defining trait of avant-garde aesthetics in *La deshumanización del arte* (1925; *The Dehumanization of Art*), inspired *Poema del cante jondo* (*Poem of the Deep Song*), a collection that García Lorca was composing while organizing the flamenco contest and drafting his promotional lecture. On January 1, 1922, he told Adolfo Salazar that this work heralded "a *new orientation*" for Spanish poetry.[142] As a stylization of popular flamenco sources, his collection was hardly original. Deep song was a popular topic among nineteenth- and early twentieth-century poets, including Francisco Villaespesa, Salvador Rueda, and Manuel Machado. What no one had done before was to render it in the heavily metaphoric language that García Lorca's *vanguardista* acquaintances in Madrid took as the emblem of new poetry. García Lorca transformed picturesque elements into a whirlwind of daring images. "Caprichos," the six sections that close *Poema del cante jondo*, evoke folkloric motifs (guitars, castanets, prickly pears, agaves, and oil lamps) through mythical references and metaphoric conceits that recall Ramón Gómez de la Serna's *greguerías*, witty aphorisms that were extremely popular among Madrid intellectuals in the first decade of the twentieth century. The guitar becomes a golden Polyphemus embracing six helpless maids (the strings); the castanet morphs into a reverberating beetle; the prickly pear, into a wild Laocoön; and the agave, into a petrified octopus.[143]

García Lorca's lecture further stressed the connections between Andalusian popular culture and the avant-garde by claiming that deep song was "an almost decisive influence" on the famous composers Claude Debussy and Mikhail Glinka.[144] Debussy and Glinka, along with Apollinaire, Pierre Reverdy, and Pablo Picasso, were cult figures among the Spanish vanguard. Glinka gained popularity in Spain as a collaborator of Sergei Diaghilev, the Russian artistic producer who toured Spain in 1916 and 1917 with his famous itinerant Ballets Russes. The company's performances, in collaboration with Picasso, Matisse, Falla, and Stravinsky, among other composers, painters, choreographers, designers, and dancers, captured all the innovations of the various "-isms" (Cubism, Futurism, Constructivism) of the early twentieth century. As Lynn Garafola explains, all aspects of these performances, from subject matter to scenic design, "felt the imprint of the quest for new forms. The ideas seeding these experiments often derived from arts other than dance—painting, avant-garde performance, and especially the 'new drama,' revolutionized by the innovative stagecraft of directors such as Konstantin Stanislavsky and Vsevolod Meyerhold."[145] In 1921, Ortega y Gasset hailed this dramatic repertoire as the best expression of the spirit of the age. According to him, dance troupes like Diaghilev's wiped out outmoded forms of art and entertainment and ushered in "a radical depuration" of scenic art.[146]

Debussy was also an undisputed icon of artistic innovation in Spain during the 1920s. A few months before praising Russian ballet, Ortega y Gasset had declared in *El Sol*: "To prefer Mendelssohn to Debussy is a subversive act; it promotes the weaker and violates the higher. The respectable public that applauds *The Wedding March* and boos the *Iberia* of the excellent modern composer commits an act of artistic terrorism."[147] Debussy, Ortega y Gasset claimed, composes for an elite audience; his compositions are too demanding for unrefined commoners who are keen on the realistic representation of human emotions. Lorca probably knew that Ortega y Gasset was echoing the central arguments of Falla's lecture "Introducción a la nueva música" ("Introduction to the New Music"), read in the Madrid Ateneo in 1915 and published a year later in *Revista musical hispanoamericana* (*Hispano-American Musical Review*). According to Falla, Debussy created a new art of sound that eschewed anecdotal elements and only existed "because of itself and for itself."[148]

García Lorca follows Falla's lead but takes his arguments in a direction that Ortega y Gasset would have rejected. While the musicologist Adolfo Salazar was seeking support for the 1922 Granada festival among Madrid's intellectual leaders, he reported to Falla that Ortega y Gasset was interested in the event but lukewarm about *cante jondo*, which did not really "speak to him."[149] Ortega y Gasset's indifference became aggressive disapproval when what Salazar calls "second-rate Europeanizers" equated the promotion of deep song with the "Africanization" of the country.[150] In response, García Lorca redrew the cultural geography that partitioned Andalusia off from the rest of Europe and the modern world by reiterating the tight connections between deep song and Europe's latest artistic innovations. Andalusian song and avant-garde music share a number of formal features, including atonality, dissonance, and lack of metrical rhythm, but what brings them together most decisively, according to García Lorca, is "the sad modulations and sober orientalism" of *cante jondo*.[151] The true source of Glinka's innovations, he argues, was the captivating tune of a guitarist he had listened to during a visit to Granada in the mid-nineteenth century.[152] And Debussy defined new theories, climbing to the very summit of European music, only after he was "made pregnant by the ancient Orient" at the Spanish Pavilion of the 1900 Universal Exhibition in Paris. Far from being the shameful ulcer that the reporter Alfonso del Mar scorned in his dispatch, the melodies of gypsy *cantaores* in Paris were the decisive stimulus for musical renovation.

In proposing Andalusian song as the inspiration for the latest and most sophisticated European musical trends, García Lorca draws again on Falla, particularly his often-repeated observation that the works of Glinka, Stravinsky, and other Russian composers featured in Diaghilev's Ballets Russes productions should be artistic models for Spanish composers.[153] When considering countries sharing eastern roots with Spain and its music, particularly flamenco, Russia was "in first place."[154] Falla's admiration for Russian music was reciprocated. In 1916, Diaghilev toured Spain and was enthralled by the striking resemblance between the Russian peasant art that inspired many of his performances and Spanish folk culture. On October 8, 1916, an enthusiastic reporter for the Madrid daily *La Correspondencia de España* (*The Correspondence of Spain*) wrote that the Russian impresario was particularly taken by "the expression, rhythm, and beauty of Andalusian popular dances."[155] With Falla as his cicerone in Seville, Diaghilev hired Spanish dancers for a cycle of works inspired by Spain's south: Falla's *El sombrero de tres picos* (1919; *The Three-Cornered Hat*), *Cuadro flamenco* (1921; *Flamenco Tableau*), and the projected but never produced *Triana* and *España*.[156]

In Falla's and García Lorca's view, then, orientalism was a new way to define Spanish modernity. In *Música y músicos de hoy* (1929; *Music and Musicians of Today*), a book that clarifies García Lorca's and Falla's musical theory, Adolfo Salazar was unambiguous about the differences between the superficial European vogue for orientalist motifs, which he perceived in urban architecture and the decorative arts, and the authentic "orientalist background" behind the musical nationalism developed by the "European races that carry in their blood exotic influences," including Russia and Andalusia. According to Salazar, Debussy, despite being a Frenchman, was an exceptional interpreter of these deep "national essences" rather than an advocate of shallow exotic fashions. He produced a music inspired by Andalusia "that can be considered, even today, a model of Spanishness for Spaniards."[157] Debussy and Falla are singled out as the progenitors of a musical "Spanish renaissance" that, in Salazar's mind, responds to Ortega y Gasset's call to renovate national culture and "invent our own future."[158]

García Lorca takes the debate farther in "Juego y teoría del duende" ("Play and Theory of the Duende"), a lecture that originated as a fragment of his *cante jondo* speech. Originally delivered before an eager Buenos Aires audience in 1933, it sets out to reveal "the hidden, aching spirit of Spain," a mission that García Lorca both connects to and detaches from the "one thousand lectures" he attended as a student at the Residencia de Estudiantes in Madrid, some of them no doubt given by the frequent keynote speaker Ortega y Gasset. García Lorca promises that "the terrible botfly of boredom" which hung over that "elegant salon" will not trespass "*this* room" in Buenos Aires. In drawing the spatial and stylistic contrast, he was defining his nation-building message within and yet against the ILE and the Residencia's program of cultural renewal. He identifies Spain's soul with something that many at the ILE would perceive to be as decadent as Don Juan: the irrational, almost demonic spirit known as *duende* in Andalusia. While Jiménez equated it with his own poetic genius, Lorca calls it something that "everyone senses and no philosopher explains," a rush reminiscent of the Kantian sublime that he opposes to angel and muse, airy figures that betoken intellectual clarity and order.[159] Oriental in origin and character, *duende* is a Dionysian force that leaps in time and space from Tartessos to ancient Greece to twentieth-century Andalusia, manifesting itself in Orphic mysteries, the contortions of pre-Roman dancers from Cadiz, and the broken chants of the legendary singer Silverio.

A genuinely Andalusian and Spanish phenomenon, this demonic spirit is not aesthetically or geographically bound since every art and every country is "capable of duende."[160] It also violates temporal borders. Through *duende*, the archaic and modern become synonymous rather than opposites. In spite of its ancestral roots, it "brings to old planes unknown feelings of freshness, with the quality of something newly created."[161] *Duende* is a "mental wind blowing relentlessly over the heads of the dead, in search of new landscapes and unknown accents . . . announcing the constant baptism of newly created things."[162] Contrary to what Ortega y Gasset and others advocated, novelty and artistic sublimation are linked rather than opposed to Andalusian Moorishness and folklore. *Duende* connects Allah with *olé* as it induces the "real and poetic evasion of this world" characteristic of avant-garde poetry: "In all Arabic music, whether dance, song, or elegy, the duende's arrival is greeted with energetic cries of Allah! Allah!, which is so close to the Olé of the bullfight that who knows if it is not the same thing? And in all the songs of the south of Spain the duende is greeted with sincere cries of *¡Viva Dios!* . . . it is a real and poetic evasion of this world," precisely the celebrated mechanism that Ortega y Gasset termed "de-humanization."[163] At once archaic and innovative, eastern and western, traditional and avant-garde, Lorca's mischievous hobgoblin unsettles and mixes interlocking sets of contraries, opening an alternative formulation of modern Spanish culture wherein Andalusia is vital rather than tribal, inspirational rather than intellectually desolate.

Three years after García Lorca's electrifying lecture in Buenos Aires, on the eve of the Spanish Civil War, the Seville-born poet Luis Cernuda published "Divagación sobre la Andalucía romántica" (1936; "Digression on Romantic Andalusia"). Cernuda's relationship with Andalusia and Seville was vexed. In 1928, he set off for Toulouse to teach Spanish at the local university because he was "fed up" with his hometown.[164] He expressed his disgust on several occasions, and yet the ideal Andalusia that he imagines in "Divagación," what he calls the "dream of a few poets," is a persistent leitmotif in his work.[165] Although Cernuda's text does not mention Ortega y Gasset or García Lorca explicitly, it can only be fully understood as a response to "Teoría de Andalucía" and "Juego y teoría del duende." It is rife with ideas, arguments, and even specific expressions and phrases from Ortega y Gasset's text. Cernuda, like Ortega y Gasset, seeks to understand the "peculiar form of collective life" that lies beneath the "absurd, external, and repugnantly facile *andalucismo*" that Ortega y Gasset derided.[166] His findings correlate with those of Ortega y Gasset. Underneath the alluring picture originally captured by nineteenth-century foreign travelers, Cernuda sees a deeper truth about the region, a "certain intoxicating atmosphere that silently bathes this land."[167] Andalusia is an oriental paradise aloof from the deadening rationality of the "horrible modern cities."[168] Inebriating like alcohol and opium, the land rejects intelligence and breeds sheer physical sensuality. Seville, its epicenter, is a golden ruin that seems to have fallen into lethargy.[169]

Cernuda's description echoes Ortega y Gasset but only to oppose his beliefs and conclusions. The poet's Andalusia is as oriental and exotic as the philosopher's, but these features are not seen as the antithesis of creative originality.[170] Exoticism, Dorothy Figueira affirms, is a "mode of self-definition" that allows a collectivity to attain self-understanding through separation and differentiation. The exotic, she adds, is "seen as a function of the 'Other,' alterity, the 'Female,' *différence*, and subalterneity."[171] Exoticized Andalusia fulfilled this function in the nationalistic imaginary crafted by prominent twentieth-century Spanish intellectuals, from Giner de los Ríos and Pío Baroja to Menéndez Pidal and Ortega y Gasset. As Spain's orient, Andalusia was perceived as a fascinating yet archaic enclave incapable of innovation and change. Like García Lorca, Cernuda targeted this assumption, deploying colorful images of the south to dislocate cultural hierarchies, particularly those that left Andalusia hopelessly trapped as modernity's primitive, oriental, feminized, backward "Other." To be sure, Cernuda's Andalusia is pitted against Castile and its myths: the Christian Reconquest, he affirms, brought "impure additions" to the "spiritual axis of Andalusia," that is, the Arabic heritage of al-Andalus.[172]

But Cernuda eventually breaks with these limiting oppositions. Boundaries between exoticizing self and exoticized other become hazy and eventually evaporate. In his fanciful cultural history, Andalusia is not the mystification of foreigners, but rather the work of a "devilish spirit, a roguish Ariel" that traveled from south to north in the Middle Ages and inspired Gothic architecture, where "idealism mixes with cunning buffoonery."[173] An avatar of García Lorca's *duende*, this spirit crosses national, geographic, and cultural divides. Tired of its "Nordic somnolence" and displeased with nineteenth-century industrialization, the spirit scampers from north to south, brewing in his wake "a storm called romanticism," a literary phenomenon that is no longer a foreign fiction, but rather the result of cultural reciprocity and complicity.

Like this impish genie and García Lorca's *duende*, Cernuda revels in trespassing borders, commingling in a defiant act of critical revelry what Ortega y Gasset saw as opposites: Andalusian orientalism and cultural innovation. Through his iconoclastic lens, Cernuda sees his friend García Lorca not just as an avant-gardist, but also as an ancestral "bard of Oriental Andalusia"; and the cohort of Andalusian poets who gathered around him, including José Moreno Villa, Manuel Altolaguirre, and Vicente Aleixandre, as the creators of a dreamed south that he labels "Spain's north," a latitudinal term that here means a poetic and spiritual reference point.[174]

This Andalusia, which has nothing to do with the garish fashions of what Alberti called "vulgar *Andalucismo*," is a locale that Jiménez, García Lorca, Falla, and Cernuda, among other writers and artists, imagined within and yet against the liberal-humanistic project of renovating Spain culturally during the early twentieth century. Caught between fantasy and reality, myth and history, Andalusia was less an actual place than a rhetorical frame to rewrite the ILE-inspired, Castile-centric project for a new Spain. This multifaceted image of the region dismantled definitions of cultural modernity as an eminently Western phenomenon, complicated views of an exotic south, and opened alternative understandings of the modern nation. These alternate gateways, which led to diverse yet complementary ideas of Spain, were violently blocked after the Spanish Civil War, when Andalusia was again garbed in cheap folklore to act as flashy propaganda for Franco's regime.

Chapter 3

✦

Andalusia and Franco Spain

On May 5, 1939, the day after nationalist Spain's victory parade, Francisco Franco entered Madrid's Santa Bárbara church in royal style, under a canopy, to attend a thanksgiving mass. In a carefully staged ceremony, the triumphant general was surrounded by relics of Spain's crusading past, including the battle flag of Las Navas de Tolosa, a hilly enclave in northeastern Andalusia where Alfonso VIII of Castile and his allies defeated the Moors in 1212, pushing the *Reconquista* decisively forward. As Franco reached the high altar, he presented his sword to Cardinal Isidro Gomá, the officiating priest, who laid it before the Christ of Lepanto, a symbol of the legendary victory of the Spanish Empire over the Ottomans in the sixteenth century.

These memorabilia were hardly out of place. To his loyal supporters, the generalissimo was a holy crusader, the glorious savior of a Christian nation threatened by barbaric hordes of godless Marxists. The Spanish Civil War, Cardinal Gomá wrote in a 1937 pastoral letter in support of the rebel army, was "a true crusade in favor of the Catholic religion," a second Reconquest against "red" Spain.[1] Branded "anti-Spain," the rural landless anarchists of the deep south, the growing proletariat in urban areas, and the liberal intellectuals and professionals who survived the war but could not flee became strangers in their homeland, much like the sixteenth-century Moriscos. Those who were not executed, incarcerated, or sent to concentration camps had to live in a country covered over by crosses and uniforms, a place where no sphere was immune to Franco's sweeping ideological mobilization.

Unlike his wartime allies Hitler and Mussolini, Franco did not usually seek consent through massive rallies and inflamed speeches. The uncharismatic leader, who was naturally quiet and reserved, relied instead on the pervasive power of the Roman Catholic Church to form the minds and souls of his subjects. Patriotism, social discipline, and blind respect for class hierarchies were enforced from the pulpit and in the schoolroom under the exclusive control of ecclesiastical authorities. Falange, the Spanish fascist party, contributed to the consolidation of the new order, but its goals and assumptions did not differ from those of the regime's religious and military leaders. All supporters of the new regime embraced the mythology of Reconquest,

Counter-Reformation, and sixteenth-century Empire and traced the roots of a united country back to the Spain of Ferdinand and Isabella. The yoke and arrows, an emblem of religious and territorial unity during the reign of the Catholic kings that was appropriated by Falange as a party insignia, was dutifully stenciled on the walls of occupied towns and cities and printed in posters, pamphlets, and periodicals distributed in rebel Spain during the Civil War. A reminder of the subjugation and expulsion of the Muslims, the omnipresent icon reinforced the metaphorical connection between al-Andalus and the liberal and working-class constituents of the Second Republic.

If "reds" were the new "Moors," Franco, who was often portrayed in visual propaganda astride a white horse, was the reincarnation of Santiago Matamoros, Saint James the Moor Slayer, who is believed to have led medieval Christian troops on a white stallion. The glorification of Catholic victories over Islam persisted during the early Franco years in order to legitimate the military coup and indoctrinate Spaniards of all ages. Not coincidentally, one of the most popular comics in the postwar period was *El Guerrero del Antifaz*, a medieval champion of Christian values against sadistic Arab enemies. As in the fifteenth century, Spain was now a centralized Catholic nation with one language, one supreme ruler, and one God.

Andalusia seems to have embodied all that the Franco regime wished to suppress. A hub of anarchist activity since the early twentieth century, it was one of the regions most battered during the war. Following the Russian Revolution in 1917, the large estates of the rural south became battlefields where landless peasants fought against the oligarchic elite who would later support Franco's coup. During the *trienio bolchevique*, or "three Bolshevik years" (1918–20), rioting farmworkers destroyed property, terrified landlords, and alarmed moderate and conservative politicians in Madrid. Localized bursts of revolutionary activity persisted through the Civil War period.[2] Stunned by the virulence of peasant unrest in the Andalusian sierras, observers referred to Spain as "the Russia of the West."[3]

Like revolution, Andalusia's turbulent political history was a specter that Francoists were determined to bury. As a platform for agrarian reform, the *andalucismo* of the 1920s and 1930s rejected radical anarchist tactics but promoted a federalist, socialist state that clashed with the conservative centralization advocated by the rebels. The *andalucista* leader Blas Infante not only supported the cause of the poor day laborers in the south, but also idealized the region's Arab past, which was the symbolic antithesis of nationalist Spain. Madrid's Institución Libre de Enseñanza, demonized by right-wing pundits as the source of all national evils, radiated cultural images of Andalusia that were also incompatible with the basic tenets of the new regime. Jiménez, García Lorca, and Cernuda's modernist visions of their homeland clashed with the archaizing ethos of Francoism. The summary executions of Infante and García Lorca during the war represented the brutal suppression of the idea of a plural, progressive Andalusia that would be open to international influences and committed to social egalitarianism.

Exile, censorship, and murder swept the liberal and socialist views of the south off the peninsula, but the post–Civil War years fostered the Andalusization of the nation initiated by the Primo de Rivera dictatorship. Infante's pan-Andalusian doctrine survived 1939, albeit fitted out in the trappings of Hispano-Arabic brotherhood in order to justify Spain's continuing colonial presence in Morocco. A leading officer in Africa, Franco crafted a dual identity: ruthless scourge of the Riffian rebels and able chieftain of the more than 75,000 Moroccan mercenaries he recruited to fight against the irreligious Republic.[4] As both heroic crusader and friend of the Muslims, the Caudillo often made public appearances escorted by the Guardia Mora, Moorish horsemen in native costume.

Curiously, the general's wartime enemies abetted his Arabophilia by depicting the wretched Moroccan peasants who joined the rebel army for a pittance as the second coming of the Moorish invaders who took over Spain in 711.[5] These penniless seasonal workers, driven to pick up rifles and bayonets by bad harvests and workplace closings caused by the very nationalist uprising they served, were characterized by leftist leaders as "savage Moorish hordes, drunk with sensuality, who pour forth to wreak horrendous violations of our daughters and our wives."[6] These sentiments were more suitable to defenders of sacred Spain than to those who claimed to oppose colonialism, exploitation, and misery.

Franco's more nuanced rhetoric oscillated between repudiation and celebration of the Islamic world, a strategy that intersected with his ideological manipulation of cultural images of Andalusia already in circulation before the war. The "vulgar *Andalucismo*" that Alberti and his fellow poets of 1927 feared and derided in the 1920s (see chapter 2) informed nationalist propaganda efforts after the Civil War. The new status quo encouraged what some labeled "national *flamenquismo*," a tongue-in-cheek variation on national Catholicism, the dominant ideology that now defined Spanish identity in terms of religious fervor and militaristic discipline. For decades after the war, national *flamenquismo* flooded the airwaves with catchy *coplas* and saturated movie screens with iconic *folklóricas*: charismatic gypsy dancers in ruffled, polka-dot dresses.

However, the idea of Andalusia, like the regime itself, did not remain unchanged. Its symbolic value and meaning shifted as the Franco state, a feudalistic structure in the 1930s and 1940s, became a fast-growing economic power within a free-market system in the 1960s and 1970s. Without adhering to strict chronology, this chapter distinguishes three phases in the development of images of Andalusia under Francoism.

First, the autarkic period after the Civil War isolated Spain from international cultural and economic flows. Government efforts to purge the nation of foreign influences led to regressive educational policies, harsh censorship, and a weakened domestic market. Shortages, unemployment, and inflation bred malnutrition, rampant infant mortality, and widespread disease, especially among the landless peasants of Andalusia. These bleak living conditions in the 1940s were countered by a culture of evasion built on an Andalusian fantasyland. Blockbuster musical films starred fiery *folklóricas* living in a pastoral south that was devoid of scarcity and oppression. An opiate of the people, these movies perpetuated the orientalist representation of Spain as Andalusia and contributed to Franco's retrograde cultural policy, which emphasized Spain's difference from the rest of Europe as an essentially rural society that was impervious to modernization and change. The genre's appeal persisted throughout the Franco years, although it dimmed in the 1950s and 1960s when greater political and cultural freedom changed perceptions of the south.

Second, in the *desarrollo* (economic development) years beginning in the early 1950s, the Franco government established military and economic agreements with the United States and opened the country to foreign investment and tourism. National Catholicism was toned down in order to render Spain's difference from Europe as a marketable commodity, not a cultural trait. Andalusia was gradually transformed from an archaic land populated by dancing gypsies to an appealing destination for sun-starved northern Europeans. Popular musical comedies about mass tourism and the widely read works of the right-wing publicist José María Pemán will illustrate the continuity between postwar conservatism and the new rhetoric of progress, prosperity, and liberalization. Pemán fervently opposed the real and symbolic enemies of throne and altar in the 1920s and 1930s. During the development era he turned into a master ventriloquist, embracing those enemies (Islam, the working class) and emptying them of contentious substance. In his dreamed Andalusia, floating far above class conflicts and legislated by folklore and ritual, the discrepancies between right-wing myths and the evolving realities of consumer culture are posed, but are then blurred into an illusory liberalism that forces a return to traditional beliefs and hierarchies.

Third, during late Francoism, from the mid-1960s to the dictator's death in 1975, authoritarianism eroded; state censorship relaxed; and a culture of protest arose among university students and an increasingly organized working class. While right-wing reformers like Pemán continued to try to reconcile tradition and change in an imaginary rural south, opponents of the regime revived progressive versions of Andalusia that had lain dormant for decades. Andalusia became a symbolic battleground between reform and *ruptura*. The iconic left-wing magazine *Triunfo* (*Triumph*) emerged as the main adversary of the myths and fantasies spread by the official press and media, particularly national *flamenquismo*, a term coined by its frequent contributor Francisco Almazán Marcos. The pages of *Triunfo* rescued García Lorca's musical orientalism and Infante's views on al-Andalus to cement a regional identity that reconciled ethnicity with class consciousness. The magazine's contributors rejected abstract theories and attributed the region's cultural distinctiveness to chronic underdevelopment and the cumulative effect of centuries of marginalization, oppression, and colonization. Unlike the autarkic period, in this period, the orientalist lens revealed rather than hid the south's economic and social woes, connecting it to the Third World rather than an anachronistic Arcadia. Despite its support of Andalusian political and economic emancipation, *Triunfo*'s collective proposal lost traction and collapsed during the transition to democracy, which favored neoliberal rather than Marxist and popular-democratic models. As a self-governed territory within the federalized post-Franco state, Andalusia embraced Infante's legacy but downplayed his socialism. Orientalism was promoted as a tourist attraction, not an alternative view of history and material reality.

Silver Smokescreens

Heeding Mussolini's proclamation that "cinema is the best weapon," nationalists supported the production of folkloric musicals, also known as *españoladas* or *andaluzadas*. They were one of the major film genres during the early post–Civil War period, along with historical dramas and religious films. In a country plagued by high illiteracy but with "more cinema seats than any other European country, the Spain of the forties and fifties," historian Raymond Carr observes, "was a nation of cinema addicts."[7] While the strategic value of cinema seems obvious, the use of female gypsy stars to consolidate an authoritarian nation-state shaped by bishops and generals seems paradoxical. The films' flamboyant protagonists fly in the face of the feminine ideal advocated during the Franco years: the passive, docile, obedient mother and wife. Rather than Catholic angels of the home, *españoladas* featured transgressive femme fatales who challenged established moral codes and rules of conduct. Despite these discrepancies, the films fulfilled two important ideological roles. First, they asserted Spain's difference from Europe (with Spain coded as gypsy, oriental, and Andalusian) at a time when cultural and economic isolation was favored and enforced. Second, they staged a symbolic rebellion, providing the oppressed masses with a momentary emotional release while confining social conflict to the silver screen.

Españoladas complemented national Catholicism in the creation of a feudalistic order. Clichéd representations of an idealized premodern south unsullied by liberalism, anarchism, and Marxism promoted national unity under a strong paternalist, antirevolutionary state. This fantasy world coexisted uneasily with the harsh realities of exploited farmworkers and criminalized gypsies. The 1943 code of the militarized Guardia Civil stipulated close surveillance, not to say routine persecution, of gypsies. The *andalucismo* favored by the regime was, as the novelist Manuel Vázquez Montalbán put it, "a willful affirmation of *Spain is different*," a 1960s tourist slogan that both transformed and capitalized on Spain as Europe's internal orient.[8]

Very much like the Hispanicized al-Andalus invented by the Spanish Arabists (see chapter 1), gypsified Andalusia manifests a persistent desire both to self-exoticize national identity and to erase its living source.

Españoladas redeployed all the exoticism and picturesque local color found in Romantic literature from Beaumarchais's *The Barber of Seville* (1775) to Prosper Mérimée's *Carmen* (1845). If French fictions about Andalusian gypsies were inextricable from European orientalism, Spanish versions were caught between identification and rejection. Exoticized gypsies eternally wander a symbolic no-man's land between "like us" and "not like us." At once despised outlaws and national emblems, they play out the country's ambiguous status as simultaneously orientalized and orientalizing.[9] Lou Charnon-Deutsch writes that whenever Spanish nationalism is on the rise, the "Otherness of the disenfranchised group" is "maximized" to define authenticity against foreign influences.[10] In eighteenth-century Spain, Madrid's aristocracy embraced *gitanismo*, or the love of gypsy manners and customs, to assert their patriotism against French fashions and ideas. Brazen countesses in mantillas and inebriated dukes clapping to flamenco dancers epitomized Iberian resistance to Gallic influences, particularly after Napoleon invaded in 1808, and the terms "patriot" and "enlightened" became almost mutually exclusive.[11] Boundaries between exotic stereotypes and national self-images remained blurred throughout the nineteenth century. Two years before the publication of Mérimée's *Carmen*, the gypsy cigar-maker was already featured as a national type in *Los españoles pintados por sí mismos* (1843–44; *The Spaniards in a Self-Portrait*) (figure 3.1). What makes gypsies icons of national authenticity is their resistance to progress. They are, as one of the contributors to the collection wrote, impervious to "that arrogant matron called civilization" like the imaginary Andalusia they inhabit, a primitive land untouched by modern social upheaval.[12]

The Francoists, who were sworn enemies of the Enlightenment and democracy, had much to gain from promoting this sort of cultural primitivism. As Andalusian types leapt from illustrated *costumbrista* anthologies and the musical theater stage to the silver screen, they perpetuated an idea of Spain that perfectly suited nationalist efforts to turn back history's clock. To maintain Spain's insulation from cultural and social change required fierce government control. The early postwar solutions to social inequality were austerity, repression, and autarky. Known as the "hunger years," the 1940s and 1950s burdened the working class with strict protectionist measures against imports, spawning a massive black market and spiking prices of staples like bread and flour. This misguided economic self-reliance was combined with agricultural policies that favored those who had supported the military revolt in 1936. In southern Spain, land confiscated for agrarian reform during the Republic was returned to former landowners, who subjected day laborers to unregulated working conditions sanctioned by the authorities. To defuse open unrest, popular films buried oppression and material deprivation under

Figure 3.1. *La gitana*, from *Los españoles pintados por sí mismos* (1843–44).

a bucolic façade of dancing gypsies and singing peasants, happily plowing the fields of benevolent bosses.

La blanca paloma (dir. Claudio de la Torre, 1942; *The White Dove*) and *Macarena* (dir. Antonio Guzmán Merino, 1944), for example, are melodramas set in a land devoid of poverty, unemployment, and inequality. Rural life is peaceful, disturbed only by romantic passion and rowdy local fiestas. Female subordination to a patriarchal society and the oligarchy's failure to absorb working-class mobilization are resolved in rags-to-riches plots, often involving the betrothal of the female protagonist to a landowner or nobleman.[13] A variation is the narrative of stardom. Films like *El sueño de Andalucía* (dir. Luis Lucia, 1951; *The Dream of Andalusia*) apply the romance format to lower-class, ethnically marked protagonists who rise to fame and fortune through singing, dancing, and bullfighting. In all cases, real economic and social conditions in the south are hidden from view under a thick veneer of clichés. As the *folklórica* star Imperio Argentina confessed in 1962, Spanish cinema had yet to show the "real Andalusia."[14]

The use of folkloric cinema to deflect working-class protest and push a conservative agenda did not start with Franco's regime. Since its earliest manifestations in the 1920s, the Spanish musical featuring flamenco song and dance had been an asset, not a challenge, to right-wing interests and the

Restoration's Catholic elite. In 1919, a group of wealthy Madrid investors created, with King Alfonso XIII's blessing, Atlántida SACE, a film production company that provided formulaic, escapist entertainment for the poverty-stricken and increasingly rebellious popular classes. The new company pursued both economic and moralizing goals, and its first box-office hit was an adaptation of an operetta, or *zarzuela*, *La verbena de la Paloma* (dir. José Buchs, 1921; *The Fair of the Virgin of the Dove*), whose popular themes and songs elicited instant identification from lower-class spectators.[15] Along with musical comedies and *zarzuela* remakes, rural dramas set in Andalusia soon became a silver screen staple. What brought these two genres together was the melodramatic use of music and the restaging of the popular national types of nineteenth-century *costumbrismo* (bullfighter, bandit, gypsy). The success of silent films such as *Currito de la cruz* (dir. Alejandro Pérez Lugín, 1925; *Currito of the Cross*), adapted from a 1921 bullfighting novel, encouraged the production of talkies that further exploited Andalusian folklore and customs.

In the 1930s, Cifesa, a major film company with strong conservative tendencies, released a series of musicals featuring a cheery southern countryside where exploitation and class struggle are nowhere to be seen despite the tense climate that plagued rural Andalusia. A good example is *Morena clara* (1936; *The Light-Skinned Gypsy*), starring Imperio Argentina and directed by her husband, Florián Rey, one of the two outstanding Spanish directors of the time along with Benito Perojo. The film tells the interracial love story of Trini, an Andalusian gypsy caught and tried for stealing hams, and her prosecutor, Enrique. Although the film timidly denounces anti-gypsy prejudice, like earlier domestic productions, it exposes moviegoers to an anesthetic fantasy where social conflict is happily resolved without challenging social and racial hierarchies.[16] When Trini moves to the prosecutor's house to work as a servant and then seduces him, the message is that knowing and respecting your place in society leads to harmony and a full life as one happy, loving family living under the same roof. Still a stock gypsy in some ways, the robber-turned-housemaid protects her benefactors against their enemies using sorcery: the "Pharaoh's charm," a mixture of song and spell, underscores her oriental ancestry. But by this point Trini is no longer a transgressive element; the assimilation of the ethnically marked outlaw to bourgeois order powerfully disavows racial and class tensions as it negotiates Spain's symbolic ties with orientalized Andalusia. This mix would ensure the genre's permanence and prominence in Franco Spain.

If Republican Spain briefly challenged the genre with such documentaries as *¡Pasaremos!* (1936), which covered uprisings in rural southern towns, they were no match for the popular *andaluzadas*. *Morena clara* reaped record box-office revenue from audiences on both sides during the Civil War. The Republicans banned it only in 1938, when the director was found to have accepted an invitation from Nazi propaganda minister Joseph Goebbels to collaborate in a series of German-Spanish coproductions. With nationalist approval, Rey was joined by his wife, Imperio Argentina (with whom Hitler was infatuated), and Perojo in Nazi Berlin, where they made five folkloric musicals, four set in Andalusia and one in Spanish Morocco. Perojo directed *El barbero de Sevilla* (1938; *The Barber of Seville*), *Mariquilla terremoto* (1938; *Mariquilla the Earthquake*), and *Suspiros de España* (1939; *Sighs of Spain*); Rey directed *Carmen la de Triana* (1938; *Carmen of Triana*) and *La canción de Aixa* (1939; *Aixa's Song*). Andalusian folklore and orientalized settings, appropriate for international consumption, tallied with German perceptions and economic interests in the expanding Latin American market. For nationalist Spain, the films were marketable commodities as well as an important means of identity formation.

Carmen and the Caudillo

Rey's *Carmen la de Triana*, an adaptation of Mérimée's novella *Carmen*, is emblematic of the process of identity formation. At first described as perhaps Moorish or Jewish, Mérimée's Carmen is, as Sander Gilman explains, "the quintessential other"; such "overlapping images of Otherness" are "only possible from the perspective of the French narrator" for whom violent, passionate Carmen stands for everything that he, an educated antiquarian from Paris, is not.[17] In Rey's version, the gypsy is not an outsider against whom a sense of self is defined but an icon of collective identity that mediates Spain's uneasy relation with inherited images. Beyond its value as a highly marketable commodity, the film reconfigured orientalist perceptions of Spain without undermining the religious and heroic principles of the nationalist side. Like the Caudillo himself, who was styled as both crusader and friend of the Moors, Rey's Carmen strategically reconciled seeming opposites to build a new cultural order.

Set in Seville in the summer of 1835, the film revolves around the love triangle between Carmen, a sultry gypsy who lives with a band of smugglers; Antonio Vargas Heredia, a famous toreador; and José Navarro, an upright military officer. After a brawl with a rival dancer at a tavern, Carmen is escorted to jail by José. He falls for her wiles and lets her stop for a change of clothes at her house, where she seduces him. His infatuation with her makes him betray his fellow soldiers, and, now a wanted fugitive, he joins the smugglers. When Carmen's affection for him wears off, a betrayed and frustrated José repents and warns his former comrades-in-arms of the smugglers' planned ambush. He dies tragically, his lost honor restored. During his funeral ceremony, the martyr's dead body is venerated, while a repentant Carmen gazes at the scene from behind a wrought-iron grille.

This filmic version of the myth is clearly motivated by immediate cultural and political concerns. The army is brought to the forefront as the embodiment of "the power of the law, its enforcement, the enactment of justice, and its repressive capacity to discipline and punish, but also to reward and honour those sacrificed in the name of the nation."[18] Discipline and punishment lead not to Carmen's sacrificial death as in the French version, but to her redemption. Characterized in the novella as a sorceress, whore, and even the devil, in the film she becomes a contrite penitent who is reformed rather than sacrificed. This transformation enacts a ritualistic union between two apparently antagonistic female types: the free-willed oriental temptress and the pious and self-abnegating role model promoted by Franco supporters. Changed by trauma and bloodshed, the lively dancer is relocated from the backdrop of palm trees and Islamic architecture at the local inn where she regularly performs to the dungeon-like chamber where a lifeless José is honored by his fellow soldiers.

The film's camerawork elicits ambiguous feelings toward the purged sinner. In the closing sequence, the camera moves past Carmen into the funereal scene. A reverse shot confronts us with her anguished face covered in tears, her hands gripping the bars that separate her from José's corpse (see figure 3.2). This final close-up, a mournful Carmen behind bars, emblematizes the rigid control of potentially subversive exoticism, encouraging the spectator to identify with moral lawfulness and military power from a position of submissive reverence and repentance. At a visual level, the sequence objectifies and contains the protagonist, aligning the spectator's gaze not only with Carmen's perspective, as it has throughout the film, but also with the weeping faces around the martyred soldier.

The soundtrack further enforces ideological control. The Andalusian *coplas* that express the star's wit, charm, and playful eroticism throughout the film give way to sacred hymns, evocative of her subdued passion and penitence as she mourns José's passing. Her heart, described as "black like coal" in her performance of "Los piconeros" ("The Coalmakers") early in the film, is submitted to a ritualistic burning in line with the affective demands of the conservative status quo. In the end, black is not the color of illicit desire, but rueful mourning, symbolized by the veil that drapes her face in the final shot.

Though it lacks any overt political content, the film contributes decisively to constructing and determining the actions of the new subjects of Franco Spain. The scene that introduces the spectator into the funereal chamber, the space of martyrdom, encourages respect for the army as the agent of justice and moral rectitude as much as caution against the snares of passion, instinct, and unlawfulness. After all, José is dead. The ecclesiastical side of the authoritarian order is forcefully represented by the religious tunes that replace Carmen's songs. While the regime favored Andalusian *coplas* as alienating forms of entertainment, their sentimental themes of tragic love and loss could be a transgressive ad-lib in a strictly scripted society. Vázquez Montalbán reports that exhausted housewives and mothers in postwar Spain sang popular tunes about unfulfilled female passion not as commercial hits devoid of social meaning, but as protest songs "against their condition as Carmens

Figure 3.2. Still from Florián Rey's *Carmen la de Triana* (1938). Copyright © 1988 Video Mercury Films, S. A.

of Spain waiting for husbands condemned by History" either to an early grave or a life of oppression and silence.[19] The ceremonial religious rhythms in the film leave no room for surreptitious resistance.

Therefore, Rey's Carmen does not, as some critics have suggested, oppose a myth of female, southern, oriental Spanishness to the myth of Christian Spain; she conflates them. As Eva Woods argues, the movie re-signifies Carmen "as an angel of the home, converted into the female body of National Catholicism."[20] Years later, in the 1950s, the popular *copla* "Carmen de España," usually sung by the musical film star Carmen Sevilla, captured this ideological manipulation with great precision:

> Carmen of Spain,
> brave,
> Carmen in a gypsy dress,
> but Christian and decent.
> . . . .
> I am Carmen of Spain,
> and not Mérimée's.[21]

Understandably, some conservative voices openly denounced the use of such a debased foreign stereotype for nation-building. Writing in the journal *Radiocinema* in January 1939, one critic complained that a movie featuring a "Spain seen by a Frenchman" and inhabited by Andalusian bandits and fortune-tellers should not be "propaganda for the Spanish Empire."[22] This concern was widespread among those Franco supporters who refused to reconcile southern orientalist images with their idea of a hyper-Catholic, imperial Spain that had strong fascist tendencies. Ernesto Giménez Caballero declared in *Arte y Estado* (1935; *Art and State*) that Spain should collaborate with Mussolini's Italy to create a cinema inspired by the Latin Roman Catholic tradition and define itself against imported fictions based on folklore.[23]

However, not everyone committed to the nationalist cause rejected *españoladas*. Another contributor to *Radiocinema* felt *Carmen la de Triana* proved that foreign and authentic representations could coexist: the movie, which did not "stink of *gabacho*," destroyed Mérimée's fake "Espagne" with José's self-sacrifice and Carmen's softened character.[24] In essence, this Andalusia is closer to the world of Christian crusaders than to the marginal underworld of gypsy smugglers and criminals. Along the same lines, a review in the right-wing newspaper *ABC* argued that the main character, extricated from her "surrounding atmosphere, so mystified by the French author," is "a thousand times more desirable than the original cigar maker."[25] The director, Florián Rey, concurred. In a less-than-convincing terminological maneuver, he rejected the label *españolada*, synonymous with inauthenticity, while defending his use of folkloric elements to capture the true "spirit" of Spain.[26] Labels aside, what made his movie compatible with conservative ideology was its domestication of a mythical female icon of uninhibited social and religious transgression.

Rey's reversal of Mérimée's fiction reaffirmed the patriarchal order of nationalist Spain and paved the way for subsequent adaptations. Unlike pre–Civil War *españoladas*, where the Carmen type often threatened the social stability in an otherwise peaceful countryside (e.g. *Rosario la cortijera*, 1935; *Rosario the Country Girl*), the films produced after 1939 frequently featured loyal gypsies falling for or even marrying an army officer.[27] *Carmen la de Ronda* (dir. Tulio Demicheli, 1959; *Carmen of Ronda*) is a case in point. Set in the south during the War of Independence against Napoleon, the movie relates the story of Carmen, played by superstar singer Sara Montiel, and José, a French officer who deserts and joins the Spanish rebels for her love. They die in each other's arms, riddled by French bullets, in an act of sacrifice that leads to a decisive victory over the invaders. To the Spanish spectator, José's treason, prompted by Carmen's seductive power, reflects heightened antiforeign patriotism, not transgressive rebelliousness or shameful betrayal. As mass entertainment, such movies dramatized passivity to the authoritarian state, repression of revolutionary tendencies, and blind support for the military leader at a time when the Axis-inspired fascist model had died out and Spain's economic survival hinged on potentially disruptive foreign influences. The film suggests that these influences can be assimilated (José) or rejected (the French army), but they must never extinguish the true national self (Carmen).

Off screen, actresses who played Carmenesque roles reinforced this message. Foremost among them was Lola Flores, an extremely popular singer, actress, and entertainer whose meteoric career roughly coincided with the Franco years. Like Rey's Carmen, her iconic star persona balanced fervent Catholicism with a reputation for sexual excess. Her love life included rumored affairs with Gary Cooper, Aristotle Onassis, and Ricardo Montalbán, making her an object of fear and fascination for ordinary women doomed to a life of cooking, cleaning, sewing, and child-rearing under the dictatorship. A successful *folklórica*, Flores projected national culture abroad while offering illusory release to repressed female fantasies at home.[28]

At once a transgressive figure and a patriotic icon, Flores was also racially ambiguous. Although she was only part gypsy, she identified strongly with gypsy culture, married a gypsy, and often performed gypsy roles in Andalusian comedies and musicals. She opened her memoirs: "I am not gypsy, even though the truth is that I am not too sure about it. Because in my bones I feel essentially like a gypsy, a total gypsy, a gypsy from head to toe."[29] As a prototypical "white gypsy"—a white or mostly white performer parading as gypsy—she foregrounded difference while integrating it within the status quo. As Eva Woods remarks, the ethnic and cultural diversity associated with the figure of the white gypsy is a "mirage"; the dissimilarity represented in film and song is contained, creating the fantasy that "society's main antagonism" is in its margin, within itself; that nothing exists apart from this society.[30] Nicknamed both "Lola of Spain" and "La Faraona," or the Pharaoh, Flores personified the regime's conflation of traditionalist and orientalist images of the nation.

Flores's star performance as Trini in a 1954 color remake of *Morena clara* plays out this symbolic negotiation. A humorous prologue traces the ancestry of the gypsies back to the Egyptian pharaohs and then rolls into the familiar Pygmalion plot: Trini's social transformation and moral redemption upon joining the household of Enrique, who is a respected prosecutor. Together, the orientalization of the protagonist as Andalusian, gypsy, and Egyptian and her domestication solidify official versions of Spanish national identity. Trini's ethnicity, gender, and class complement rather than oppose the normativity against which she is defined. Her difference translates as authenticity in a political and cultural context that emphasizes Spain's singularity. Her submission to law and order stresses authoritarianism—the all-powerful Franco government can silence or assimilate any opposition, big or small.

Lola's life mirrored Trini's. From the 1930s to the late 1970s, she fashioned herself as a shrewd, oriental temptress as carefully as her identification with the establishment and its leader. Along with Estrellita Castro and Carmen Sevilla, among others, she was known as a *tonadillera de Franco* (Franco's folkloric singer), often performing for the generalissimo on special occasions.[31] Quick-witted and irreverent, she was the wildest of the cohort, which makes her repeated admission that she was *muy franquista* all the more useful from the official viewpoint. In the 1960s, she was the star performer at the Royal Palace of La Granja receptions, held every July 18 to commemorate the rebel rising against the Republic in 1936. Her recollection of the 1961 gathering illustrates her place in Francoist cosmology. Pregnant with her third child, Antonio, she felt sick after her performance and wandered off. A concerned Franco found her in tears and gently consoled her in the "beautiful gardens, full of fountains and soldiers from the *Guardia Mora*."[32] This bucolic setting reconciles apparent opposites: celebration of a victorious Catholic "crusade" under the watch of cavalrymen in Muslim attire, while a fatherly knight rescues the "Pharaoh," who is both the antithesis of docile femininity and a pregnant damsel in distress. The snapshot is crisscrossed with contradictions resolved by Franco's patriarchal authority. Through the iconic Lola Flores, alternatives to accepted gender and racial models are recognized to the extent that they support the principles of the nation and state, foremost among them the Caudillo's uncontested power. Both in life and art, Flores's staged female resistance may temporarily suspend draconian gender pressures and constraints but ultimately must concede the limits of propriety, morality, and decency. Likewise, her orientalized identity, a nod to the country's Moorish past, is a mass-media version of the colonial myth of Hispano-Arab brotherhood, acknowledging Spain's ties to the Muslim world only to reinforce its Catholic essence (see chapter 1).

Perhaps the biographical detail that best exemplified Lola Flores's balancing act between exoticism and traditionalism was her induction into the Order of Isabella the Catholic in 1962. Men who are appointed to this order are called *caballeros*, or knights, and women are called *damas*, or dames. The cross-shaped medallion, inscribed with the twin mottoes "To Proven Loyalty" and "For Isabella the Catholic," is an emblem of the unbreakable alliance of church and throne. Created in 1815 by King Fernando VII, the order rewards "allegiance to Spain" as shown by exceptional services, especially those "provided for the prosperity of territories in America and overseas."[33] In the early nineteenth century, when the Spanish Empire was losing its grip in the Americas, this official accolade reflected an urgent need to promote direct military action. A century and a half later, Spanish preeminence across the Atlantic was conceived in cultural terms. Renouncing the dream of regaining political control, the Franco regime embraced *Hispanidad*—a transatlantic community united by the Catholic religion and the Castilian language—as the foundation of foreign policy in Latin America.[34]

These values proved highly compatible with the papier-mâché Andalusia of Spanish musicals. Beginning with the 1930s Berlin coproductions of Perojo and Rey, which were intended for both domestic and Latin American consumption, nationalists mobilized the cinema to further cultural pan-Hispanism.[35] Famous *folklóricas* like Lola Flores helped the cause. She often performed in the Americas to attain international recognition and a heftier paycheck. In 1951, she signed a contract with the Galician producer Cesáreo González that made her a fortune—6,000,000 pesetas, roughly the equivalent of $20,000,000 in today's U.S. currency. Over the next decade, a glamorous Flores dominated the popular press headlines on both sides of the Atlantic, an increased visibility that turned her into a celebrated ambassador of Andalusianized *Hispanidad* worthy of the Order of Isabella the Catholic. Between 1953 and 1964 she starred in six films, including *La Faraona* (dir. René Cardona, 1956) and *La gitana y el charro* (dir. Gilberto Martínez Solares, 1964; *The Gypsy and the Mexican Cowboy*), that combined overworked gypsy clichés with Mexican folklore. Arrayed in polka-dot dresses with castanets and guitars against a background of dusty agaves and sombreros, a self-assertive woman, often named Carmen or Carmela, is restored to the confines of domesticity by her Mexican suitors. In *La gitana y el charro*, a Mexicanized version of *Morena clara*, Flores plays the archetypical feisty gypsy, doomed to a life of crime among thieves and bandits until a respectable landowner whisks her away on his horse. Moments of comic release and a healthy dose of singing and dancing punctuate the plot's twists and turns. Other movies followed an almost identical pattern, casting Flores as the rebellious, seductive, yet honorable gypsy, a character both highly marketable and ideologically productive.

Flores's performing and public personae, which were almost indistinguishable, composed an allegory of the Andalusia confiscated by the regime. The successful *folklórica* turned Dame of the Order of Isabella the Catholic married market commodity with nationalist propaganda, tallying an orientalized, folkloric south with Francoist nation-building and cultural diplomacy. The connection persisted, albeit in modified form, after the dictator's death in 1975. In the 1980s, Flores appeared on-screen as Isabella the Catholic in the Monty Pythonesque historical comedy *Juana la Loca, de vez en cuando* (dir. José Ramón Larraz, 1983; *Joanna the Ocassional Madwoman*) (see figure 3.3). The movie lampoons the mythical court of the Catholic kings through comic repartee and erotic episodes, often involving the hypersexualized princess Juana. Symptomatic of the post-Franco transition's rejection of pre-1975 symbols and ideals of womanhood, *Juana la Loca* thoroughly debunks historical heroes and traditions held sacred during the Franco era. Indeed, a gypsified Isabella of Castile with a strong Andalusian accent may seem as subversive as the bisexual Christopher Columbus featured in the burlesque *Cristobal Colón de oficio descubridor* (dir. Mariano Ozores, 1981; *Christopher Columbus: A Discoverer by Profession*).

But even in *Juana la Loca* archetypical Francoist imagery flashes. In one of the funniest scenes, Isabella tells the Grand Inquisitor, Fray Tomás de Torquemada (Quique Camoiras), that she has never bathed because she is "clean, pure, chaste, and *olé*." The demeaning joke, capped by a jubilant *olé* more

Figure 3.3. Still from José Ramón Larraz's *Juana la Loca, de vez en cuando* (1983). Copyright © Constán Films, S. L.

fitted to the bullring or flamenco stage than to a medieval queen's chamber, inevitably recalls Flores's conflation of Andalusian, gypsy, and traditional Spanish identities during the dictatorship. Like all parodies, the mock gypsy queen evokes the model. Even as the performer adapts to the new uncensored freedom, she preserves old stereotypes, which look forward and backward at the same time. For all its irreverence, Flores's performance in *Juana la Loca* surreptitiously contradicts the film's ideological intent by establishing the continuity of Andalusian archetypes before and after Franco's death.

Andalusian Mediations

Continuity and change also defined the view of Andalusia promoted by the leading pro-regime writer José María Pemán Pemartín, a reputable chronicler and observer of culture and society under Franco. Born to a wealthy family of lawyers and politicians from Cadiz, he studied law but soon devoted himself to journalism and literature. A prolific poet, dramatist, and essayist, he was the most influential voice of conservative Spain for more than four decades. The young Pemán rose to fame under the Primo de Rivera dictatorship as a persuasive ultra-right publicist and politician. In 1928, he was appointed to supervise the drafting of a new constitution that drastically increased the crown's legislative and judiciary power and limited parliamentary representation. When the monarchy fell to pieces in 1931, he joined a group of diehard antiliberals in founding Acción Española, a counterrevolutionary bloc that fought to restore the bond between throne and altar. The group's repeated calls for a return to traditional, monarchical Spain echoed Marcelino Menéndez Pelayo's conviction that anti-Catholic liberalism and Europeanization were corroding the country's unity and strength.[36] Pemán propagated these views through the organization's periodical, also called *Acción Española.* There he maintained, among other things, that Descartes did not break with religious worldviews but continued them. Published in April 1936, just a few weeks before the outbreak of the Spanish Civil War, "Revisión del Descartes escolar" ("Revising Schoolbook Descartes") builds on the work of the Catholic philosopher Jacques Maritain to stress the poetic, even oneiric, origin of rationalism, depicting Descartes not as a cold thinker but as an impassioned mystic, who gathered his insights from divine epiphanies.[37]

This revisionism characterized Pemán's efforts to head off the renovating influence of the Institución Libre de Enseñanza. As president of the Commission of Culture and Education, created by the nationalists shortly after their rebellion began, he spearheaded a vicious campaign against the cradle of "unbelieving and anarchic generations." A few months after the Civil War's outbreak, he sent a circular letter that characterized the Republic's "revolutionary hordes" as the ILE's "spiritual children"; he called on those who wanted to redeem the blood spilled by nationalist martyrs on the battlefield to "combat resolutely the system that has honored and elevated evil wrongdoers for more than a century."[38] His followers did not disappoint: thousands of cultural workers branded enemies of the nation were removed from their posts. Books deemed subversive, from the French *Encyclopedia* to Marxist treatises, were burned. Schools and universities were purged of *institucionismo.*

Pemán pushed his cultural agenda on the stage. His highly popular dramas, including *El divino impaciente* (1933; *A Man of Divine Impatience*), *Cisneros* (1935), and *Noche de levante en calma* (1935; *Windless Night*), combined historical, religious, and Andalusian themes to promote royal authority and Catholic values as the true essence of Spain. *Cuando las Cortes de Cádiz* (1934; *At the Courts of Cadiz*), written and first staged during the Second Republic and later adapted for the big screen during Francoism (*Lola la piconera*, 1951; *Lola the Coal Girl*), anticipates the alliance of reactionary thought and Andalusian folklore that national *flamenquismo* consolidated. Set in Cadiz during the War of Independence against Napoleon in the early nineteenth century, the play is a virulent attack on liberalism, which is depicted as alien to the soul of the Spanish people. The protagonist, Lola the Coal Girl, a gypsy dancer, is seduced by the Frenchified Spanish politician Luis de Acuña, a member of the Cortes that drafted Spain's first constitution in 1812. Driven by his selfish political agenda, he causes Lola's downfall and execution by the French. The play is a stern reminder that liberal politicians are self-serving and egotistical. They are more interested in hollow oratory than in the suffering of anonymous patriots, and they can scarcely represent the popular will. Spain's true roots and values, incarnated by Lola, are opposed to parliamentary freedoms, which are harmful rather than liberating and serve foreign (French) interests. The analogies between 1812 and 1934 were hard to miss. Spaniards were encouraged to learn from their past and turn away from the deceitful promises of left-liberal politicians, perceived as cloaked traitors. In contrast, the Andalusian *pueblo* and its customs are glorified as the authentic embodiment of the nation.

Andalusia remained the center of Pemán's symbolic universe during the Franco years. Little in his version of his native land is his own invention; it is not place, but commonplace—a parade of dancers, bullfighters, indolent agrarian workers, Holy Week penitents, and clapping revelers at local fiestas. His originality lies in the adaptability of his view, which crossed from mass cultural media to highbrow academic debates without compromising its right-wing character. Pemán could utter a philosophical meditation and sing a *copla* in the same breath. He was revered by his fellows at the Spanish Academy, which he directed in the 1930s and 1940s, and by folklore divas like Lola Flores, who was eternally grateful for a rather trite verse he dedicated to her in 1957: "Whirlwind of colors / There is no flower in the world / That the wind moves better / Than Lola Flores." Like her, he contributed decisively to Andalusia's incorporation in the regime's socially conservative project, though his repertoire was more varied and polyvalent. Shuttling from history book and newspaper column to stage, big screen, and, in the 1960s, television, he harnessed his imagined Andalusia to the shifting yet essentially conservative contours of Franco Spain.

Pemán had some brushes with Francoist censorship due to his strong monarchist views. His private diary reveals his anger at Franco's refusal to relinquish power to the legitimate heir to the throne, Don Juan de Borbón.[39] He was also frustrated with other loyalist groups, especially the *falangistas*, who were lukewarm about the role of the Catholic Church in the new state. However, he shared enough with the regime to prove a lasting asset. His pages on national history and identity are mediations more than meditations; social and cultural transformations never contradict what he calls the "most unchallengeable and nuclear" Spanishness. From his preferred "observation post," Andalusia, he anchored Francoism's ideological shifts to lasting antirevolutionary values.[40] Whether bucolic utopia, Catholic haven, or tourist destination, Pemán's Andalusia is a place where social agitation is conspicuous only by its absence, and history is experienced in parenthesis: within yet separated from specific material conditions.

Pemán's first systematic theory of Andalusia, "Andalucía, la eternamente vencedora" ("Andalusia, the Eternal Victor"), appeared in the conservative newspaper *El Debate* in 1928.[41] It produced a formula that long outlived its defining moment, bequeathing a set of themes and tropes that resurfaced at key moments during the dictatorship to support antiquated beliefs and structures. In Pemán's view, true Andalusia is rooted in Tartessos, not in a foreign invention by Mérimée. Bullfighting, dancing, and southern indolence are the legacy of the ancient civilization. Like an incorruptible grain of salt, Andalusia's spirit has flavored successive waves of invaders—Romans, Visigoths, Arabs, and Castilians. Some mixtures turned out more savory than others. While Pemán reduces the Arab presence to a handful of mercenaries who quickly surrendered to the magnetic charm of the natives, he delights in the robust stoicism the Romans brought, which persists to the present. Seneca could be found, not in philosophy books, but in the sententious wisdom of old Andalusian peasants.

Startling in its similarity to Ortega y Gasset's language in "Teoría de Andalucía," which had been published about a year earlier, Pemán's article is its ideological antithesis. If they agree on typical southern traits, Ortega y Gasset sees them as residues of antiquity that must be expunged from modern, Europeanized Spain, while Pemán sees them as the root of national authenticity. To him, Andalusia is a conservative haven devoid of social tensions, where agrarian workers are consummate stoics who do not worry about things they cannot change. Their imagined acceptance is extremely valuable for someone who wants to preserve retrograde values and elitist structures. Pemán prescribed stoicism to endure the hardship of autarky in the 1940s and the recession that came with economic liberalization in the late 1950s and early 1960s. In "Estoicismo y economía" ("Stoicism and Economy") published in *ABC* in September 1959, shortly after the First Stabilization Plan opened the country to foreign capital, causing recession and unemployment, he urged the average "stoic Spaniard" to dig deep and "fasten your seatbelt." While such "social tailoring" is unpleasant, it is "less pleasant to see one's pants fall off" in front of the modern world.[42] He also accommodates stoicism with Christian idealism and self-denial. Poverty and impotence should be embraced happily and gratefully. He would develop *el Séneca*, an Andalusian bumpkin, to popularize these views in dozens of articles published in *ABC* from the 1940s to the late 1960s, and on state television from 1964 to 1970.

If "Andalucía, la eternamente vencedora" mediated elitist ideas of authority, hierarchy, and order to subdue the laboring masses, Pemán's "Los amigos moros" ("Our Friends the Moors"), written during the Civil War, reconciled anti-Islamic Catholicism with the Moorish soldiers fighting on the nationalist side.[43] Pemán believed that Western civilization is the only civilization; it is synonymous with classical heritage and Christianity and is antagonistic to liberals, Africans, and Asians. He warned repeatedly against the oriental threat, which came in different guises: Buddhism, communism, materialism, and atheism. "Damned be the Orient where / even the air is adultery," he wrote in his most popular play, *El divino impaciente*.[44] He abhorred *nigricia*, or the imitation of black customs, which he perceived in the popularity of jazz and the "Africanized flesh" of tanned beachgoers. Yet his racism was assimilationist rather than exclusionist.[45] He thought the teachings of civilization could redeem inferior races, as in 711 and 1936, when, in joining forces with true Spaniards, the Moors were decisive in saving the country from barbarism and decadence. Bringing the logic of Arabism and Africanism to his middlebrow readership, Pemán argued that the medieval Hispano-Arab and the pro-Franco Moroccan mercenary were admirable not because of their Islamic culture, which he judged cruel, sadistic, and superficial, but because they contributed to preserving western Christianity. His famous "Poema de la Bestia y el Ángel" (1938; "Poem of the Beast and the Angel"), a thinly veiled allegory of the Civil War, claims that the Moors are heroes only because they fight for God "against the infidel enemy," who, mutatis mutandis, is now the atheistic red.[46]

Soul for Sale

If the goal after the Civil War was uprooting all internal enemies, the priority in the 1950s and 1960s was economic modernization and keeping the demands for change from urban workers, students, clandestine political opposition, and even ecclesiastical authorities within acceptable limits. Unlike some prominent rightist intellectuals, Pemán realized that pushing Andalusia as a stark contrast to modernity would not count for much in an increasingly material and secular world. His friend Florentino Pérez Embid, the highest censorship authority under the uncompromising minister of information and tourism, Gabriel Arias Salgado, tried this approach. Pérez Embid's "Pequeña teoría de Andalucía" (1963; "Little Theory of Andalusia") laments the effects of urbanization and economic development and lauds a traditional rural life that only existed in the minds of conservative writers. Since reality did not match rhetoric, he affirms that Andalusia is "a poetic category."[47] Favoring abstractions over material conditions, he quotes the pro-regime poet Joaquín Romero Murube: "The vibration of light: this is the secret of Andalusia. Light translated into rhythm and expressing all our feelings, all our words. What is the secret of our cities and countryside if not this luminous enchantment that surrounds us?"[48] Nowhere in view is the suffering Andalusian people who Rafael Alberti, in exile, inveighing against Franco's Spain, called "serious, pure, and heartbroken / in the lands of light; / Poor unemployed / peasants, laborers of hunger / wandering along pathways."[49]

Pérez Embid's text proved to be the swan song of the antiquated conservatism of the 1940s, when official doctrine favored pastoral stasis over mechanization and technological progress. No longer an isolated stronghold, Spain opened to the global market, joining the United Nations in 1955, the International Monetary Fund in 1958, and the World Bank in 1959. In 1962, a World Bank report encouraged Spain to burst the autarkic bubble by liberalizing trade and attracting foreign investment, specifically through tourism, and instructed the government to promote Spanish beaches as an attractive destination for sun-starved northern Europeans.[50] Manuel Fraga Iribarne, the newly appointed minister of tourism and information, was happy to oblige. He masterminded a propaganda campaign under the slogan "Spain is different," which rolled out in 1964. It consolidated a new phase of economic and cultural *apertura*, or opening, to Western cash and customs. A deluge of promotional material featuring iconic images ranging from gypsy dancers to hooded Holy Week penitents refashioned Spain's idiosyncrasy—some might say backwardness—as a commodity. The cultural traits that had excluded the peninsula from the rest of Europe were now an attractive trademark. It was as if Franco was now ready to sell what he had sought to save in 1936. The marketing gimmick succeeded, and foreign capital began to pour in. By the end of the 1960s, more than 20,000,000 visitors per year accounted for over 9 percent of the gross national product.

Prosperity came at a high moral price. The newcomers' customs and attitudes clashed with the restrictive principles of national Catholicism. Bikini-clad blondes flooded the Mediterranean coastline year after year, and Spanish men were hard-pressed to heed benighted rants to preserve national authenticity such as "Let our friends, our servants, our girlfriends be Spaniards. Don't let customs other than ours live in the blessed land of Spain."[51] Along with a seemingly unending source of revenue, tourism created its own mythology that was centered on Don Juan Turístico (Don Juan the Tourist), an average Joe in search of adventure who came to beach resorts to chase Nordic females.[52] Traditionalists were outraged. The Catholic newspaper *¡Ya!* branded the loose morals of tourists "anathema to healthy Spanish custom." The bishop of the Canary Islands saw in the bikini "a symbol of the delinquency and degeneration of today's woman."[53] Despite these puritanical protests, the new myths created by the tourist boom played right into the regime's hands. The country's image was renewed, and what conservatives considered to be the nation's eternal values were perhaps compromised but not destroyed. *Apertura* meant opening previously shut doors and windows, not abandoning the house.

Representations of Andalusia in the mass media played a crucial role in this symbolic negotiation between old and new. Sunny southern beaches, welcoming locals, and cheap prices were a holidaymaker's paradise and a breeding ground for sexual permissiveness. This picture-perfect yet morally decadent setting, the fodder of promotional brochures, acquired a tamer look in domestic films produced in the 1960s. Moviegoers were exposed to an Andalusia caught between the demands of economic expansion and an allegiance to national essences—between moneymaking fun-in-the-sun and respect for timeless patriotic values. This dilemma's most recognizable face and voice was the actor and singer Manolo Escobar, the son of workers who migrated from the rural south to Barcelona; he made it big in showbiz and ended up marrying a German tourist. The prototypical Don Juan Turístico in life and art, he reconciled national Catholicism, national *flamenquismo*, and the "different" Spain of the consumerist era.[54] His signature role was the blue-collar worker with exceptional singing abilities who faced an agonizing choice between tradition and modernity, with the latter often represented by his love for a northern tourist or the dream of a successful career as a pop star. In the end, he manages to have it both ways; he benefits from the new opportunities, carnal or commercial, afforded by foreigners without relinquishing his integrity and moral superiority as a Spaniard. In *Un beso en el puerto* (dir. Ramón Torrado, 1966; *A Kiss in the Harbor*), he plays a rural gas station employee, also named Manolo, who is dazzled by the allure and glitter of the tourist boomtown Benidorm. After he is fired for singing on the job, he spends his days crooning through high-rise buildings and along golden beaches and seducing gullible foreigners ready to fall in his lap. Eventually, he steers clear of endless flirtations and embraces old-fashioned family values. The message in this and similar films reinforced the regime's ideological orthodoxy.

Although Escobar's movies retain the early Francoist image of Andalusian Spain, the contexts seem to empty it of enduring significance. Like the *folklóricas* from the 1950s, he is remembered for his inflamed nationalism. His hit single "¡Y viva España!" (1973; "Long Live Spain") still swelled the patriotism of thousands of soccer fans celebrating Spain's FIFA World Cup win in 2010. Crowds chorused the hit as an aging Escobar, attired in a red-and-yellow suit and flanked by the team on a stage set up in Madrid's Puente del Rey, closed the victory ceremony. However, when his songs were woven into rags-to-riches plots set in the age of tourism, their goal seemed more to simply entertain, not to indoctrinate or stir chest-thumping patriotism. Framed as commercial spectacle for consumption, Escobar's "brand of authentic Spanishness" was, in the words of one perceptive critic, "staged performance, a game, even a hoax, the truthfulness of which is irrelevant to its value."

In 1952, Luis García Berlanga's film *Bienvenido Mr. Marshall* (*Welcome Mr. Marshall*) dramatized this tension in its depiction of an impoverished Castilian town hurriedly made over into an Andalusian fantasyland to attract foreign aid from the U.S. secretary of state, who never shows up. It implies that in putting Spain's soul up for sale, its society becomes a hollow husk, an empty commercial label barely disguising the gaping "ontological void" left by traditional certainties.[55] The trick is never letting the imposed mask slip, lest it reveal the absence of a face.

And yet, *Bienvenido Mr. Marshall* was officially declared of "national interest," a sign that existentialist cynicism is more obvious to today's postmodern scholar than to the millions of Spaniards for whom the imposed stereotypes and moralistic constraints of the Franco regime were hardly null and void. A nihilistic reading of development-era Spain fails to account for persistent government efforts to save the soul beneath the skin. For regime supporters, opening up did not mean selling out. New conceptions of the nation-state were still very much rooted in conservative principles that no one took lightly. In a general climate of cultural tolerance and relaxed censorship, the 1963 censorship guidelines, Normas Cinematográficas, still enforced extreme prudery, instructing filmmakers to avoid topics that might infringe on "the Catholic Church, its dogma, its morality, and its cult, the fundamental principles of the state, dignity, homeland security, and everything that might undermine the authority of the Head of State."[56] Banned subjects included divorce, abortion, birth control, prostitution, and deviant sexual behavior. In 1966 a new law abolished censorship of the press, but ideological control was still felt in state-run television. Its official publication, *Tele/Radio*, affirmed that "it is not permissible, neither legally nor morally, to elude in one way or another the vital obligation to shelter the people's morals."[57]

Pemán, who had become a TV celebrity in the 1960s thanks to the success of the sitcom *El Séneca*, marshalled his arguments in new configurations to convince a more mobile and educated middle class that imported hedonism and economic prosperity could coexist with traditional values. For instance, he assured readers of *Gaceta Ilustrada* (*Illustrated Gazette*), a Catholic version of *Paris Match* or *Life*, that capitalism was essentially Christian. In a rather naive reading of Cold War oppositions, he conflated economic and spiritual reactions against Marxism, forcing an unholy alliance of market forces and religious principles.[58] Another Catholic periodical, the cultural monthly *El Ciervo* (*The Deer*), quickly disarmed Pemán's flimsy argument, stressing the inherent immorality of mass consumption and capitalist accumulation. A system that placed greed over justice and market demands over real human needs could hardly respond to "evangelical premises."[59]

A bit out of his element among economic abstractions, Pemán was at his most convincing in Andalusia, observing changing conditions as if in quarantine. In "El Séneca y los turistas" (1951; "Seneca and the Tourists"), the laconic peasant intones that the best way to attract foreign investment is by holding on to traditional roots and values. French holidaymakers passing his farm on their way to the beach see only bulls in his herd of milk cows but he refrains from correcting them. "We should not try to be civilized and industrious," he observes. "They ask for *toros bravos* [brave bulls] and we should not tell them they are *vacas de leche* [milk cows]." Rather than rejecting the "black legend" and "dressing in pink," he encourages Spaniards to look the part and cash in. The timeless and the timely can coexist in harmony and preserve morals. Like "young widows who come out of mourning too quickly," suggesting frivolity, Spain may lose its spiritual worth (and a great deal of revenue) by trying to imitate foreign customs.[60] Conversely, accepting foreign expectations about national identity need not damage or contradict essential values.

Time Travel

Pemán's travel book *Andalucía* (1958) develops these insights. One of the sixteen guides to Spain that Ediciones Destino commissioned from well-known authors (e.g., Josep Pla, Pío Baroja, Dionisio Ridruejo) from 1943 to 1977, *Andalucía* suspends the region between fact and fiction. It provides specific details about culture and society, creating an image informed by firsthand observations yet watermarked by the timeless south sublimated by Pérez Embid. Its more than 500 pages are packed with illustrations, photographs, and maps, but they provide no conventional travel guidance about hotels, restaurants, shops, and not-to-miss entertainment venues. If the common travel guide bridges home and abroad, Pemán's rendering of his native land is, as he puts it, "intimate and personal."[61] Closer to Washington Irving than Baedeker, he encourages an orientalist view that caters to tourist expectations while justifying conservative understandings of the country's past.

Half guidebook, half lyrical recollection, *Andalucía* has a dual purpose: turning the south into a desirable tourist destination without disrupting its traditional roots. Capturing the spirit of *desarrollismo* (developmentalism), it toes the line between consumer demands and conservative principles. It opens with a summary of Pemán's 1928 article, "Andalucía, la eternamente vencedora," and rather than placing the region on the map, traps it in a time warp. Metaphysical meditation meets tourist experience a few pages later, as Pemán, wending through centuries-old palaces, cathedrals, and mosques, takes the reader back in time to the civilizations that layer the region's culture. Architectural landmarks, from Seville's Giralda to Cordoba's Mosque-Cathedral, testify to eight centuries of Arab presence in Andalusia, though Pemán sees classical and Christian roots in the region's culture. Speaking of the Giralda, he focuses on the Roman and Visigothic cornerstones on which the Moorish minaret was built. Under the interlaced red and white horseshoe arches of the Cordoba Mosque-Cathedral, he directs our attention to the "forest of Roman columns" on which they rest, an emblem of the inflexible determination with which "Lucan's and Seneca's Cordoba" persists through the ages.[62] Even what is inarguably Muslim about this monument—the civilization that built it—owes its grandeur to Roman influences. The Umayyad Caliphate was a beacon during the Middle Ages and produced an architectural marvel like the Mosque-Cathedral only due to "its distance from Baghdad and its settlement on the splendid Roman Baetica."[63]

Pemán's observations on architectural syncretism also downplay the Islamic component of the Alcazar of Seville, one of the city's most representative sites. Built by the Almohads in the twelfth century, it was expanded by the Castilian king Peter the Cruel in the fourteenth century. His *mudéjar* additions imitate Moorish workmanship, from the latticework arches that grace dozens of balconies and entryways to the intricate plasterwork that covers interior walls with arabesque ornamentation. Against all evidence, Pemán claims that Peter's work is not an homage to the taste of the conquered Moors but manifests an autochthonous style. The Alcazar and Islamic culture, he argues, have little in common. The same applies to Andalusia, where the label "Arab" "is excessive." Peter the Cruel, he concedes, "was an 'orientalist'" but practiced "an Andalusian orientalism," which differed substantially from that of Baghdad.[64] Paradoxically, this orientalism de-orientalizes, detaching Andalusia from the Muslim world to reveal its indigenous character.

In Pemán's hands, orientalism also mediates between Spain's history and the international marketplace. Assuming the role of travel agent, Pemán sells Andalusia's Islamic legacy as exotic fare for avid European tourists who do not want to visit the orient. Andalusia offers northern visitors all the benefits and none of the inconveniences of journeying to Asia or North Africa. The fare is cheaper, and the customs more familiar. In an "Orient where there is no need to fast during Ramadan," they can stroll down from Granada's Alhambra gardens, sit in a nearby restaurant, and order *boeuf à la mode*, or French pot roast.[65] Pious visitors can proceed to the crypt of the Catholic kings in the cathedral and fulfill Charles V's printed request of a Lord's Prayer for the souls of his grandparents.[66] Granada, a curious hybrid of Islamic theme park and Catholic enclave, shores up an increasingly precarious alliance between antiquated values and modernization epitomized by the tourist industry. Pemán's *Andalucía* does not idealize an organic community frozen in time, like the typical *españolada* film, nor does it portray it as a commodity bereft of spiritual connotations like a Manolo Escobar comedy. Instead, it is a halfway house between immovable spiritual principles and economic and social development—between myth and reality.

Reality can be distasteful at times, but Pemán is ready to harmonize it with his idealized perception. His guide registers social unrest in the rural south only to minimize or deny it, but while holidaymakers reveled on the coast or gaped at Islamic buildings, agrarian workers in the late 1950s faced bleak conditions. Rural migration to urban centers and the mechanization of agriculture reduced their number but not their age-old struggles with unemployment and exploitation. Salaries in 1960 were proportionately lower than in 1936.[67] With inflation averaging over 10 percent annually, the disproportion between wages and prices made it impossible for families to meet their daily needs, causing widespread malnutrition, chronic diseases, and child underdevelopment. As one historian put it, the province of Malaga, the "glamorous tourist destination that would be known as the Costa del Sol, could more accurately have been called the Costa del Hambre (Coast of Hunger)." From 1960 to 1961, only three years after Pemán published his idyllic portrayal of the region, unemployment increased in Malaga from 23,000 to over 27,000 "even though the hemorrhage of emigration to Europe had already begun." The dispossessed peasantry in the towns that dotted the coastline were "caught between semi-feudal conditions and rampant capitalist greed, with a fascist bent."[68] Younger generations fled to become janitors, waiters, and cleaning ladies in Madrid, Barcelona, Valencia, and other major cities. The villages of their parents and grandparents languished: streets were unpaved, lands were uncultivated, and municipal services were sorely lacking, in brutal contrast to the image of peace and prosperity disseminated by the authorities.

Pemán edited out all these desperate details. Even when broadening his range to include social issues, he keeps the lid on dissatisfaction. During his visit to Carmona near Seville, he remarks that the idle peasants in the town square might suggest a "social problem of unemployment, which does not correspond with reality." No, the apparent apathy is merely stoicism. In his opinion, Andalusian character is rooted in Roman attitudes; specifically, the Olympian indifference championed by Cicero and Seneca. Work comes and goes, but Carmona's day laborers keep calm and always find time to sit on a park bench and take in "the sun, the wind, time, and life."[69]

The pages he devotes to La Chanca, a poor neighborhood in the southeastern province of Almeria, delete all traces of neglect. He senses the "moderate vitality and good sense of humor" of the ghetto's inhabitants, although they are nowhere to be seen in the accompanying photographs. The "half Stoic, half Morisco" community is said to spend its days "singing and laughing," oblivious to the tragic living conditions brutally depicted in critical reporting of the 1950s and 1960s, including Carlos Pérez Siquier's photo study, housed at the Reina Sofía Art Museum in Madrid, and Juan Goytisolo's book *La Chanca* (1962), which states that in an environment where "poverty is queen," the locals lived the "enslaved existence of men subjected to savage colonial exploitation."[70]

Social protest makes a fleeting, if anachronistic, appearance in Pemán's account. Conflating the dispossessed agrarian worker and the ostracized medieval Morisco, he joins their voices across time in the mournful notes of flamenco deep song only to trivialize it. The depth of deep song refers to "something dark and confusing," not to the suffering caused by the loss of a culture, land, and freedom.[71] The truth in flamenco is not social or historical but purely lyrical. As Pemán states elsewhere, Andalusian songs manifest a fatalism that places complaints and grievances outside of time and space. Discontent never responds to scarcity, hunger, or any other "vulgar" need; it is explained by "cleaner and more aristocratic" psychological processes, which he leaves tantalizingly undefined.[72] Flamenco is thus depoliticized and depleted of social significance. Rather than a call for civil rights, the lyrics voice an eternal spiritual pain untouched by utilitarian concerns. In flamenco, as in life, Pemán contends, drawing straightforward connections between poetic abstractions and real and pressing human concerns is a mistake. *Andalucía* faithfully observes this caveat.

Pemán continued to deflect the working-class unrest that accompanied the economic changes in the 1950s and 1960s through el Séneca, the ideal inhabitant of the region imagined in *Andalucía*, who is meant to voice "the opinions and commentaries of many peasants. I have called him el 'Séneca,'" Pemán wrote, "because the name of the famous Stoic philosopher from Cordoba has remained in Andalusia the paradigm of moral and sententious wisdom."[73] Like flamenco, this wisdom sublimates material interests out of existence. For el Séneca, the bread-and-butter demands of the workers he supposedly represents are better dropped and forgotten. Against collective bargaining for better conditions and wages, he holds up an artisanal idea of work as a labor of love. Like art, work is an exercise of "elegance and freedom" that should not be straitjacketed by "regulations and trade unions."[74] The antithesis of the unionized worker, el Séneca embraces negation over negotiation. If there is no problem, why seek a solution?

Pemán sniffily disdained problems of which others were painfully aware. In response to mounting pressure, the government promulgated a Law of Collective Agreements in 1958, allowing limited bargaining in the workplace. Comisiones Obreras (Workers' Commissions) emerged as a working-class organization that rejected the paternalist official unions controlled by Falange and operated at the grass roots to negotiate demands in response to the immediate needs of its affiliates. Although these demands were economic rather than political, they opened unprecedented space for dialogue in civil society, encouraging the development of democratic processes and models of citizenship. At the same time, the 1959 Stabilization Plan triggered a lasting recession. Income fell and unemployment rose with deflation. Some workers emigrated to Europe; others took their demands to the streets. Labor protests and strikes overflowed the nation's cities, more than doubling in number from the early 1960s to 1974, when almost 2,300 were reported.[75] The aftershocks of urban agitation were felt in rural areas, including the sherry-producing region of southwestern Andalusia, where Pemán's family was heavily invested in vineyards.[76]

In reaction, Pemán mediated between state and society through the small-screen adaptation of el Séneca, which aired at prime time on national television from 1964 to 1970. A flamenco jingle introduced viewers to a traditional Andalusian patio, where el Séneca (Antonio Martelo) delivered his wisdom with a strong southern accent to a group of town notables: the mayor, the priest, and the schoolteacher. The *costumbrista* set was impervious to social conflict. Like the travel guide *Andalucía*, the studio conjured up an imaginary land that muted and replaced contestation with an unthinking acceptance of ancestral customs. The episode "El Séneca y los juguetes" ("Seneca and the Toys"), which aired on January 26, 1965, at 9 P.M., spelled out the connection between Andalusian folklore and social peace. In line with state paternalism, el Séneca sees syndical practices and calls for political rights as children's toys, but of course Pemán dresses up his reactionary message with backhanded praise. If the masses are like children, it is not because they are immature, unsophisticated, and whimsical but because their imagination and wisdom exceed the limits of parliamentary and syndical representation, just as childlike ingenuity is ultimately unsatisfied by dolls and figurines. The people's "mysteries and fantasies" are fleshed out by bullfighters and flamenco singers; politicians and union leaders are simplistic toys that curb popular creativity. "Pan y toros" ("bread and bulls"), an anti-Enlightenment motto from the nineteenth century, captures the type of social order that Pemán's mouthpiece advocates, where sustenance (*pan*) comes first and entertainment second—if not *toros*, then "religious pilgrimages, dances, ferias, and things like that" but "most definitely not elections and trade union meetings."[77] In lauding unchanging rituals as authentic manifestations of collective consciousness, Pemán performs an insidious form of censorship, exchanging debates in the public sphere for mindless participation in recurrent ceremonies that arrest any notion of social, historical, and political progress. In el Séneca's world, the people have the power to dance, clap, and cheer but not to govern themselves.

Popular will is acknowledged, then canceled. In fact, el Séneca's role as the voice "of many peasants" was precarious at best. An *hombre de pueblo*, or townsman, he is loath to be considered part of the *pueblo*, the people, a sovereign entity and historical agent that, according to Pemán, always stirs up unwanted social turmoil and revolution. Being down to earth precludes any desire to make the law of the land. "I don't mind being poor, humble, and hard-working," el Séneca avers, "but 'pueblo,' God forbid!" Just as Pemán's orientalism minus orient reconciles traditional Catholic values and Islamic legacies with market forces, el Séneca's *pueblo* without the *pueblo*, his passive alternative to organized labor and representative democracy, balances the restive popular will with the corporate desire for stability.

Territory of Strife

In the face of an uncertain political future, with the aging dictator and his regime living on borrowed time, representations of Andalusia became a tug-of-war between conflicting political and intellectual factions. Reformed Franco loyalists evolving toward moderate liberalism saw Pemán's formula as the ticket to democracy, but it satisfied no one pushing for a complete break with the hoary structures of the regime. Pedro Laín Entralgo belonged to the first group; Manuel Vázquez Montalbán, to the second.

With just a few amendments, Laín, a prominent fascist intellectual and former rector of University of Madrid, accepted Pemán's south as the foundation for a renewed Spain. In August 1974, about a year before Franco's death, he delivered a speech at a conference honoring Pemán in Cadiz, rehashing a proposal he had formulated almost three decades earlier in *España como problema* (1949; *Spain as a Problem*). That controversial book advised the Civil War victors to trade exclusionary rhetoric for a commitment to rebuild the nation through debate and dialogue with the vanquished. Reaction would be cautiously abandoned without fully embracing antipatriotic liberalism; a conciliatory stance would transcend ideological divisions without sacrificing the country's Catholic roots. At the time, supporters of Francoist orthodoxy, most notably Florentino Pérez Embid and Rafael Calvo Serer, stubbornly resisted Laín's pleas for pluralism. Calvo Serer's devastating rejoinder, *España, sin problema* (1949; *Spain without a Problem*), which was awarded the Francisco Franco National Literature Prize shortly after its publication, viewed the Civil War not as a semicolon in Spain's history, but as a period—the resolution of centuries of dispute over the nation's essence.

Laín's speech at the Pemán conference, "La Andalucía de Pemán" (1974; "The Andalusia of Pemán"), can be read as a postscript to *España como problema*, a response to the clamor in the street, the countryside, and the shop floor. The solution to national problems was neither state repression nor abstract discussions about Spanishness. In 1974, as in 1949, Laín's strategy was to integrate dissidence with orthodoxy, but he saw the conflict differently: as a clash between the raw social realities faced by ordinary people—unemployment, lack of basic political rights, class conflict—and purely intellectual notions of collective identity, conservative or liberal. Both exegetical and programmatic, "La Andalucía de Pemán" builds Spain's post-dictatorial future on the writer's view of his homeland. For someone like Laín, who envisioned top-down reform rather than grassroots revolution, the selfless stoicism that Pemán assigns to Andalusians has high political value. What many saw as lethargic apathy is the key to success in work and life. Fine wine-making, like "all great things," thrives on the "very Andalusian" policy of letting things take their course. Laín was quoting Pemán and implying that fighting Francoism might not be as effective as taking a back seat.[78] In this political context, Pemán's words suggest that anti-regime protesters should let their sour grapes ripen into liberating liquor by doing nothing.

If Pemán's Andalusia was melting into thin air during the last years of the dictatorship, Laín recovered it as a blueprint for the future. Although Pemán opposes his myth of the south to industrialization, labor demands, strikes, and even the suntan lotion desecrating the beaches of legendary Tartessos, Laín celebrates two qualities that support an ethical model for a changing society. First, he sees an "ecumenical pact" between tradition and modernity in the protagonist of Pemán's comedy *El río se entró en Sevilla* (1963; *The River Flooded Seville*), a landowner who needs help from those with technological know-how to preserve her crumbling estate. Second, he promotes the "lazy conception of progress" displayed by ancestral peoples like the Andalusians, who have been through it all and know that advancement is illusory.[79] The message is gradualism: replacing the worn pieces of the old system through agreements and concessions across class and ideological divides. The ruling elite should adjust to the new times and the rising demands for "political freedom, social justice, and technical efficiency."[80] The working class should view promises of material gain with irony and consider work not as a bargaining chip for social advancement, but as an end in itself. A "man in the Andalusian manner," detached from misguided revolutionary calls, abandons any hope of living in the best of all possible worlds like a "simple animal, satisfied and happy." His fatalistic attitude is crystallized in traditional flamenco *coplas* of pain and sorrow.[81]

Laín's Andalusia harmonizes the demands of a restive society through internal structural transformation. Instead of reawakening red Andalusia, post-Franco Spain required an exemplary south, "creative and open to pacts, accepting and original, new and essential."[82] In the end, this rhetoric corresponded quite closely with practice. Francoism collapsed, not through the revolutionary struggle of the masses, but through consensual arbitration among political elites and the military. After the dictator's death, the organized opposition chose reform over rupture, accepting the legitimacy of the regime's structures while working to transform them. Following the logic of "elite convergence," communist leaders recognized the monarchy and the flag in exchange for legal status as a political party. Most drastically, by the time the socialist party came to power in 1982 its leader, Felipe González, had eliminated its Marxist rhetoric, turning it into the "most conservative 'socialist' party in Europe, adopting more restrictive economic and fiscal policies than the preceding center-right UCD governments."[83] Democratic stability was consolidated through a choreographed elite settlement in which ordinary citizens were deemed, not actors, but stoic spectators like el Séneca.

The problem with this model is that "el Séneca does not exist," to use Manuel Vázquez Montalbán's words in the leftist magazine *Triunfo* (*Triumph*) in 1972. He is a mask that hides "the true face of the Andalusian people" and, by extension, the Spanish nation. An "eternal spectator," his occasional mockery of established rules of conduct and moral prudishness is a poor substitute for the "radical, real, truly questioning criticism" that would have jeopardized elite orchestration of the transition to democracy.[84] According to Vázquez Montalbán, Pemán's character, the mouthpiece of a "useless liberalism," falsified the realities of life and the needs of ordinary citizens under authoritarian rule while robbing them of the power to express themselves in the public sphere. This assessment captures the link between genuine opposition to the regime and the demystification of Andalusian reality that other contributors to *Triunfo* took seriously and developed in hundreds of articles in the 1960s and 1970s.

Left-wing intellectuals ranging from Alfonso Carlos Comín to Antonio Burgos channeled political dissatisfaction in their uncompromising reportage of southern underdevelopment. While they focused on social questions, they did not neglect popular culture as a site of struggle and resistance. Walking the high-tension wire between theory and practice, they mobilized Andalusian culture to denounce economic stagnancy and class inequalities. Pemán and Laín used folklore to dull critical consciousness; *Triunfo* presented it as a sphere that said "no" to bourgeois power in order to build socialism. As

Stuart Hall explains, this is "why 'popular culture' matters" from a Marxist point of view. Otherwise, we might not "give a damn about it."[85] For instance, flamenco is valued in *Triunfo* not for its musical qualities or fatalistic outlook, but for its capacity to redefine the people as an active social bloc pushing against the blindness and exclusions of the dictatorship, most of which remained unaltered after 1975. This collective intellectual effort, a road not taken during the post-Franco transition, died with the magazine in 1982, just a few months before the electoral victory of González's reformed socialist party, which represented the inversion, rather than the culmination, of the spirit underlying *Triunfo*'s Andalusia.

The magazine, founded in 1946, was originally devoted to the performing arts, and its stories often featured *folklórica* stars, such as Lola Flores and Carmen Sevilla. A slow yet relentless change in editorial policy began in 1962 with the relaxation of the censorship laws. Under the direction of José Ángel Ezcurra, the publication included articles on international affairs that indirectly questioned the regime. The magazine looked at the Second Vatican Council, whose call for the separation of church and state aimed a fatal blow at national Catholicism, and Third World decolonizing movements, which resonated with the calls for basic political rights and freedoms that beset the dictatorship during its last phase. Along with such progressive publications as *Cuadernos para el diálogo* (*Papers for Dialogue*), *Destino* (*Destiny*), and *Cambio 16* (*Change 16*), *Triunfo* emerged as an alternative to the official press.[86] What set *Triunfo* apart was its unstinting attention to the challenges of the rural poor in the south. It was the wrecking ball pitted against an obfuscating folkloric fantasyland.

Triunfo's early perspective still tints Joaquín Romero Murube's 1963 article, "Sevilla." Heavily illustrated with photographs of gorgeous parks and astonishing monuments, it depicts a "world that seems unreal, but is not." Social interaction among *sevillanos* of all classes is circumscribed by the *feria* (fair), where happiness is the norm, and the "anxieties of the modern world" are nowhere to be seen, mainly because the author is "afraid to walk down certain paths."[87] This idealizing view did not prevail in *Triunfo*.

The Marxist thinker Alfonso Carlos Comín defined the magazine's common goal to recover a "real Andalusia" that was ignored by, and unknown to, official Spain, in four groundbreaking articles published in July 1967.[88] His objective approach shattered Pemán's glorification of misery and Ortega y Gasset's orientalist view.[89] According to Comín, all "theories of Andalusia" are hollow rhetorical exercises that hide reality behind generalizations and abstractions.[90] They either ignore poverty and misery or blame it on innate apathy. Inspired by Juan Goytisolo's *Campos de Níjar* (*Countryside of Níjar*), Comín cites reports from the World Bank and the UN's Food and Agriculture Organization to show that land accumulation, inefficient crop management, and lack of capital, not oriental fatalism, were responsible for Andalusia's third-world status.

Comín also targeted the optimistic rhetoric of *desarrollismo*, which ignored the fact that prosperity was far from evenly distributed. Official figures and statistics emphasized Spain's rapid economic growth, which was the fastest in the Western world from 1960 to 1973. With the GDP rising at an average annual rate of 7.2 percent and the rural population sharply dropping, cabinet members eagerly celebrated the "Spanish miracle." The miracle left a few martyrs along the way. Comín burst the triumphalist bubble by showing that the government's investment in southern "poles of development" in Huelva, Cadiz, and Linares in the 1970s actually increased regional economic disparities. Fledgling shipbuilding, chemical, and auto assembly industries could hardly absorb the rural workers left unemployed by the mechanization of agriculture.[91] The 1959 Plan of Economic Stabilization might have propelled Spain into the world market, but it left the southern peasantry struggling to make ends meet in the barren latifundia of Seville and Cordoba and the disease-ravaged *chabolas* (shacks) clustered around Madrid and Barcelona. Comín offers "anti-postcards" of these slums to show that state-sponsored economic modernization did nothing to end the marginalization of Andalusians.[92] He concludes that ending repression will require new forms of analysis and social engagement that can answer the question "Where is Andalusia?" without recourse to "new metaphysical interpretations."[93]

Comín's interest grew out of a Marxist commitment to stimulate class consciousness among the Andalusian poor and to defy Francoist mystifications and sociopolitical structures, but his materialist approach, which reduces ethnicity to class, threatened to render his question, "Where is Andalusia?" moot. Rejecting abstractions might reveal raw socioeconomic truths, but it might also dissipate communal ties based on nation or region. "The working men have no country," Marx and Engels famously stated in *The Communist Manifesto* (1848), so in theory, Andalusian identity and working-class consciousness are mutually exclusive.[94] Marxist nationalism is defined by class, not culture: the working class is "national, though not in the bourgeois sense of the word."[95] From this perspective, the cultural and linguistic traits that distinguish the oppressed masses of Andalusia from those in Galicia or Ireland, among other traditionally agrarian, unevenly modernized communities, are of no interest. Material needs rather than patriotic feelings are the foundation of nations and regions. Comín agreed. He believed that Andalusia could play a key role in undermining Francoist fictions but as a site of class struggle, not as a singular culture.

Other *Triunfo* contributors, notably Francisco Almazán Marcos and Antonio Ramos Espejo, followed Comín's lead but tried to nuance his economic determinism. They knew that detaching culture from reality leads to decadent escapism; but they also rejected blinkered approaches to society unchallenged by the imagination. Finding support in the writings of the Italian Marxist Antonio Gramsci, they viewed folklore not as a picturesque deformation of lived experience, but as a challenge to "'official' conceptions of the world."[96] Gramsci faced a similar "southern question" in 1930s Italy and acknowledged that much of the culture called "popular" is actually conservative and fatalistic. He also believed that art which does not mystify material conditions could generate a "national-popular" movement that would unite committed thinkers with peasants. Rather than a wholesale rejection of folk culture, he proposed finding those currents that were "in contradiction to or simply different from the morality of the governing strata."[97]

Triunfo writers saw such a current in flamenco. Francisco Almazán, a schoolteacher "purged" from the Francoist educational system due to his leftist ideas, contributed several articles wresting flamenco from "national *flamenquismo*," a term he coined to describe the debased folklore of the Franco era. Against the cheery performances of Lola Flores and Manolo Escobar, he counterpoised the "dark sounds" of deep song, manifesting pain and hunger. Citing Gramsci, he contends that flamenco is not just amusement, but a form of protest against underdevelopment and oppression. In this light, it reveals aspects of reality ignored or hidden by those who write history "from above," like, Almazán writes, "Laín Entralgo." *Coplas* of love, tragedy, and sorrow register an emotional response to material adversity, allowing the illiterate masses to build a conception of the world nowhere found in "grandiloquent history."[98] To recover these lost voices, Almazán abandons an archeological approach to flamenco as a relic or rarefied pure essence and instead considers it as a many-sided, evolving historical phenomenon. As both a traditional form of expression and a consumer product, flamenco can only challenge official Spain by infiltrating the "bourgeois, technocratic, TV culture of consumer society."[99]

Almazán mourns the lost tradition of *cante jondo* that Lorca and Falla sponsored in the Granada contest in 1922 (see chapter 2). Like the enemies of national *flamenquismo* in the 1960s, they sought to rescue deep song from frivolous commercialization, but their project was elitist rather than national-popular. They imagined a preindustrial community where pure Andalusian folk songs were still uncorrupted by commercial interests. Thought to originate from "the people," this archaic tradition could only be preserved from adulteration by an educated minority. Almazán shared García Lorca and Falla's concerns about the commodification of art, but he rejected their elitism and cult of aesthetic purity. Real change and regeneration could come only from subaltern minds and voices, not sophisticated artists and intellectuals. He wanted aesthetic purity to be obliterated by new content inspired by current realities: forced migration, precarious employment, exploitation, and rural poverty, among other social problems of late Francoism.[100] Instead of inspiring an avant-garde movement controlled by a select few, he argues, flamenco singers must play the same role in Spanish society that politically committed songwriters like Bob Dylan, Pete Seeger and the Weavers, and the Staple Singers played in the United States during the turbulent 1960s.[101] Almazán saw signs of this burgeoning flamenco counterculture in the songs of José Menese, Enrique Morente, and Manuel Gerena, who quickly became spokesmen for a generation of displaced Andalusian workers in Barcelona. Eschewing the fatalism lauded by Pemán and Laín, they heralded a culture of protest unobstructed by what another *Triunfo* critic called "playfulness, drunkenness, exact rhythms, and aesthetic beauty."[102] The focus was now on real people, real circumstances, real pain, and real challenges:

> The trains are leaving tomorrow
> They are loaded with immigrants
> They cry because they leave behind
> Great sorrow and pain.[103]

Flamenco fought misrepresentations of Spanish society by voicing discontent. It also shattered Francoist myths of national unity by anchoring a distinct Andalusian ethnicity. Reacting against the belief that authentic deep song can only be found among gypsies, magazine contributors revived Blas Infante's orientalist hypothesis about the origin of *cante jondo*. Flamenco, the Andalusian patriot had argued in the 1930s, was the unofficial record of generations of oppressed ethnic groups, from the sixteenth-century Moriscos displaced from al-Andalus to the twentieth-century laborers marginalized in Andalusia. In the 1960s, this understanding of folk music conflated class consciousness and cultural distinctiveness to consolidate a national-popular solution to socioeconomic underdevelopment. In "Flamenco: Del cante jondo al flamenquismo" (1966; "Flamenco: From Deep Song to *Flamenquismo*"), the critic José Monleón states that committed *cantaores* like Gerena build on the trauma of the Muslims and Jews of medieval Iberia to contribute to a silenced history of a centuries-old "illiterate and dominated collectivity." More than simply an expression of dissatisfaction, the flamenco tradition is the people's history.

The truth about flamenco, Almazán wrote in 1969, can only be understood in the broad context of the "triumph of the Cross over the Crescent."[104] Echoing Infante, he implies that Andalusian underdevelopment and its emotional effects, registered in the lyrics of traditional songs, originated with the Christian Reconquest of al-Andalus. Unlike Infante, however, he and other *Triunfo* writers did not see al-Andalus as a gateway to distant mythological origins or a timeless "Andalusian Ideal." Their orientalism was tactical rather than essentialist; it emphasized class and social dynamics, not unchanging metaphysical conceits like the spirit of the people or the soul of the nation. Instead of innate racial or spiritual traits, what unites Andalusians and the expelled Arabs of al-Andalus is an outlook based on structures of economic exploitation and cultural subjugation that remained largely unchallenged from the Middle Ages on.

The most systematic rewriting of Infante's orientalism is found in the essays of Antonio Ramos Espejo. His view of Andalusia was shaped by his stint as a young reporter in Rome in the 1960s where he learned about what Gramsci called the *questione meridionale* in the 1930s, the marginalization of the underdeveloped Italian south, which was still a reality thirty years later. He also picked up a copy of Goytisolo's *Campos de Níjar* in a local bookstore, and it became his reference and model, especially when writing about Andalusia.[105] The Francoist press, he wrote, always looked at the south through rose-tinted glasses, dismissing the hunger, illiteracy, and disease that plagued places like La Chanca in Almeria as "subversive inventions by Goytisolo and others."[106] Ramos Espejo takes these "inventions" as his starting point to reach a Gramscian compromise between cultural and material analysis. Unlike Goytisolo, however, he is not motivated by existential dilemmas and artistic choices.

Goytisolo's *Campos de Níjar* (1960), *La Chanca* (1962), and his essay "Tierras del Sur" (1967; "Lands of the South"), which was printed as the prologue to the Italian edition of *Campos de Níjar* that Ramos Espejo found in Rome, confront what Goytisolo derides as "Sunnyspain" with the harsh social and economic reality of the south, which he portrayed as an archaic, almost North African realm. The inspiration for his contemptuous social criticism, Andalusia was also the object of a deeply personal orientalism that was essential to his self-fashioning as an oppositional writer during the dictatorship and beyond. Goytisolo's later identification with Islam and the Arab world in art and life, a pose he adopted to challenge the nationalistic myths enshrined by Franco, originated in the Andalusian countryside.[107] "What I am as a writer now," he wrote in 1984, was determined by his contact with the Almeria desert and its people in the 1950s, an experience "that will recur, years later, in African lands."[108] However, after several trips to Andalusia, Goytisolo grew disgusted with the atmosphere of fear and oppression there. "It is difficult to express the bitterness and gloom," he wrote in his memoirs, "with which I would decide not to return, thus depriving myself of the warmth and sense of belonging that by instinct, and in compensation, I would search out and find in North Africa."[109] As in his Andalusian narratives, his approach to the Arab world from *Reivindicación del conde don Julián* (1970; *Vindication of Count Don Julian*) to *Makbara* (1980) is to stage an assault on despised national affiliations.[110] Looking at his own writing through Edward Said's orientalism, he wrote that in his "mental world," "empirical reality and direct observations" are secondary; the "traditional Europe/Islam antinomy (though situated on a different and even inverse scale of values) none the less maintains its irreducible character."[111] Goytisolo's orientalism manifests a personal quarrel with an imposed cultural identity. In appropriating what is deemed exotic, his authorial voice echoes the Napoleonic savant writing about Egypt and the Romantic poet fantasizing about the Alhambra. Thinking that an obviously imaginary creation can influence reality is, in his own words, an "inept supposition."[112]

Triunfo writers dismissed literary self-creation. Like Comín, Ramos Espejo focused on Goytisolo's engagement with economic backwardness, seeing orientalism as a means to awaken critical consciousness about southern underdevelopment, not as the object of desire of a "bourgeois with a bad conscience," as Goytisolo described himself.[113] To do so, Ramos Espejo assimilated and adapted Blas Infante, who was another major influence on him. In articles and photo-reportage published shortly after the dictator's death, when Spain's political future was still gestating, he used Infante's *andalucismo* as the lens through which to view Andalusia's social needs and future challenges. But the lens had to be refocused.

After partial home rule was granted to the regional government of Andalusia, constituted in 1978, Infante's legacy became the center of a bitter dispute between centralist and nationalistic *andalucistas*. Ramos Espejo sided with the latter, represented by the Socialist Party of Andalusia (Partido Socialista de Andalucía, or PSA), the self-appointed true heirs of Infante. Weighing in on the matter from *Triunfo*, he criticized the Socialist and Communist parties and the right-wing Union of the Democratic Center for trying to deny Andalusia nationality status.[114] The PSA rank and file perceived self-determination within a federal state, the political model Infante had supported in the 1930s, as the only viable solution to the south's chronic underdevelopment. Their leaders warned that anti-Marxist socialists in Madrid and their delegates in Seville would stunt social and economic reforms in Andalusia. Southern regionalism had to be, as Antonio Burgos put it in *Andalucía, ¿tercer mundo?* (1972; *Andalusia: Third World?*), a *regionalismo del subdesarrollo*, or regionalism of underdevelopment.[115] José Aumente, a founding member of the PSA, concurred. Writing in *Triunfo* in 1976, he underlined the "absolute coincidence" between Andalusian identity and working-class interests while other regionalist nationalisms in Spain were "manipulated" by the bourgeoisie. "True national consciousness," he wrote, "is the product of the working and agrarian masses, the only ones capable of providing it with real content."[116] Following the Basques and Catalans, the PSA galvanized regional consciousness by denouncing collective oppression. For Andalusians, oppression was not simply ethnic, linguistic, or historical but, most importantly, economic. A perennially peripheral region, almost an internal colony, Andalusia was a source of cheap labor and raw materials but never a center of robust industrialization like Madrid, Barcelona, and Bilbao.

Ramos Espejo developed this perspective in the early 1980s, when the newly created Andalusian autonomous community was in the throes of self-definition. To reject cultural labels devoid of socioeconomic content, he revised the aspect of Infante's work that had been most prone to an idealist interpretation: his view of al-Andalus. He literally followed Infante's footsteps to Fes, where the exiled King Boabdil of Granada died after the Christian Reconquest, and the town of Aghmat in southern Morocco, where al-Mutamid (1040–1095), the last king of Seville, who was displaced from his homeland by illiterate Almoravid invaders in the eleventh century, is entombed. In 1924, Infante made a pilgrimage to these historical sites to reconnect with "the spirit of our land," which had been lost when the vibrant culture of al-Andalus was destroyed.[117] He saw Aghmat as the Mecca for Andalusians on both sides of the Straits of Gibraltar—as a "Holy Land" where their common history, silenced and driven underground for centuries, lies dormant. Infante's genealogy conflated al-Andalus and Andalusia in racial and metaphysical terms, privileging the idea of an unchanging collective soul over a materialist conception of history.

Ramos Espejo chronicled his journey to Aghmat in "Con los descendientes de Al-Motamid" ("With the Descendants of al-Mutamid") and "Boabdil cabalga de nuevo" ("Boabdil Rides Again"), published in *Triunfo* in July and December 1980, respectively. Juxtaposing photographs of Infante and Ramos Espejo in Morocco, the articles cite Infante's observations on Andalusia as a bridge between Spain and the orient. "Con los descendientes de Al-Motamid" focuses on the practical side of Andalusian-Moroccan relations, particularly Infante's proposed coalition of underdeveloped oriental nations fighting Western colonialism. "The enslaved nations of Afro-Asia," Infante had written in 1930, will never break their chains until Andalusia galvanizes a "great synthesis between Orient and Occident."[118] Cited in Ramos Espejo's article, these words resonated with the debates and discussions of the Bandung Conference (1955), which had promoted cultural and economic cooperation between formerly colonized nations in Asia and Africa amidst Cold War tensions. They also flesh out what Burgos labeled *regionalismo del subdesarrollo*, stressing Andalusia's ties with the anticapitalistic Third World. Unlike Infante, however, Ramos sees these ties in materialist rather than idealist terms.

In "Boabdil cabalga de nuevo," Ramos Espejo decisively pushes forward his materialist understanding of Andalusian history and identity. He interviews flesh-and-blood descendants of the exiled Andalusis without summoning up what Infante called "a buried psychic construction."[119] In Fes, he finds the progeny of King Boabdil and the expelled Muslims who gathered in the city's Andalusian neighborhood. What links them to their lost homeland is not just the memory of their ancestors, but the crafts they learned from them: "The Andalusians of Fes are the most reputed tanners, blacksmiths, leatherworkers" in the world, challenging myths of southern/oriental apathy and laziness while establishing trans-Mediterranean ties through workmanship.[120] In Ramos Espejo's view, al-Andalus brings Andalusia and Morocco together as a workforce, not as an ethereal *Volksgeist*. Class, not spirit, is the basis of unity across the Straits of Gibraltar.

The democratization period undermined these materialist and working-class conceptions of Andalusia. Major schisms among the proponents of Andalusian self-determination emerged during the first free national elections in Spain in forty-one years, held on June 15, 1977. The PSA lost ground to centralist parties, particularly the Spanish Socialist Workers' Party (PSOE), which was shelving its Marxist rhetoric, a gesture that reflected the marginalization of left-wing ideology during the "third wave" of global democratization (1974–91) that swept Latin America, eastern and southern Europe (including Spain and Portugal), East Asia, and sub-Saharan Africa.[121] With the arrival of democracy, the PSA and PSOE socialists began to speak different languages. While Aumente and his colleagues continued to advocate a nationalist agenda centered on the working class, the PSOE leader Felipe González was seduced by global neoliberalism and the idea of a fully Europeanized culture and society. Eventually, moderate Europeanizing reformism and Madrid-based Andalusian regionalism won out, tying the future of the newly created autonomous community to the PSOE, which has controlled the presidency of the Junta de Andalucía from 1978 to the present. Shortly before the historic elections of 1977, a despondent Antonio Burgos saw this political dependency as a form of "colonization," a new reconquest of the south by the north.[122] It did not mean that Infante's legacy or the memory of al-Andalus ceased to be marks of identity, however. The Andalusian regional government declared Blas Infante the "Father of the Andalusian Nation" in 1983, and it has tirelessly promoted the Andalusi past, although confining its oriental character to the cultural sphere. Emptied of political and economic significance, these contradictory symbols coexist with bouts of anti-Muslim xenophobia and sometimes become folkloric trade for tourist consumption, echoing Franco's national *flamenquismo*.

Chapter 4

✦

The Persistence of Myth: Post-Dictatorial Andalusia

After General Franco's death in November 1975, Spanishness needed redefining. Almost forty years of close association with an authoritarian regime had damaged it considerably—beyond repair, some felt. Francoists had used the notion of an unbreakable Spain to defend themselves against internal and external enemies. After the dictatorship's demise and the transition to democracy, the country shattered into the seventeen autonomous communities under a single political nation created by the Constitution of 1978. This new territorial arrangement abolished Franco's crushing centralism but perpetuated its basic protocols of identity formation. Old government structures disappeared, but habits of thought remained.

The constitution divided the autonomous communities into two groups. Catalonia, the Basque Country, and Galicia, the "historical nationalities" which had their own languages and home-rule status granted prior to the Civil War, were put on a fast track to self-government. They needed only to notify Madrid before they established their own parliaments and supreme courts. The other fourteen autonomous communities could take this route if more than half the votes in a regional referendum endorsed it. With this distinction, the constitution implicitly acknowledged that the transfer of power to the regions was based on historic rights and language and cultural differences. The race for autonomy quickly turned into a search for distinct historical identities, which were scaled-down versions of Francoist patriotism. Anthems, shields, and flags began to crop up from every corner of the peninsula in support of the newly useful local pride.

Andalusia, the only region that joined the fast-track path to self-government, was under great pressure to justify its distinct status. Its referendum, held on February 28, 1980, overwhelmingly endorsed autonomy, but few people had any clear idea of what "Andalusian nationality" was, so historians, linguists, and anthropologists readily concocted it. If Catalans, Basques, and Galicians exercised their vernaculars in classrooms and public spaces, Andalusians celebrated their own phonetic idiosyncrasies, often grasping at linguistic straws and proclaiming the Arabic origin of their accent, stopping just short of declaring the existence of an Andalusian language. Similarly, if Catalan, Basque, and Galician children were tested on their region's past, their Andalusian counterparts had to take a History of Andalusia course in high school, an artificial editing of Spanish history. The backbone of the new *andalucismo* was the notion of *hechos diferenciales*, or "differentiating facts," the term used by competing nationalisms to jockey for increased autonomy within the Spanish state.[1] An *hecho* is a given; it is not subject to debate or interpretation or change, and it paves over contradictions and dissent. Like all the autonomic nationalisms, *andalucismo* submitted to the same monolithic rhetoric it wished to challenge.

The Catalan philosopher Xavier Rubert de Ventós criticized this new paradigm, branding post-dictatorial Spain "the country of *forms*" or a "formal democracy," where modes of address are more important than the messages they deliver.[2] The paradigm emphasizes chauvinistic differences among the new political actors rather than the real needs of the communities they represent. The new semi-independent regions emptied the national myth of its conservative content but kept its form. According to Roland Barthes, "myth is not defined by the object of its message, but by the way in which it utters the message: there are formal limits to myth, there are no 'substantial' ones."[3] Myths place complex reality and human acts in a closed system of unquestionable beliefs. Things and events acquire the "simplicity of essences" and become facts, or *hechos*, whose meaning goes without saying. Myth is "*depoliticized speech*," Barthes concludes; it freezes social relations rather than describing or trying to change them.[4] Rubert de Ventós sees autonomic nationalisms hardening into myths, promoting museum-exhibit identities (or *hechos diferenciales*) fixed in glass cases with explanatory cards, and arresting impulses to interrogate the old apparatus's institutions and its economic policies. Myth is the price for choosing reform over revolution, the tax exacted for integration in the global capitalist market.

With the transition to democracy, models of collectivity based on class eroded. With memories of the violence and trauma of the Civil War and dictatorship, talk of social justice and wealth redistribution disappeared from political discourse in Spain. Wary of messages that could reopen old wounds and obliterate pacts and agreements between the old Francoist leadership and the new political elite, peripheral nationalisms merely mirrored the status quo mandated by the 1978 constitution. In Andalusia, nationalist affirmation became the pretext for political devolution, rather than for ending economic underdevelopment, as the PSA leaders and *Triunfo* contributors had wished. Leftist nationalisms influenced by Third World liberation movements and Marxist ideology met a similar fate in other regions. The Galician People's Union (UPG) and the Catalan Liberation Party (FAC) gained only marginal support, and the terrorist tactics of the Basque Country and Freedom movement (ETA) led to its ejection from parliamentary politics. Majority parties, conservative and progressive alike, talked only about modernization and integration with Europe. When the PSOE was voted into national power in 1982, it had discarded its Marxist past and convinced Spaniards that free trade was the key to prosperity; when at long last Spain joined the European Community in 1986, defining Spain's national identity against market forces and Western modernity was seen as a liability. That year unemployment reached a staggering 22 percent in Spain. The country's economy had grown at the highest rate in Europe during the mid-1980s, but the goal was not redistribution of wealth or the provision of social welfare. Economic growth in absolute terms was the ticket to the club of "advanced" nations.

The regionalist formulations of the Andalusian branch of the Socialist Party, which was still in power in 2018, did not contradict Madrid-based officials' push for first-world status. The 1981 Statute of Andalusian Autonomy listed the "consolidation of Andalusian identity" as a main goal of the regional government, the Junta de Andalucía.[5] But the amended 2007 version wrote this identity into the narrative of European integration: "The European Union is the point of reference of the Autonomous Community, which assumes its values and will ensure the fulfilment of its objectives."[6] One casualty was the left-wing idea that nationalism was a phase Andalusians had to pass through on their way to socialism. *Triunfo* contributors like Alfonso Carlos Comín and Antonio Ramos Espejo had believed that class should inform a regionalist political framework. Andalusians should first identify the forces of change and then compose a platform to streamline and institutionalize them. However, home rule was imposed by decree, not revolution or popular mobilization, thereby depleting it of social content. The 1978 constitution put the cart before the horse, abolishing grassroots efforts to change the region's political landscape.

In 1974, the Marxist psychiatrist Carlos Castilla del Pino published an article under the provocative title "Andalucía no existe" ("Andalusia Does Not Exist").[7] According to him, from a materialist perspective, the word "Andalusia" is meaningless, since the Left aims to organize and to liberate the working class whether in Ghana or Granada. From a cultural point of view, a regional identity "either exists or it does not"; it cannot be fabricated "as if in a laboratory." Transferring administrative powers in the areas of commerce, culture, and education does not require a distinct regional consciousness, and fostering one merely to justify political independence may be counterproductive: unmoored from socioeconomic conditions, "consciousness" can become "ideology," a lifeless creed that disempowers the people by standardizing their beliefs and emotions. In 1990, the left-wing Catholic priest José María de los Santos, a founding member of the PSA, agreed with Castilla del Pino, arguing that separating regional identity from the real world of labor relations and material conditions can only "mythologize Andalusia."[8]

The Junta de Andalucía proved them right. Since the 1980s, it has sponsored "laboratories" that promote regional identity from above without addressing economic deficiencies and messy class relations. Though it is the largest and most populous autonomous region in Spain, Andalusia is still ranked low in Spain and in Europe in terms of its per capita gross domestic product and rate of unemployment. The transition to home rule did not change its economic structure, which is still dependent on agriculture and tourism. Most arable land remains in the hands of a few rich families, whose priority has never been investing in industry or creating jobs. According to data provided by Eurostat, the European Union's statistics agency, Andalusia had the highest unemployment rate in the entire eurozone in 2016, 31.5 percent.[9] The regional government compounds these problems with mismanagement. Political leaders, including the longtime Junta president Manuel Chaves, are under investigation for corruption and embezzlement of public funds, including a missing $19,000,000 in European funds intended to aid the unemployed. More damning has been the government's tendency to favor the expansion of the ruling party's political base over regional prosperity. For example, between May 1993 and August 1994, the Junta invested over $269,000,000 in public funds to save thirteen bankrupt and largely unviable firms, including Suzuki Santana, a Japanese-owned automobile manufacturer in Linares (Jaen). The amount represented 83 percent of the Junta's total annual budget for industrial investment. The political analyst Alfred Montero points out that the results "were politically useful for the Socialists, but fiscally costly and ultimately unimportant to most of Andalusia's firms."[10] Although the Junta's industrial policymaking made little sense from a purely economic perspective, it appeased angry union leaders and dejected workers, and it promulgated a populist message that had high electoral returns. In 1994 Chaves won a second consecutive time, and he would be elected to the presidency four more times, remaining in office until 2009.

Autonomy has been more discourse than development—more formality than reform. Claims to a separate identity materialized in public school curricula, museums, exhibitions, and cultural events, and they took the media by storm. The regional television station has been particularly useful in spreading the post-Franco *fiebre autonómica*, or "autonomy fever" in Andalusia, which has the highest TV-viewing rate of autonomous communities in Spain. These venues filtered the regionalist message of scholars, who from the 1970s on devoted themselves to unearthing a lost Andalusian nationhood. Borges once wrote that the distant past, "infinitely malleable and agreeable, far more obliging than the future and far less demanding of our efforts," is the "famous season favored by all mythologies."[11] He precisely describes the modus operandi of the crafters of southern specificity. History became a quarry from which to dig the indigenous stones to support cultural parity with Catalans, Basques, and Galicians. The proceedings of the First Conference on the History of Andalusia, held in Cordoba in 1976, filled eleven hefty volumes. In the next few years, several histories of Andalusia penned by prestigious college professors hit the bookstores.[12] University library stacks filled with new periodicals devoted to Andalusian studies, notably the prestigious *Revista de Estudios Andaluces* (1983–present; *Review of Andalusian Studies*). Newsstands made room for *Sur* (*South*), *Ideal*, and *El Correo de Andalucía* (*The Andalusia Post*), new dailies headquartered in the south and featuring entire sections on southern speech, culture, and symbols, especially the new green-and-white flag. The *Gran Enciclopedia de Andalucía* (1979; *Great Encyclopedia of Andalusia*), sold in weekly installments in Andalusian capital cities, Madrid, and Barcelona, included an atlas with linguistic and geological information and entries on Andalusia's art, geography, history, and politics, among other subjects. In his contribution to the volume, the anthropologist Isidoro Moreno, one of the most active crusaders for regional particularity, declared categorically that Andalusians have "common traits" that can foster a "strong feeling of auto-identification."[13] The debate went straight to the origin, features, and historical development of a distinct Andalusian identity without questioning its existence.

The consensus held that newly autonomous Andalusia's identity must be rooted in Blas Infante's *andalucismo*. In 1983 the regional parliament named Infante the "Father of the Andalusian Homeland," an official recognition that enhanced his iconic status in post-dictatorial Andalusia but did not confer wholehearted acceptance of his controversial political ideas. The preamble of the 1981 statute evokes him as the "precursor of the fight for self-government" and the "right to autonomy of all Andalusians," justifying the Junta, but not mentioning his socialist ideas or his views on land reform and redistribution. Likewise, Infante's orientalism was edited out to assure Andalusia's full integration into the European Community, which was emphatically ratified by the 2007 version of the regional charter. As Infante's readers would recall, he claimed that Andalusians, who were closer to their Mediterranean neighbors to the south and east than to the French, English, and Germans to the north, "cannot, and will not ever be Europeans." Europe, he explained, is the cradle of crass material interests, while in Andalusia, heir to the refined culture of al-Andalus, individuals are not just "cogs in a machine."[14]

Prominent scholars writing after the transition to democracy encouraged Andalusians to shed Infante's anti-European maurophilia and move with the times. In 1983 the historian Claudio Sánchez Albornoz, who was famous for his rebuttal of Américo Castro's notion that Spain was born from the joint efforts of medieval Jews, Muslims, and Christians, attacked the equation of Andalusia with al-Andalus. According to him, identifying with the Moors falsifies history; the bulk of today's Andalusians are descended from northerners who settled during the Reconquest. Moreover, the creators of the nation "engendered modernity" by defeating the sadistic leaders of al-Andalus, a host of barbarians who routinely engaged in massacres, political assassinations, and acts of religious intolerance toward Christians. If Andalusians want to welcome progress, they must shelve their "Islamizing fantasies."[15]

Serafín Fanjul, a professor of Arabic at the University of Madrid, echoed these comments a year later in the daily *El País* (*The Country*). He wrote that the "current search for the Arabic roots of Andalusia" amounts to cultural blindness. The region's history, language, and popular customs have little, if anything, in common with the Arab world. Andalusians worship pork, speak a modern version of Latin sprinkled with just a few Arabic words, and are descended from the Christians who drove out the Moors centuries ago.[16]

Believing that, without the Moors, Andalusians might as well be Castilians with an accent, the Junta nonchalantly swept aside any contradictions that its identity politics might pose. For example, linguists affiliated with the Junta stated in *El Correo de Andalucía* in 1979 that southern pronunciation owes its distinctive features to Arabic influences that the Castilian conquerors could not delete, a theory that has since been discredited.[17] They argued that the aspiration of the *j*-sound in words like *jamón*, making it sound like the English *h* in *ham*, is "one of the linguistic legacies that the Arabs left among us."[18] A few months later, readers of the same newspaper were assured that by uttering words like *almacén*, *tarifa*, and *zanja*, all lexical borrowings from Arabic, they were paying homage to "Andalusian speech."[19]

Funded by the regional government, the Legado Andalusí Foundation was established in 1993 to reinforce the equation of Andalusia with al-Andalus. In 1995, it organized a cultural exhibit during the World Ski Championships in Granada that showcased the work of eleven Andalusian artists. They used different methods and media, from collages to metallic structures, to evoke the pathways, thoroughfares, and trade routes that had shaped and connected the world of al-Andalus.[20] The foundation's publications later marketed these itineraries as tourist destinations, promising a journey back to medieval Muslim Iberia. As Eric Calderwood notes, the opening pages of *Ruta del Califato: De Córdoba a Granada* (*The Route of the Caliphate: From Cordoba to Granada*), first published in 1998, describe travel in Andalusia "as a passport to the past, but they cast the city of Granada as something even more dramatic: a bridge beyond language, culture, religion, and subjectivity itself."[21] Travelers were encouraged to visit and use their imaginations to revive the relics of an ancient civilization. The intercultural, transcendental myth of al-Andalus in official discourse became an identity-marker and a trademark: both an essential building block of regional political autonomy and a tourist attraction. In *Itinerario cultural de Almorávides y los Almohades* (1999; *Cultural Itineraries of the Almoravids and Almohads*), the Junta president Manuel Chaves defined Andalusia as a "meeting place and a link between Europe and Africa," a territory whose deep, living ties with the Maghreb are an indisputable *hecho diferencial* within Spain.[22] In this context, Andalusia's ties to the orient no longer magnify its Third World status, as Ramos Espejo proposed in *Triunfo* (see chapter 3), but provide the entry to Spain's State of the Autonomies, the European Union, and the global market.

This cultural policy was riven with profound contradictions. Most glaringly, it ignored the strong xenophobia aroused by Moroccan immigrants in Spain from the late 1980s on. Riding a bus along Andalusia's southern coast in 2006, the American anthropologist Mikaela Rogozen-Soltar was struck by the sharp contrast between a political billboard inciting regionalist pride and xenophobic graffiti scrawled on an almost adjacent cliff overlooking the Straits of Gibraltar, "equating North African immigrants to the 'Moorish' invasions of the 8th Century: '*Hay dos tipos de invasiones, uno con fusiles, otro con pateras*' ('There are two kinds of invasions, one with rifles, and one with *pateras*')," or the small motorized vessels in which traffickers take African immigrants to Spain.[23] Many Moroccans have risked and lost their lives trying to reach Spanish shores in these overcrowded boats. As Manuel Chaves was celebrating Andalusian-Moroccan brotherhood in a Legado Andalusí travel guide, thousands of bodies were washing up on the southern coast. Andalusian citizens have witnessed these tragic events with indifference and perhaps a perverse sense of relief, since Moroccans are perceived "not only as guests but also as hosts who have come to reclaim what was theirs." As the embodiment of "the non-European, African and oriental aspects of Spanish national identity," they are a problem "not because of their cultural differences, as many argue, but because, like the *Moriscos*, they are not different enough."[24]

The official response to Islam and African immigration over the past twenty years further belies the idea of Andalusia as a transcultural "meeting place." Following European Union directives, the regional and national governments have dutifully sealed Spain's southern border with advanced radar surveillance and an eight-mile barbed wire fence around the city of Ceuta. Southern Spain has become, in Juan Goytisolo's words, a barrier against the "dreaded invasion of the *barbarians*."[25] This fear also explains why political and religious leaders have opposed petitions to transform the Mosque-Cathedral of Cordoba into a place for Muslim as well as Catholic prayer. For many Andalusians, Islam and Western civilization are only compatible in tourist brochures.

Andalusia's ambivalence regarding its African neighbors and Islam points to the Junta's failure to reconcile what Blas Infante saw as opposites: European integration and the Moorish legacy of al-Andalus. Persistent efforts to reconcile these two realities fly in the face of evidence, creating a deeply contradictory self-image that recalls the nationalism that developed in postcolonial enclaves like India. Partha Chatterjee sees Indian nationalism caught up between debasing, alien, colonial intruders that are nonetheless accepted as a model and rich, affirming, ancestral religious traditions that are nevertheless seen as antithetical to modernization.[26] Although considering post-dictatorial Andalusia a former colony is far-fetched, Chatterjee certainly exposes a rift that the regional government has tried to pave over for almost four decades. Its method has remained essentially the same: presenting identity as myth. Myth, Barthes explains, "does not deny things, on the contrary, its function is to talk about them; simply, it purifies them, it makes them innocent," editing them to fit a prearranged story line.[27]

This strategy has shaped a variety of scripted events and media broadcasts that amalgamate Andalusian identity, Muslim heritage, and European modernity through careful exclusions and equivalences. Three examples show the strategy's intricacies: the inaugural program of the Andalusian television channel, Canal Sur, broadcast on February 28, 1989; the Andalusian Pavilion at the 1992 Universal Exposition held in Seville; and the Museum of Andalusian Autonomy in Coria del Río (near Seville), which opened its doors in July 2006. All three of these examples reinforce the notion that Andalusia's history and culture should be consumed as spectacle. In replacing class consciousness as the foundation of regionalism, cultural difference is packaged as an object of admiration and remembrance, not something actively performed. In addition, cultural traits become commodities in complicity with the regional government's "touristification" of Andalusia, a marketing strategy that complies with post-Franco Europeanizing neoliberal politics.

Ethnocentric Television

As a fast-track region, Andalusia was granted the right to operate its own television channel.[28] Approved by royal decree in 1988, Canal Sur (South Channel) was a public agency that aimed to raise consciousness of Andalusian identity, a main objective of the regional government as outlined in its statute. The renowned novelist Antonio Muñoz Molina once called the channel "the official platform of Andalusianization."[29]

Juan Luis Manfredi, the network's director of external relations from 1989 to 1991, explained this process in terms that reinforce its similarity to mythmaking. Myth begins with a concept and then organizes reality to confirm it. Whatever does not fit the paradigm is either ignored or assimilated.[30] This argument guided Manfredi's presentation of Canal Sur to the readers of Seville's daily newspaper *ABC*. Without any trace of irony, he announced that the channel was modeled on U.S. television networks like BET, Univision, and EWTN, which focus on audiences defined by race, religious affiliation, gender, or ethnicity. For instance, he applauded Latino channels for not reporting on such global events as the Bosnian War (1992–95) "unless the American mediator's name is García or one of the pilots who bombarded Pale is a Fernández."[31] Canal Sur's strategy thus reinforces local perspectives, but it also risks omitting important information. Carried to the extreme, Manfredi's regionalism would allow him to report on an expedition to Mars only if the astronauts hailed from Jaen, Cordoba, or Seville.

Besides its narrow-mindedness, which is more apt for proselytizing than communicating, what makes Canal Sur a mythical frame is its audiovisual structure. Television, like myth, turns contingency into meaning. While images on the screen seem to capture the world in all its richness, formulas and genres act as templates that predetermine viewer expectations.[32] Television is an effective indoctrination tool that can "give a life to ideas or images, but also to groups" who can be mobilized for political, cultural, and economic ends.[33] Of course, as the media studies scholar Ron Lembo points out, responses to television are "understandable as power effects, but not *only* as power effects."[34] Television may mean different things to different viewers at different times; their social, economic, and cultural background and the specific circumstances in which viewing takes place affect the viewers' interpretation of what they see on the screen. Watching alone or in company, after a long day at work or on the weekend, with undivided attention or while multitasking, will affect how messages are received and processed.[35]

Individual viewer response aside, Canal Sur's inaugural telecast in February 1989 meant to use television's power to give life to a group. The Junta president José Rodríguez de la Borbolla delivered the network's statement of purpose on screen: to bind together a community that moves forward without sacrificing local values and traditions. By watching Canal Sur, Andalusians would "know themselves better, reinforce their markers of identity, and become a well-integrated people capable of speaking up in Spain, Europe, and the world." This message, accepted as fact, was echoed ad nauseam during the rest of the telecast. Only two guests, the songwriter Joaquín Sabina and Antonio Muñoz Molina, defied it. When asked whether he would include Andalusian themes in his future records, Sabina responded that regional identity should not demand a chauvinistic narrowing of perspective. He considered himself no less Andalusian for writing songs about Madrid and Buenos Aires. Muñoz Molina was also skeptical about confining art to national or regional topics. Writers and intellectuals should regard their birthplace as a point of departure, not a final destination, he said. These critical voices were drowned out by an audiovisual display that encouraged consent rather than discussion.

The variety-show format mixed addresses by regional and local authorities, interviews with celebrities, and performances by well-known singers and dancers. In equating region-building with television watching, the on-screen spectacle replaced civic debate and turned citizens into passive viewers. Spectacle, Guy Debord writes, is not just a collection of innocent images, but a "social relationship between people that is mediated by images" and supplants genuine political activity based on critical thought.[36] The effects of editing, lighting, and camera angles complemented the show's central message and glossed over potential contradictions, particularly the use of Francoist kitsch (national *flamenquismo*) and the impact of Andalusia's Muslim past on the present. In the first case, montage was used to cleanse the singer and actor Manolo Escobar of his ties to the dictatorship. Directors cut to his performance of a song riddled with clichés during two short speeches, one by the poet Julio Alfredo Egea, who stressed Andalusia's European character; and the other by the journalist Joaquín Caparrós, who greeted Canal Sur as a new beginning for people like himself who had to leave their homeland to pursue a lucrative career. These juxtapositions reworked Escobar's music, which had been an icon of Francoism, in the service of a narrative of democracy, opportunity, and progress.

More problematic was incorporating the region's Moorish heritage. The risk was double: reviving romantic legends that separated orientalized Andalusia from western Europe, on the one hand, and evoking xenophobic responses to Islam and contemporary African immigration, on the other. An ideological powder keg, al-Andalus as *hecho diferencial* was conveyed through images, not discussion. Visual language conflated the Islamic past with the post-Franco present: every transition to a commercial break was announced by computer-animated graphic designs simulating Arabic tilework. But it was the choice of shooting locations and their cinematic presentation that most forcefully thrust the Moorish past into celebratory accounts of modernization and autonomy.

Broadcast live from network headquarters in Seville, the program included eight taped segments, each corresponding to an Andalusian provincial capital: Almeria, Cadiz, Cordoba, Granada, Huelva, Malaga, Jaen, and Seville. While the live element performed the consolidation of regional identity, bringing together disparate fragments, the recorded videos fleshed out its content. Four segments (Cordoba, Granada, Jaen, and Seville) were set at Moorish architectural landmarks. In a fifth segment, Manolo Escobar's song "Viva Almería" conjoined tired stereotypes with references to the Alcazaba, a tenth-century Muslim citadel overlooking that southwestern city: "Almeria, paradise of love / your women are flowers. / Your *Alcazaba* of light / and your Andalusian charm. / You are a Moorish queen / for all Spaniards." Beyond this trite allusion, encrusted with male chauvinism, the Andalusi heritage is neither noted nor discussed, either here or in the other taped segments. It is only through camera movement, lighting, and shot framing that its symbolic relevance for the new Andalusians is underlined.

The section on Cordoba opens with low-angle shots of the ceiling of the great Mosque-Cathedral. Looming over the viewer, its magnificent friezes, domes, and stalactite decorations inspire awe. The monument envelops guests who tirelessly laud Canal Sur as a beacon of innovation and progress; shots of its horseshoe arches and filigreed walls intermittently return to the foreground in alternation with a flamenco performance. Bereft of historical meaning, the grand religious structure is just a prop that is both an ideological support and a stage set. As décor, it is silent about the conflicting memories, histories, and identities it contains. Emptied of its cultural complexity, it props up a contemporary image of the region that blends Moorish roots, folkloric traditions, and a modernizing outlook without any apparent contradiction.

This blithely stitched-up formula recurs throughout the program. The segment on Granada starts with a long shot of the Alhambra. Low-key lighting surrounds the fortress in an aura of mystery reminiscent of orientalist fantasies. The camera slowly pans out to singer Miguel Ríos and journalist Tico Medina, who address the audience from the Albayzín, Granada's old Muslim quarter. UNESCO declared it a world heritage site in 1984 as a "rich repository of Moorish vernacular architecture,"[37] and the quarter's narrow streets with charming Arab-style shops and tea rooms have become a magnet for tourists. Ríos and Medina highlight its suitability to welcome Canal Sur, but neither they nor the other two guests, the city's mayor and the writer Francisco Ayala, explain why. They do not mention the UNESCO distinction or the quarter's kitschy re-creation of Muslim culture, let alone the political and legal battles, still raging at the time of broadcast, between the Albayzín neighborhood association and the Islamic Community in Spain, which proposed building a mosque in the quarter in 1984. The religious organization, which saw the building as a return of Islam to al-Andalus, could not complete the project until 2003. To elide unwanted tensions, allusions to Granada's rich and live Muslim legacy are made only silently by the camera, which pans smoothly across the Alhambra's walls during transitions among speakers.

The slot dedicated to Seville also makes the Andalusi past a banal cultural trait and tourist attraction, not the starting point for a serious discussion of the contradictions and ambiguities inherent in Andalusia's regional identity. The opening shot is a panoramic view of the city by night. Contrast lighting underscores the Torre del Oro, a thirteenth-century Almohad watchtower, and the Giralda, a twelfth-century minaret that now serves as the cathedral's bell tower. Architecture again establishes location in the next scene, which takes place in the Plaza de España, a Moorish revival square built for the Ibero-American Exhibition of 1929. As discussed in chapter 2, the plaza epitomized the Andalusization of Spain during the Primo de Rivera dictatorship (1923–30); the television program dons the old orientalist mask to harmonize tradition and modernity and to overcome the marginalization the mask created in the first place. Again, camerawork establishes a sense of continuity between exoticism and modernity, joining together what the European mind had previously separated. The shots of Islamic-style monuments function as cutouts of a romanticized, traditional, folkloric south pasted into a contemporary myth of renewal and progress. During the central five-minute scene, several low-angle shots of the Plaza de España are linked without transition to three messages: first, the city mayor announcing the upcoming 1992 Universal Exposition in Seville, described as a showcase of twenty-first-century technology; second, the avant-garde painter Luis Gordillo and award winning actor Juan Diego praising the forward-looking spirit of southern culture; and third, a *sevillana* celebrating gypsy dancing and urging viewers to clap incessantly: "*Tócala tócala tócala toca las palmas . . .*" ("*Clap, clap, clap your hands . . .*"). The scene ends by cutting to the Giralda by night. The camera zooms out, eventually fading to black, as "*Tócala, tócala*" rings in the background. As in the previous segments, montage creates an audiovisual continuum that erases potential contradictions in the regionalist narrative.

Specifically, the juxtaposition of Islamic architecture and folklore with messages of transformation, development, and change compels viewers to accept the autonomous community's Europeanizing aspirations and its *hechos diferenciales*, especially the legacy of al-Andalus and popular culture, as a single, unbroken thread.

This mass-media *costumbrismo*, a spectacle that dictates rather than debates collective identity, persists in *Andalucía Directo* (*Andalusia Live*), a prime-time television show that Canal Sur has aired Monday through Friday since 1998. For more than two decades, this popular magazine program, among the most viewed on the channel, has relied on the immediacy of live television to create a false sense of participation that clashes with the ritualistic festivals and unchanging customs and traditions it tends to focus on, including annual religious pilgrimages, local *ferias*, food fests, and other iconic events throughout the region. Its format, *el directo*, or live television, which was also the format of Canal Sur's inaugural telecast, convinces spectators it is bringing them the abstract entity "Andalusia" as it really is, without mediation. *Directo* means "live," but it also means straightforward, immediate, and sincere. By equating *live* with *real*, live television draws viewers in, but as the critic Jane Feuer points out, "liveness" is an invisible filter used "to suppress contradictions."[38] It presents a mirage, a fabrication, a myth that hides and denies nothing but defangs reality of conflicting meanings or connotations, making it look innocent. The network's pilot and *Andalucía Directo* not only coalesce disparate, often contradictory, content into a whole, but present it as the true, live face of Andalusia.

Cultural Exhibitionism

Expo '92, the Seville Universal Exposition, also staged Andalusia and Spain's triumphant reentry into Europe after the forty-year dictatorship and a short transition to democracy. In less than twenty years, Spain had consolidated a parliamentary system and a consumer economy, leapfrogging from the shoulders of its northern neighbors to stand as a full member of the European Union and NATO. Together with Barcelona, host of the 1992 Summer Olympics, Seville became the showcase of this transformation. For six months, between April and October 1992, it was the shining face of the post-dictatorial nation and the brave new world it had just entered. As Tony Bennett astutely argues, universal expositions aim to overlap national and modern time "by projecting the host nation as among the foremost representatives of the time, and tasks, of modernity."[39] Pulling Expo '92 off involved a certain degree of historical rewriting for a country traditionally associated with backwardness. Starting in the eighteenth century, Spain was deemed an inquisitorial land ruled by a host of sadistic rulers and relegated to the periphery of enlightened, capitalist Europe. To northern observers, Spanish and modern time split in 1492, when the country became an empire but did not cast off traditional notions of religious order and social privilege.

The Expo changed this perception by inviting visitors to see 1992 as the culmination of a process that began in 1492. Its official theme, "The Age of Discoveries," celebrated Columbus's "discovery" of the Americas as the first episode in an unfolding narrative of progress and scientific advancement. The seafarer was grouped with Copernicus, Galileo, and Newton, not with bloodthirsty conquistadors and Catholic inquisitors. Thematic exhibition halls, such as the Pavilion of the Fifteenth Century and the Pavilion of Navigation, stressed that the maritime technologies that took Columbus across the Atlantic Ocean laid the foundations for today's telecommunications and means of transportation. Without galleons and compasses, we would have no telephones or faxes, let alone jets capable of covering thousands of miles in a few short hours. Globalization and cosmopolitanism would be unrealized utopias had the "encounter" between the Old and New Worlds (the euphemism organizers used for "conquest and colonization") never occurred. At the Expo, 1492 was the dawn of the modern age, not the birth of a benighted empire. As the exhibition's official catalog asserts, it is "from Spain, in 1492, that sprung the grandest historical enterprise undertaken by Europe."[40]

Spain's ties with Andalusia, Spanish America, and the Islamic world, haunted by colonialism and orientalism, also had to be revised. One strategy was obliteration. When world's fairs are held in peripheral nations, annexation to modernity requires that the host "be shorn of all that is local and limiting," Tony Bennett writes.[41] Accordingly, uncomfortable portions of the national past, including the conquest of America and the expulsion of the Moors and Jews, were dutifully extirpated from Expo '92 brochures and sites, including the Spanish Pavilion. Its exhibition rooms showed no traces of bloodshed and conflict. Moors, Jews, and Christians coexisted during the medieval period, and the colonization of the New World was depicted as a peaceful encounter of two different civilizations. "Without the mention of gold or silver, of religion or blood," one critic stated, visitors left "with the confusing impression that Spaniards traveled to the Indies on a strictly academic mission, that is to look for useful plants and to offer new agricultural techniques and domestic animals to the native people."[42] For a site of historical memory, the pavilion truly seemed amnesiac.

The past was also mythologized. In some cases, colonial history was rewritten rather than simply ignored in order to aid and abet the host's first-world status. The notion of *Hispanidad*, used by Spanish liberals and conservatives after 1898 to defend and promote Spain's cultural leadership after the loss of empire, took a new lease on life.[43] In 1983, King Juan Carlos invoked a "common past, language, and culture" as the foundation of a "community of Hispanic nations" that would "perform a mediating role in world society, between the north, an industrialized center, and the south, or periphery."[44] Expo officials used these commonalities as proof of Spain's continued influence in the Americas, a powerful argument to end the country's centuries of marginalization within western Europe.

Similarly, the legacy of al-Andalus was marshalled to present Spain as a mediator between Europe and the Arab world rather than the nation that came into being after expelling the Moors in 1492. Just as the Expo's purified Spanish imperialism would broker modern transatlantic relations, Andalusia's Muslim past would put the region in an "ideal geo-strategic position to participate in projects of international cooperation and transferal of technology to developing nations, especially those in Spanish America, north Africa, and the western Mediterranean."[45] Translated from officialese: Andalusia may exhibit its oriental face, but only to assert its potential utility to the capitalist West. This orientalism is public relations, not intercultural brotherhood. The quote is taken from a government dossier that laid out the plan for the Pavilion of Andalusia. Needless to say, the Islamic connection had to be handled with extreme care. Embrace it, and you risk reviving dreams of romantic Spain or nightmares about the Inquisition. Cut it, and you lose the distinctive traits that make the country recognizable to locals and attractive to foreigners. The task of Expo organizers was to retain Spain and Andalusia's difference, traditionally coded as oriental, without jeopardizing their centrality to European integration.

Location, location, location! This real-estate cliché is essential to understanding the message of Expo '92 and all other world's fairs. Since the Great Exhibition held in London in 1851, the spatial organization of nineteenth-century fairgrounds built world order on the technological and scientific achievements of Western capitalism. The hosting nation, a metropolitan power (Great Britain, France, the United States), occupied the center; other industrialized countries surrounded it; the colonies and countries outside of Europe and North America were pushed to peripheral gardens and parks. Relegated to the margins, Muslim countries were treated as ethnic curiosities that brought a taste of the past to celebration of the future. Whirling dervishes, belly dancers, and Bedouin riders delighted visitors while taming the strange through spectacle.[46]

In this microcosm, Spain was closer to Libya than London. During the nineteenth century, Spain's Alhambresque pavilions, reverberating with the clapping and wailing of flamenco dancers and singers, shared quarters with the Turks rather than the French. Organizers of the 1900 Paris exhibition strengthened Spain's orientalization by building a 5,000-square-meter village named "Andalusia in the Time of the Moors" in the Trocadéro Gardens. It featured replicas of the Patio of the Lions at the Alhambra palace and the Giralda tower, which intrepid visitors could climb on a donkey. Other attractions included jousts between Moors and Christians, gazelle hunts with Arab greyhounds, and gypsy weddings.[47]

The Spanish Pavilion at Seville's 1992 Expo was a stone's throw from the real Giralda but was centrally located at the corner of the Road of

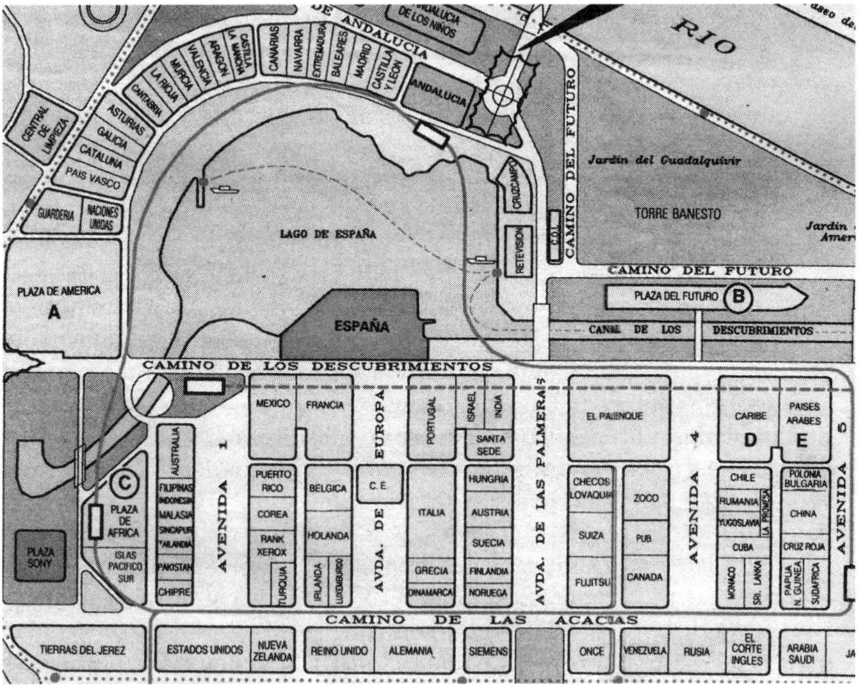

Figure 4.1. Map of the Expo '92 site.

Discoveries and the Avenue of Europe, near the Pavilion of the European Community. One side edged the Lake of Spain along with buildings representing the seventeen autonomous communities and the Plaza of America, a large hall housing the exhibits of Latin American and Caribbean countries. This spatial organization carried a clear message: Spain, a full partner in the European Union, was a composite with strong links to its former colonies in the Americas. Its unity and past imperial glory, tainted by Francoist connotations, were downplayed, but the outdated idea of the *Madre Patria* (Mother Country) still underscored its strategic value as a mediator between Europe and America.[48] The Lake of Spain is shaped like a womb (figure 4.1).

Andalusia held pride of place among the regions. Its pavilion was closest to the national headquarters and was set apart from the other pavilions, which were arranged in three clusters on the far shore of the lake. At 7,992 square meters, it was four times their average size. Its prominence may have been a nod of recognition to the host, but it also filled old orientalist stereotypes with new meanings. The image of Andalusian Spain, familiar to international eyes, was made compatible with domestic claims to modernity.

The Spanish and Andalusian pavilions were almost mirror images: large futuristic arrangements of predominantly white geometric forms that evoked ancient whitewashed villages along the Mediterranean coast. Umberto Eco wrote that the "architecture of the contemporary exposition is used to connote symbolic meanings, minimizing its primary functions."[49] What does the Spain-Andalusia nexus convey? In philosophy and linguistics, an utterance like "I bet," "I promise," "I now pronounce you man and wife" is a performative act. It "effects an action by being spoken or by means of which the speaker performs a particular act."[50] The pavilions perform in a similar way: their avant-garde designs with a pinch of ethnic flavor announce a new era that reconciles tradition and modernity without explanation, discussion, or debate. You should get the point by looking at the buildings.

The pavilions were the result of a careful process of selecting and reconfiguring stereotypical images of the nation. Spain and Andalusia both unloaded and reworked a lot of architectural baggage on their sites to perform their centrality within Europe. Nineteenth-century Spanish pavilions had catered to visitor expectations and were decked out with portals, lattice screens, and intricate arabesques that evoked Moorish architecture.[51] The first attempt to break with this orientalized self-image was the Spanish Republic's pavilion at the 1937 Paris international exhibition, designed by Josep Lluís Sert and Luis Lacasa at the height of the Spanish Civil War. A disciple of Le Corbusier, Sert's three rationalist stories housed avant-garde art by the Catalan painter Joan Miró and Picasso's famous *Guernica*, commissioned especially for the occasion. The pavilion and its contents proclaimed the Second Republic a bastion of democracy and modernity threatened by retrograde fascist forces.

Fascism triumphed in 1939 and Spain lapsed into ancestral exoticism, becoming a picturesque anachronism among European liberal democracies. However, as the Franco regime moved to integrate with the capitalist world in the 1950s and 1960s, it redefined the national image at universal exhibitions, reconnecting with Sert's modernism. At Expo '58 in Brussels and especially at the 1964–1965 New York World's Fair, the Spanish pavilions shed all traces of architectural orientalism. The poured-concrete, high-modernist structure in Flushing Meadows Park in Queens, reminiscent of Sert's creation in Paris, was meant to attract tourists while announcing Spain's change of skin. Topping all the praise heaped by the press on its restaurants, exhibits, and daily flamenco performances, *Life* magazine declared it "the jewel of the fair." Not coincidentally, U.S. tourism to Spain rose 30 percent from 1964 to 1965, the total number of visitors reaching a staggering 700,000. The Spanish pavilion's building costs skyrocketed to $7,000,000, and maintenance expenditures were double its revenues, but the pavilion succeeded in symbolically reintegrating Spain in the modern world as a burgeoning economic power and desirable tourist destination. As Neal Rosendorf points out, "the foundation of Spain's reputation as a fundamentally 'normal,' progressing Western state was firmly in place" by the mid-1960s, "the product of effort by Francisco Franco and his dictatorship."[52]

Figure 4.2. Detail of the Pavilion of Spain at Expo '92. Courtesy Herrero Arquitectos, Seville (Spain).

If the Francoist display in New York threw gypsy dancers and geranium-spangled courtyards into hypermodern architectural design, the Expo '92 pavilions harnessed tradition and change as doubles rather than opposites joined haphazardly. Both Andalusia and Spain chose white marble walls: not local color but a clean slate, albeit marked with references to Moorish architecture. The Pavilion of Spain, with its multiple volumes joined by patios and shaded walkways and capped by an impressive bronze dome reminiscent of the Umayyad Dome of the Rock in Old Jerusalem, had the stately elegance of a mosque (figure 4.2). The interiors, intended as an oasis from the scorching Andalusian sun, featured traditional elements of Arabic-Andalusian architecture, including latticed windows, arcades, and canopies.

The use of orientalist markers to express the new and improved Spain also prevailed in the Pavilion of Andalusia. Predictably, its official theme was "Andalusia, Tradition and Change." The project, funded and overseen by the regional government, was launched in 1989 with an architectural competition that asked participants for "a unified image" of a modernized region that was fully integrated with Spain and the European Community. The winning bid, submitted by the architect Juan Ruesga Navarro, was celebrated in an official press dossier as a "visual metaphor" wedding past, present, and future.[53]

Figure 4.3. Pavilion of Andalusia at Expo '92. Copyright © Archivo General de Andalucía, Seville (Spain).

The structure consisted of a large quadrangular base of white marble and an elliptical sandstone building cleaved by an inclined cylindrical tower of blue ceramic tile (figure 4.3). The base is meant to represent "traditional culture"; the sandstone building, "elaborate culture" (these terms are not clarified in the dossier); and the cylinder is their synthesis. Evoking dynamism, growth, and forward movement, the leaning cylinder also represents "modernity"; the allusion to the blue flag of the European Union is hard to miss.

At the same time, "the small portholes that perforate its surface evoke the tower-houses of Arab culture."[54] The Arabic theme continued in the rooftop restaurant and a balcony overlooking the Expo site and the city of Seville, "inspired by the watchtowers" along the coast from "Arabia to Cadiz."[55] The reference here is to Islamic fortifications, extremely common in al-Andalus, that were used as rest areas but also as signal towers, using smoke to transmit messages. They were varied in their layout, and often imitated Parthian and Byzantine models.[56] The architectural language of the pavilion consciously blends the antitheses of previous universal exhibits: Moorishness and Western modernity.

Selective use of the Islamic past to project an Andalusia that is modern yet distinct continues inside the pavilion. As the Expo's official guide states:

> The purpose of the exhibits and contents of the Pavilion is to publicize an Andalusia that seeks to partake in the dynamism of the

> modern world without sacrificing its identity markers. Thus, the theme, "Andalusia, tradition and change," is more than a felicitous phrase already suggested by the architecture of the building; it is the expression of a deeply felt desire to be part of modernity and still be who we are.[57]

The desired balance, perceived as the resolution of a paradox or dilemma, is the unifying thread in an otherwise dizzying display combining ancient pottery and biotechnology, Baroque sculptures and sports cars. Like Canal Sur's first telecast, the pavilion (coincidentally the network's current headquarters) represented regional identity as the amalgamation of diverse cultural and historical traditions. Entering its gates, visitors could see that who Andalusians are relies on who they were—or were supposed be. The first floor housed the permanent exhibit "La memoria productiva" ("Productive Memory"); according to the proposal submitted to the Junta de Andalucía, it represented the "transformations and continuities that relate the diverse periods and cultures of Andalusian history."[58] In other words, it parsed and imposed order and meaning on the past, fitting a mixed collection of artworks into a coherent, unified story. Paintings, book manuscripts, sculptures, and archeological remains—including such outstanding pieces as the *Lady of Baza*, a fourth-century B.C. statue of a seated Iberian goddess, and the Roman bronze of a nude boy known as the *Ephebus of Antequera*—were grouped under four broad labels as stages in a continuum: "Tartessos," "Betica," "al-Andalus," and "Andalusia." The display windows were built into a wall running parallel to a corridor that led to the large exhibition hall. The wall was divided into four sections corresponding to the four historical labels. Each section contained typical architectural details but in the same color and texture to stress continuity (figure 4.4). "Tartessos" was evoked by an arrangement of stone plinths and mortar; "Betica" imitated the Roman defensive walls that once surrounded cities like Cordoba; in the "al-Andalus" section, a limestone façade was crowned by two coupled horseshoe arches, reminiscent of the Cordoba Mosque-Cathedral and the Alhambra; "Andalusia" stressed Islamic-Christian transculturation with a *mudéjar* three-lobed arch and an adobe brick wall framing Baroque sculptures of Mary and Jesus, a nod to Holy Week festivities.

At the end of the hallway, visitors were ushered into a modern gallery celebrating contemporary Andalusian artists, writers, and composers: drawings and manuscripts by Federico García Lorca and Rafael Alberti, sheets of music in the hand of Manuel de Falla, and even a bullfighting cape autographed by Picasso. The avant-garde painters Luis Gordillo and José Guerrero represented post–Civil War art.

"La memoria productiva" was an odd conflation of modern optimism and postmodern pastiche, an accumulation of different styles without original substance. Fredric Jameson explains that pastiche mobilizes a schoolbook

Figure 4.4. Section of "La memoria productiva" exhibit at the Pavilion of Andalusia, Expo '92. Copyright © Archivo General de Andalucía, Seville (Spain).

knowledge of history but robs us of "our historicity, of our lived possibility of experiencing history in some active way."[59] The point becomes clear if we compare the face of al-Andalus in "La memoria productiva" to Blas Infante's gesture of donning the old Moorish mask to bring something new into a region plagued by poverty and social injustice. Infante had faith in the power of the Andalusi past to revolutionize the present; he saw it not as a fixed point in history, but as a new point of departure. In contrast, the exhibit confines the past to a single story line progressing inexorably to the triumph of regional autonomy within the context of advanced capitalism. This framework makes history a fetish or a commodity and squelches the Muslim legacy's power to challenge, question, reconceive, rewrite, or even disrupt the very idea of Andalusia. Infante's mask is no more authentic than the fake mosque wall in the Andalusian Pavilion, but it has a radical creativity—a historicity—the exhibit lacks. The memory of al-Andalus at the Expo is productive only in a commercial and bureaucratic sense: to glorify prepackaged, palatable views of identity, community, and history.

Although pastiche is often described as a heap of fragments combined in an aleatory fashion, "La memoria productiva" covered its gaps to promote the two aspects of Andalusia's new image stressed in the Junta's press dossier.

First, Andalusia is a "cultural unit with its own identity," despite its rich historical diversity. Second, it is a region on the move, leaving behind "age-old economic backwardness."[60] Visitors symbolically reenacted this path as they walked down the straight corridor into the central gallery. Historical and cultural discontinuities were paved over, and the southern avant-garde was presented not as a deviation from Western notions of modernity (a plausible interpretation of Lorca and Falla's work, as I suggest in chapter 2), but as a springboard catapulting fairgoers to the pavilion's second floor, which emphasized material progress with displays of local advances in biotechnology, telecommunications, and naval industry. The third floor gift-wrapped Andalusia as a tourist destination. A ten-minute movie entitled "Vehículo de fantasía" ("Vehicle of Fantasy") bombarded spectators with dazzling bird's-eye shots of emblematic sites, and a travel agency close to the screens made sure that no prospective tourist left the building without purchasing a vacation package.

The pavilion, a baffling blend of museum, technological park, and tourist bureau, attested to the regional government's efforts to build an evolving, unitary image of Andalusia. It also suggests the triviality of this endeavor; its ultimate value was a marketing ploy to sell a commodity. Identity is accorded meaning and value only when it serves a globalized society of free trade and banal cosmopolitan conviviality where diversity must be domesticated, often by reducing cultural differences to sale items.

This odd combination of identity formation and commercial hype is also apparent in the electronic encyclopedia of Andalusia, an interactive database that fairgoers could consult from different spots in the pavilion. Comprised of thousands of videos and photographs, it guided users through the geography, folklore, and history of the region. The overall picture reinforced the message of the exhibits. Like "La memoria productiva," the encyclopedia gave visitors a vicarious sense of control while forcing them to choose from a set of predefined menus: "The Environment," "Folklore and Fiestas," "Culture," "Traces of Mankind," and—you guessed it—"Tourism." In fact, the electronic encyclopedia might have been the best expression of identity in post-Franco Andalusia. As an authoritative source (an encyclopedia, no less), it seemed to provide irrefutable proof of regional distinctiveness. Its hypermedia technology reinforced and presented the construction of the autonomous community as a participatory, democratic project. However, identity-making was no more interactive on the screen than in reality. The encyclopedia's program ran on a computer that was not networked; it was self-contained, and users could only follow preprogrammed paths. Clicking on a link or choosing a new image did not require contribution from the user; you could not search, for example, "Poverty," "Unemployment," or "Political Corruption." In short, the electronic encyclopedia replaced thinking and historicity—our capacity to freely represent and explore our experiences and questions—with predefined texts and images. It exemplifies mechanisms whereby "one does not construct a unique self but instead adopts already pre-established identities" by following computer commands.[61] Isn't this the face, the interface, of myth in the digital era?

Museumized Autonomy

After the Expo, the government of the autonomous community kept fostering a message in which Andalusia existed independent of Andalusians. Official cultural agencies and centers invited citizens to participate in events and activities devoted to region-building, not to generate open debate, but to recover, edit, and mobilize the past as a one-way path to political autonomy, the final stage of Andalusian history. In this narcissistic paradigm, the people were reduced to silent spectators admiring the triumphant consolidation of home rule. They might also play the part of tourists in their homeland. An official report from 1992, commissioned by the Junta and coordinated by the eminent sociologist and urban planner Manuel Castells, proposed to revamp the Expo site as a technological park. It stated that continued regional development and democratic stability depended on tourism based on "*active and participatory* leisure activities."[62] Policymakers respected the letter, if not the spirit, of the proposal. Jogging into the twenty-first century, the tourist industry and participatory democracy continued to buoy up the autonomic government, as citizenship and consumerism became increasingly indistinguishable.

The French poet Stéphane Mallarmé said, "Everything in the world exists in order to end up in a book."[63] To paraphrase, for the Junta, everything in Andalusia exists to end up as a statute of autonomy or a tourist brochure. The difference between the charter and the promotional tool is not as great as might first appear. Both depict the region as an empty stage rather than a people's theater open to critical voices. Browse the tourism portal, www.andalucia.org, designed and operated by the Andalusian government since 2000, and you will find iconic destinations, such as Cordoba, Granada, and Seville without people—ghost towns. Photo galleries feature deserted streets and squares, churches with empty pews, beaches bereft of bodies, and even restaurant tables without diners. This sustained trend to remove Andalusians from official images of their autonomous community is not simply an aesthetic choice or a rule of photo composition. Among all the tourist advertising materials created by the Andalusian government from 1978 to 2008, 74.4 percent contained empty scenes; 20.4 percent featured tourists; and only 5.1 percent show Andalusians.[64]

Now open the 2007 Statute of Autonomy, and you will experience the same uncanny feeling: an Andalusia without Andalusians. "Throughout history," the charter's preamble states, "Andalusia has forged a robust and solid identity that makes it a singular community, settled from time immemorial in a differentiated geographical enclave, a space of encounter and dialogue among diverse civilizations." Identity emanates primarily from the territory, not from its current inhabitants, who are characterized as passive recipients of a "valuable social and cultural patrimony" and the rights granted in the 1978 constitution.[65] Presented with a fait accompli, they have no real capacity to exert power in their environment, which, mirroring the slides on www.andalucia.org, the language portrays as an uninhabited land awaiting the arrival of eager tourists: "Andalusia, settled in the south of the Iberian Peninsula, is a territory with a varied landscape, including important mountain ranges and the Guadalquivir valley. Bounded by an extensive coastline along the Mediterranean Sea and the Atlantic Ocean, it is a bridge between Europe and the African continent."[66] The critic Eugenia Afinoguénova astutely remarks that the 2007 statute "reads like a tourist guide" that personifies territory at the expense of its citizens. "Andalusia," the only recognizable political agent in the text, doubles as a trademark, a slogan that designates a consumable product, not a collective, democratic project.[67]

This depersonalization of identity also privileges the institutional over the social, narrowing the definition of "democratic" to mean the existence of an autonomous government in the region. The form, not the substance, of the community matters most. Seen as a process that has concluded, political self-determination is divested of what validated it in the first place: the people and the past. Talk of economic underdevelopment, one of the pillars of Blas Infante's historical *andalucismo*, petered out after the transition to democracy, when the Spanish government and the European Union lavished financial resources on the newly created autonomous community. Since 1986, Andalusia has been the top recipient in Spain of European Union funds intended to stimulate employment and promote infrastructure, research, and industrial development in the poorer parts of the eurozone. Following the massive public expenditures related to the Expo, the Junta received 180 billion pesetas (over $121,000,000) per year from 1994 to 1999, amounting to 27.2 percent of all European Union money coming into Spain.[68]

The demise of what Antonio Burgos called the *regionalismo del subdesarrollo* (regionalism of underdevelopment) has also shaped official interpretations of Andalusia's history. After the transition, al-Andalus lost the revolutionary power it had in Infante's writings and the pages of *Triunfo*. Slowly drained of historical and cultural meaning, it has become a fetish rather than a legacy for investment in the present and future. Outbursts against African immigrants and religious intolerance, including the 2004 ban on Muslim prayer in the Mosque-Cathedral of Cordoba, have made al-Andalus a cultural minefield. And yet, Andalusi architecture is still over-represented in Junta-produced tourist guides, posters, and audiovisual materials. A recent study shows that 26.5 percent of the images tagged "historic heritage" in government publications between 1978 and 2008 feature Muslim artworks and monuments.[69] Their goal is not to define the relationship between a community and its past, but to market a brand—to offer the visitor "the romance of the east with the comforts of the west," to paraphrase a promotional slogan from 1930.[70]

The touristification of Andalusia in the democratic period is a telltale sign of a community whose history and territory are valued only to attract tourists and to justify the region's political apparatus. This official view attained material form in the Museum of Andalusian Autonomy (Museo de la Autonomía de Andalucía), a rather remote, uninspiring, and almost obligatory field-trip destination for Andalusian schoolchildren. It opened a year before the approval of the 2007 statute, which declared the region's "nationality" status and secured the fullest level of autonomy allowed under the Spanish constitution. The museum is a multistory, split-level structure containing two main galleries, a bookstore, a multimedia room, and office space for the Center of Andalusian Studies, which is the official managing agency. The museum is in the so-called Precinct of Andalusian Autonomy outside Coria del Río, about twelve miles from Seville. Blas Infante chose this site in 1931 to build his iconic House of Joy, where he spent his final days before he was seized and executed by Francoist rebels in 1936. Bought and restored by the Junta, the house became part of the museum complex in 2010.

Taken together, the house and museum turn the tangled story of Andalusia's move toward self-rule into a straight line. Visitors must follow a prescribed course from the House of Joy to the permanent exhibit inside the museum. Text-based timelines on the walls of both buildings mark a succession of selected events advancing inexorably toward the desired goal of regional political autonomy. Everything that happened from the first stirrings of Andalusian nationalism during the First Republic (1873–74) to the approval of the amended statute in 2007 is presented as a relentless march toward self-determination. The drafting of a federalist constitution for Andalusia in 1883, the adoption of the white-and-green flag as a national symbol at the 1918 Assembly of Ronda, the activism of the Juntas Liberalistas during the Second Republic (1931–36), and renewed efforts to attain self-government after the 34-year hiatus of the dictatorship are read as contributions, real or imagined, to the consolidation of Andalusia's autonomous government. History is viewed as a concluded process that can only be memorialized, never challenged or questioned.

Blas Infante is placed at the center of this epic. He existed, you feel, so that the Junta de Andalucía could be created. The illusion is heightened by a life-sized hologram of the patriot, who fades in and out of view to guide visitors through his house. Moving from the study where he stayed up listening to flamenco until the small hours, to his bedroom, now plastered with graphs and tables listing important historical events, to the music room, where he composed the regional anthem, you feel compelled to egg him on to continue his work, so the Andalusians of today can live as a "historical nationality" within the Spanish state. Eloquent tour guides on the public payroll drive the point home. Like the Expo pavilion, the museum mythologizes nationalism in post-Franco Andalusia by freezing history and presenting autonomy as a fully accomplished fact that demands admiration.

All aspects of the visit are made to fit into the grand plan of autonomy. The current political system is enshrined as the perfect manifestation of the region's past and people. History and citizenship are carefully staged to specify region-building as the source of present-day institutions. The first thing visitors notice is the Moorish style of the House of Joy, which itself is a translation of *Dar al-Farah*, Infante's original Arabic name for the house. The martyred patriot clearly intended his house to glorify al-Andalus and its links to modern Andalusia. An example of Moorish revival style, its design combines a plain exterior, reminiscent of Andalusi farmhouses, or *alquerías*, and an exquisitely ornate interior. Filigree decoration on tilework, intricate Arabic calligraphy, cusped arches, and coffered ceilings whisk visitors back centuries to the opulence of the caliphate. Walls frescoed with orientalist scenes more literally stress southern Spain's close ties with the Arab world.

Following Infante's lead, the curators mobilize al-Andalus as an *hecho diferencial* that marks "why we are different" and sets regional history apart from Spain's. Ideas that might halt or derail the autonomic train are screened out. Both Infante and the curators chose to ignore that there is no sign whatsoever that the many political shapes of al-Andalus over the centuries would coalesce in a unified political body bound by democratic institutions and constitutional rights. But curators also ignored important meanings that Infante attached to Muslim Iberia, particularly its symbolic role in the creation of a federal state with strong cultural ties to the Mediterranean world, from Tangiers to Damascus, as he wrote in *La verdad sobre el complot de Tablada y el Estado Libre de Andalucía* (1931). Federalism and orientalism clash with the museum's view of an autonomous yet not fully federalized community within a parliamentary monarchy that aspires to become part of Europe, not the orient. Perhaps the most glaring contrast is between Infante's recognition of history as open-ended and the museum's petrification of it as a straight line leading inexorably to a single outcome. For Infante, the past could impinge upon the present to change it; he deemed al-Andalus a living principle that could abolish the moribund structures of Restoration Spain (see chapter 1). By contrast, the museum seals the past as a historical period that attains full significance only in hindsight, from the vantage point of the present.

"The past, as it is materially embodied in museums," Tony Bennett writes in *The Birth of the Museum*, "is inescapably a product of the present which organizes it."[71] The House of Joy museum is no exception to this rule. Its last stop, an interactive "Blas Infante classroom," corsets the patriot's biography with the master narrative of autonomy.[72] Multimedia displays emphasize his fight for Andalusian political independence, underlining his push for the adoption of "national symbols" in the region, but the displays give short shrift to his land reform proposals, his celebration of Islam, his federalism, and his political flirtations with anarchism during the Second Republic, which coincided with the years he spent in Coria del Río. The accent is on institutional consolidation, not revolutionary change or the social significance of al-Andalus for today's Andalusia. The ubiquitous Moorish references in the house are severed from Infante's socialism, which saw the Christian Reconquest's creation of large uncultivated estates, or latifundia, as the source of chronic poverty, marginalization, and oppression among twentieth-century landless workers, whom he imagined as the heirs of displaced Moriscos. Museumgoers are not exposed to these associations; the Islamic ornamentation on the walls supports the banal regional distinctiveness promoted by the regional constitution. A 2005 report by the regional Institute of Historical Patrimony declared that the house has "symbolic importance for Andalusia's contemporary history and the process of construction of the autonomous community." The official publications of the Center of Andalusian Studies, for sale in the museum's bookstore, uphold the framework of expectations. In the catalog *La casa de Blas Infante: El legado* (2010; *The House of Blas Infante: The Legacy*), the curator Bico Bermúdez writes that to talk about Infante is to talk about "Autonomy and Statute."[73] He has organized the house's space and content to connect Infante's "idea of Andalusia" to the "landmarks in the struggle for the Statute."[74] This message is adapted for younger readers in a comic book, significantly entitled *Blas Infante: Una vida, un destino* (2012; *Blas Infante: A Life, A Destiny*).

As visitors exit through the back door where Infante was seized by his executioners in 1936 and walk down a beautifully landscaped path about eighty yards long, they face the restrained, pure geometry of the Museum of Andalusian Autonomy. An unornamented white rectangle, it recalls the Expo's Pavilion of Andalusia, its precursor in many ways, but it has no Islamic motifs. The dazzling white of the exterior walls, a tabula rasa, wipes out whatever historical allusions fairgoers perceived on the façade of the Expo pavilion. Inside, the permanent exhibition retains the exterior's white in keeping with one overriding and monotonous theme: autonomy's inception, development, consummation. History appears in one-dimensional props that do not distract from the choreographed task: marching from the first and second republics through the dormancy period during the Civil War and Francoism, the popular mobilization for autonomy in the 1970s, the February 28 referendum that put Andalusia on the fast track to autonomy, the approval of the 1981 statute, and—grand climax—the declaration of Andalusia's nationality in the 2007 amended charter.

The itinerary begins with a white-lacquered replica of Infante's desk, his empty shoes carefully tucked under it (figure 4.5). Intended to pay homage to the "Father of Andalusia," it unwittingly evidences the exclusions in the idealization of the hero. His absent body is a reminder of all that has been drained from the official image. The itinerary anticipates other absences in the exhibition room, where, apart from visitors and guides, human figures

Figure 4.5. Replica of Blas Infante's desk at the Museo de la Autonomía de Andalucía. Copyright © Museo de la Autonomía de Andalucía, Centro de Estudios Andaluces, Seville (Spain).

are expunged. Mute images of Andalusians from different time periods are projected on screens along the corridor, but the installations are oddly depopulated and disturbingly uniform.

Together, they evoke an unhesitating march, with all battles, setbacks, and victories leading to the establishment of the regional government. The opening section, an assemblage of Civil War barricades, rifles, helmets, and empty boots under dropping bombs, all painted white, quickly turns into a long line of white shoes of all sizes heading in the same direction. They are supposed to represent the millions of demonstrators who took to the streets on December 4, 1977, to demand regional autonomy. A hovering bullhorn heads the ghostly parade toward independence, but no one speaks through it (figure 4.6).

In the next sequence, shoes and an empty wheelchair gather around large ballot boxes to commemorate the 1980 referendum, which led to the 1981 statute, a landmark symbolized by a pile of white television sets. TVs become laptop computers in the next segment, dedicated to the 2007 statute, which is naturally the last stop. The electronic devices encourage a view of citizens as spectators, or even users, not actors. The scenography asserts an autonomous

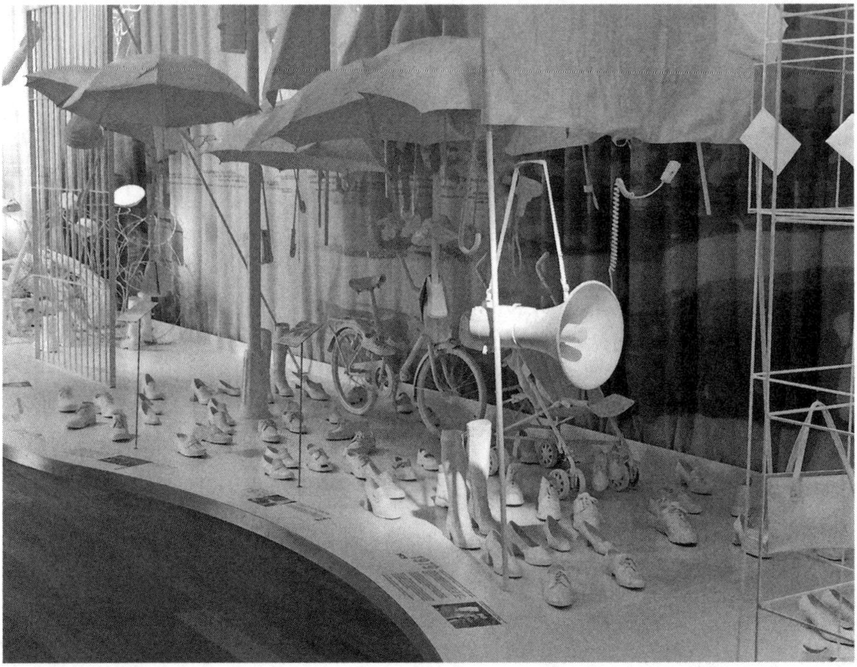

Figure 4.6. Thematic section "Un pueblo en la calle que lucha por la autonomía, 1976–1979" at the Museo de la Autonomía de Andalucía. Copyright © Museo de la Autonomía de Andalucía, Centro de Estudios Andaluces, Seville (Spain).

Andalusia whose citizens only attain significance as parts of a larger whole. The monochromatic arrangement stresses this point: freedom was achieved through the sacrifice of individuality for the sake of a collective ideal—through consensus, not discord and conflict.

Finally, visitors reach "Nombres propios" ("Proper Names"), a display of head-shots over a field of sunflowers. Most of these feature politicians who contributed to the creation of the region's independent political system, including its former presidents Manuel Chaves and José Antonio Griñán, who are now facing corruption charges.[75] An interactive screen next to the photomontage acknowledges the role of prominent artists and writers, while the remaining thematic spaces shift the focus back to regional institutions (congress, cabinet, and supreme court) and the six presidents of the Junta since its creation in 1978. Overall, the exhibit is an exercise of self-glorification, conveying at once an optimistic vision of the Junta as history's cutting edge and citizen identity as a cog in the autonomic political apparatus.

In the corner devoted to regional symbols, Infante is quoted to explain the significance of the white-and-green flag representing all Andalusians: "Green is the garment of our mountains and countryside . . . white are our whitewashed villages and ancient towns garlanded with green latticework and jasmine branches." The passage, taken from an article published in 1919, does not mention that Infante was also inspired by the green banner of the Umayyad dynasty, later modified with a central white stripe by the Almohads in the twelfth century as they tried to unify the different *taifa* kingdoms. Infante's passionate call to gather under the flag to fight for radical change and end the oppressive socioeconomic structures that have martyred Andalusians since the Christian occupation in the fifteenth century is also left out.[76] These omissions minimize the cultural influence of Muslim Iberia in today's Andalusia while echoing the Junta's tourism campaigns and the 2007 statute, where Andalusia is a landscape, not a home to an active citizenry.

Infante's revolutionary message is certainly out of place if the goal is to create a vague consensus around a definitive identity. By the same token, his economic argument, which was inextricable from his revival of al-Andalus, is at odds with the rhetoric of classlessness that shapes the permanent exhibit in the museum. It conveys form rather than content, myth rather than facts, the idea of a unified nation rather than the messy reality of clashing interests among its citizens. The one-directional pilgrimage of empty shoes that traverses the gallery symbolically forecloses alternative paths for regional development, whether past, present, or future. Just as the future is envisioned as an infinite extension of the conclusive present, those who did not march in unison toward autonomy are not mentioned. Rather than a syncopated rhythm, with reflective or discordant riffs, the past is a continuous, harmonious incantation. Party conflicts during the transition to democracy—for example, PSA challenges to PSOE leadership in the 1970s—go unremarked. Equally ignored is the *regionalismo del subdesarrollo* from the 1960s, which recovered Infante's flag, shield, and anthem as signs of identity as well as his view of history and his commitment to end southern underdevelopment. Only through the institutionalized, half-blind amnesia that pervades the museum can regional governments indulge in self-justification while 30 percent of the active population remains unemployed, and thousands have emigrated to more prosperous parts of Spain. Confronted by crisis, the Andalusian government seems to do little more than exhibit the tale of their own successful configuration.

In *Beyond the Prado*, the art historian Selma Reuben Holo celebrates how regional museums in Spain have fostered the transition from an oppressive, centralizing dictatorship to a complex pluri-national state. "Museums," she writes, have "emerged as one of the emblems and engines driving Spain into democracy."[77] The Museum of Andalusian Autonomy fits the profile, but only if we add the qualifier "formal" to the word "democracy," as Rubert de Ventós insisted we do when talking about post-Franco Spain. Democracy may be defined as a process of endless renewals, interruptions, dislocations, and readjustments, an open-ended project, always in the making, that resists a final encompassing narrative as differences beg recognition and accommodation. Like Canal Sur and the Expo, the Precinct of Andalusian Autonomy assembles history and citizenship into a narrative—a myth—that reveres a single, definitive Andalusia, a form to be contemplated rather than content to be worked through. Autonomy does not translate automatically into freedom—the kind of freedom that follows when a deliberative citizenry takes civic engagement seriously; when it considers not just the one dominant perspective on the present, but the complex ways that yesterday, today, and tomorrow interconnect; and when it knows how to tell history from a straight line.

Afterword

✦

Breaking the Spell of Identity

> Thinking involves not only the flow of thoughts, but their arrest as well.
>
> —Walter Benjamin, "Theses on the Philosophy of History"

Oscar Wilde wrote that the "one duty we owe to history is to rewrite it."[1] This process of rewriting can take place in two main ways. The first challenges previous views, not conceptual frameworks—or, as Hayden White put it, the "metahistorical element": "the precritically accepted paradigm of what a distinctively 'historical' explanation should be."[2] You can write and rewrite social, feminist, black, and national histories without questioning concepts of class, gender, race, and nationality. For the most part I have explored and explained this type of rewriting: the nineteenth-century concept of oriental Andalusia which has been refashioned and refuted, but never fully critiqued. As Edward Said wrote about the orient, this Andalusia is "less a place than a *topos*, a set of references, a congeries of characteristics, that seems to have its origin in a quotation, or a fragment of a text, or a citation from someone's work on the Orient, or some bit of previous imagining, or an amalgam of all these."[3] Romantic travelers in search of the sublime in the nineteenth century; the pro-Castilian ILE reformers and *andalucista* patriots of the early twentieth century; the nationalist *flamenquistas* and right-wing pundits of the Franco era; and the regionalists of the post-dictatorial period accepted the imagined Andalusia as a real entity, whether they revered or reviled it. Their diverse interpretations—their rewritings—differ about fundamental aspects of Andalusia, but none questions the familiar identification of the region with an abstraction, the foundation of identity politics.

The second way history can be rewritten is by challenging not *what* was said, but *how* it was said. Federico García Lorca exemplifies this approach in reworking worn clichés to blast his way into literary modernity. His Andalusia is as unprovincial as it is uncompromising; it submits to old myths while reinventing them, cutting stock images of an orientalized land populated by gypsies and Moors against the grain in order to break out of paralyzing binaries like east vs. west; archaic vs. modern; and oriental vs. Spanish. The result is a fluid poetic artifact: a flowing Andalusia of the mind that defies definition.

García Lorca's Andalusia—which was a literary landscape, not an economically underdeveloped territory—will not satisfy the pragmatic mind. Writing in the tumultuous 1960s, the Marxist thinker Alfonso Carlos Comín said that if Andalusians ever wished to break the shackles of oppression, they must first break the spell of cultural identity. Perceiving and solving real socioeconomic problems implies the rejection of fictions and theories that have never worked to benefit the people who evoked them. Andalusians must pull the wool of spiritual commonality off their eyes and regard each other as fellow exploited workers.

Contributors to the leftist magazine *Triunfo* noted in the 1970s that Comín's radical materialism throws out the baby of Andalusia with the bath water of myths about the region. The real question, they suggested, was how to break the spell of cultural fictions without discarding the idea of Andalusia. For the critics Francisco Almazán and Antonio Ramos Espejo, the way out of the dilemma was to foster a tactical rather than an essentialist approach to history and culture. In their view, flamenco and the historical memory of al-Andalus are valuable as cultural markers only if we see them as the expression of marginalization: as the "sigh of the oppressed," to use Marx's words on religion.[4] This approach demystifies Andalusia. If the region has a common culture—a common identity—it can only be understood as an effect or by-product of marginality and its causes—land appropriation and accumulation, servitude, ethnic displacement.

While the first type of rewriting keeps Andalusia as a fixed image within margins, the second type, in both its idealistic and materialistic versions, blasts them open. However, neither approach shrugs off identity as a mode of expression. García Lorca decenters and multiplies it on the written page; *Triunfo* reduces it to ever-changing material conditions. Either way, "Andalusia" is understood as entity and identity.

Even the disenchanted voices who now lament the failed cultural politics of the Andalusian government intone the unavoidable buzzword of "identity." In a 2001 article, Isidoro Moreno, a professor of anthropology at the University of Seville and one of the most active defenders of southern specificity during the post-Franco transition, condemns the Junta of Andalusia's "commodification" of the region.[5] In his view, the affirmation of Andalusian consciousness legally required by the 1981 Statute of Autonomy is a ruined project that has lapsed into the old kitsch of beaches, bulls, and *bailaoras* spiced with a dash of Moorish charm. More a tourist board than a government institution, the Junta has focused on marketing a product instead of representing a democratic community politically and historically. Fighting fire with fire, Moreno still believes that public media stereotypes can be replaced by *authentic* Andalusian-ness, which he sketchily defines as a "resistance identity" opposing the market-driven modernization and globalization that have turned Andalusia into a trademark.[6] The only solid marker that seems to remain in the post-dictatorial present is a vague class consciousness, which is more a vacuous memory of revolutionary sentiments than any actual revolution. Moreno has no problem with identity, just debased identity.

But could Andalusia be an entity without identity? Identity—from Latin *identitas*, or "sameness"—is based on synthesis and permanence and is defined by continuity over time and differentiation from others. "Continuity and differentiation," the political sociologist Monserrat Guibernau points out in *The Identity of Nations* (2007), "lead to the distinction between members (those who belong) and 'strangers,' 'the rest,' 'the different,' and, sometimes, 'the enemy.'"[7] Identity's static quality is ill-fitted to explain a region long defined as "other" by locals and foreigners alike, and where the words "stranger" and "different," especially when applied to the Moorish "enemy," often translate as "brother" and "intimate."

The interplay among Andalusia, orientalism, and the making of modern Spain—as well as my skepticism about regionalist patriotism—is more appropriately interpreted through the lens of the sublime. Frank R. Ankersmit argues that the affective ways in which we relate to the past may be explained, not through identity, but "in terms of the notion of 'sublime historical experience.' For a nation, a collectivity, a culture, or a civilization that has such a sublime historical experience, the past and an awareness of this past will become ineluctable realities."[8] Experience here is different from knowledge and is caught between history and memory. Whether we lived it or not, the past is an object of fascination preceding historiographical notions of truth and falsity, causation and representation. Historical experience may not be sensory experience, but it determines who we are and where we belong. It connects us to a lost reality, breaking us off from our present to give us a richer understanding of it. It turns loss and distance into love and immediacy. "The sublimity of historical experience," Ankersmit writes, "originates from this paradoxical experience of the feelings of love and loss, that is, of the combination of pain and pleasure in how we relate to the past."[9]

The sublime takes us to the void at the heart of identity, between what begs to be thought yet remains unthinkable. It reveals "the experience of the past underlying the language used by the historian."[10] A relentless fluctuation between affirmation and negation, past and present, the sublime historical experience is intensified by the ways Spain and Andalusia have been spliced together by orientalism over the last two centuries. More than the neat opposition of self and other posed by Edward Said, orientalism in this context is a puzzling interplay of doubles—a contradiction without resolution that produces not only "pain and pleasure in how we relate to the past," but disorientation and even vertigo.

I have felt this disorientation ever since I began reflecting critically on the cultural contradictions of my upbringing as an Andalusian, but I could not find a way to express it until I rewatched Basilio Martín Patino's televised documentary *Andalucía: Un siglo de fascinación* (*Andalusia: A Century of Fascination*) about six years ago.[11] Commissioned by Canal Sur in 1992 and first aired in 1996, its seven episodes are a breakneck tour of the myths that shaped conceptions of Andalusia in the last century, spanning roughly the same period discussed in this book. Each episode focuses on a specific motif: *Ojos verdes* (*Green Eyes*), taking its title from a love song popularized by the iconic performer Concha Piquer, deals with *copla* as a musical genre and cultural phenomenon. *Carmen y la libertad* (*Carmen and Freedom*) focuses on Mérimée's legend, tying it to the south's passionate culture and the fury of its landless workers. *El grito del sur: Casas Viejas* (*The Cry of the South: Casas Viejas*) reenacts the 1933 anarchist uprising in a small town near Cadiz, an incident that ended up with ordinary peasants bloodily massacred by the Civil Guard. *El jardín de los poetas* (*The Garden of the Poets*) documents the production of a fictional television program about the life and work of Andalusian poets of the Generation of 1927, including García Lorca and Juan Ramón Jiménez. *Desde lo más hondo I* and *II* (*From the Deepest Depth I* and *II*) look at the origins of flamenco music, its commercialization, and its most recent technological reproductions. *Paraísos*, the last installment, chronicles frustrated attempts—some real, like the Tempul Phalanstery, some imagined like Ronda's Free Community—to create utopian communities in Andalusia.

At age sixteen, I watched some of the episodes as they premiered on Canal Sur. I took them at face value as a faithful representation of a region that came into its own as an autonomous community after a century-long gestation. I remember being bored by the mock academic lectures in *Paraísos*, shaken by the massacre at Casas Viejas, and reassured that my cultural identity owed much to the poets in *El jardín* and the tunes in the flamenco episodes, which resonated with the soundtrack of family road trips, the car stereo always playing doleful cadences as we drove to the Sierra Morena or the Costa del Sol. The series' playful blend of reality and fantasy that was meant to poke fun at the truth-claims of documentary films evaded me, unfamiliar as I was with the slippery nuances of irony and satire. I took mockumentaries for historical documentaries. First came serious appreciation; then came laughter.

The second time I watched all seven episodes was in the spring semester of 2012, my pre-tenure leave, when I was gathering the source material for chapter 4 of this book. I turned to Patino's work expecting to detect the efforts of the regional government to polish the glossy modernity publicized by Expo '92 and the public media, especially Canal Sur, but instead the documentary's irreverence about hallowed symbols and images astonished me, changing my first impression. I delighted in how fabulations enshrined by the Junta were gutted in shot after shot, sequence after sequence. Stock images were offered up and hollowed out. Patino's compliance with institutional agendas was a smokescreen. In fact, *Andalucía: Un siglo de fascinación* continues his antiestablishment work of the 1960s and 1970s.

Patino's preferred technique for chiseling away at Franco's cultural monolith was collage, a style that mixes and juxtaposes footage from different sources in order to refute one-dimensional versions of reality. His documentary film *Canciones para después de una guerra* (*Songs for After a War*), made in 1971 but censored until 1976, dissolves the myth of post–Civil War peace and harmony by intercutting shots of official celebrations like the nationalist victory parade in 1939 with heartbreaking sequences of destitute crowds ravished by famine, ruined cities, and piles of corpses in the street. The soundtrack, a mix of cheerful *coplas* and fascist chants, heightens the tension between official Francoist versions of reality and what they ignored or hid. Patino's *Caudillo* (1974) uses collage to distort heroic interpretations of Franco's life. Propaganda clips of Franco as divine crusader, caring father and husband, and venerated political leader contrast with horrifying footage of war victims; people in tears mourning the loss of loved ones; refugees seeking asylum; and international celebrities, including Einstein, denouncing the atrocities of war. Through photomontage, Patino jars the ideological fabrications of the Franco regime, using documentary footage to witness the falsity of state propaganda.

But in a democratic context, collage film loses its edge as a transgressive technique. With the stodgy regime and its leader gone and the new democracy firmly established, there was no longer a sphere beyond power from which the nonconformist could react. Francoism relied on what Michael Hardt and Antonio Negri, following Michel Foucault, call "disciplinary power": it ruled by organizing society and history according to a "with us or against us" logic, and by "structuring parameters and limits of thought and practice, sanctioning and prescribing normal and/or deviant behaviors." In contrast, democratic systems turn social control into "a vital function that every individual embraces and reactivates of his or her own accord."[12] Here, "resistances are no longer marginal but active in the center of a society that opens up in networks"; they infiltrate, not simply oppose, the language of power.[13]

Andalucía: Un siglo de fascinación infiltrates under the aegis of Canal Sur, the "official platform of Andalucianization," to use Antonio Muñoz Molina's apposite words.[14] Patino playfully undermines officialdom; his irony creeps up without blocking or even interfering with the institutional narrative of Andalusia as *hecho diferencial*. Rather than deny or distort this narrative, he retells it. Part of the criticism is still achieved through contrast. The image of Andalusia assembled by the post-Franco regional governments is confronted by the working-class problems they have tended to ignore. The exoticism of Carmen, for example, is tied to labor unrest; the idea of the south as a paradise is linked to utopian socialism; and the oppression of the agrarian peasantry is dramatically displayed in the Casas Viejas massacre. Patino also breaks the boundaries between fact and fiction, integrating real and counterfeit archival documents to confuse viewers about what is authentic and what is simulated in accounts of the past.[15] But his subversion is most searing when it goes almost unnoticed as allegory, when the medium is the message, as Marshall McLuhan put it.[16]

As an aesthetic genre, allegory always elicits interpretation, casting characters and events as symbols of abstract concepts. Allegories establish a correspondence between a story, play, or picture on the one hand, and a hidden moral or political message on the other. Literary examples range from Plato's allegory of the cave to George Orwell's *Animal Farm* (1945). While allegory generally unifies concrete images and figurative meanings, it can also throw them off in opposite directions. In *The Origin of German Tragic Drama* (1928), Walter Benjamin analyzes seventeenth-century Baroque depictions of skulls, dry leaves, and decayed plants that denote death, the absence of meaning. The architectural ruin functions similarly. According to Benjamin, ruins are evidence of history turned into catastrophe: places where civilization has receded and disappeared, leaving behind meaningless fragments. "In the ruin," Benjamin said, "history has physically merged into the setting. And in this guise history does not assume the form of the process of an eternal life so much as that of irresistible decay."[17] At its most extreme, Benjamin's interpretation of ruins as empty allegories recalls the sublime experience of feeling or intuiting something that does not really exist. Lyotard argued that the sublime "puts forward the unpresentable in presentation itself."[18] "The Sublime," Žižek wrote, "is the embodiment of Nothing."[19] Both echo Benjamin's assertion that allegory "means precisely the non-existence of what it presents."[20]

Patino reveals that "Andalusia" only exists as allegory.[21] The unifying theme of *Andalucía: Un siglo de fascinación* is the futility of searching for cultural authenticity or a rooted identity in a heap of historical rubble. The backdrop of ruined buildings in several episodes beckons viewers in this direction. Rafael de Maura, the protagonist of *Ojos verdes*, is a decrepit aristocrat with a Francoist past who lives in a damp, crumbling medieval castle where he has spent a lifetime hoarding memorabilia on *copla*: thousands of records, posters, books, dancing shoes, wigs, and moth-eaten shawls and dresses. Ironically, the episode opens with a short encounter between the marquis and a government official who is planning a pavilion to display the marquis's *copla* collection at the Expo '92. This bleak confirmation that Francoism still haunts the democratic present suggests that the modern pavilion is not that different from the collapsing castle. In both places, culture is embalmed alive to elicit the passive gaze of visitors, and the fate of the modern building, the viewer senses, is anticipated by the aristocrat's ruined residence. Instead of history's culmination, the new Andalusia displayed at the Expo is one more sandcastle doomed to be washed away by the tide of history.

A similar point is made in *Paraísos*, in which three foreigners—an American professor of anthropology at Princeton, a Swiss sociologist, and a Spanish-Italian adventurer—seek to fulfill their utopian dreams in Andalusia. They join previous visionaries, fictional and real, local and foreign, who, inspired by Robert Owen and Charles Fourier's nineteenth-century doctrines, sought to create socialist communities in monastic buildings tucked away in the idyllic Andalusian countryside. These include the mysterious El Cuervo Monastery near Cadiz, the Tempul Phalanstery, and a fictitious "Humanisphery." Now lain to waste, these buildings form a ghostly parade of ruins that stubbornly refuse imposed meanings, pushing viewers to see the protagonists' dreamed Andalusia not as a romantic myth to be revived but as history's castoff.

This message comes across most forcefully in *El jardín de los poetas*, a fake documentary film about the production of a made-up television program about Andalusian literature for Canal Sur. The setting, a decayed monastery nestled in the foothills of the Sierra Morena, is presented as a fabled "garden of poets." Anachronisms, historical falsifications, and apocrypha weave a spurious literary history that orbits the ruin. Although it is a sixteenth-century building, a fictional literary scholar, comically named Sancho Berenjena (Sancho Eggplant; most likely after Sancho Panza's mispronunciation of *Quixote*'s fictitious author, the Muslim writer Cide Hamete Benengeli, as Cide Hamete Berenjena), assures viewers that Ibn Hazm, an eleventh-century Andalusi writer, found inspiration in it for his famous treatise on love, *The Ring of the Dove*. Fake documentary footage goes on to show the development of Andalusian culture against the backdrop of the run-down monastery. As a music school for the blind in the 1930s, it hosted García Lorca, who recited poetry and played the piano for residents. Other members of the Generation of 1927 are connected to the monastery in a film attributed to a fictitious disciple of Gerald Brenan, the famous British Hispanist and author of the historical classic *The Spanish Labyrinth* (1943) and *South from Granada* (1957), a beguiling account of a demobilized English soldier who "goes native" in an Andalusian village. Next, a clip from No-Do, the Francoist newsreel, shows the monastery as a headquarters of the Sección Femenina, the women's branch of the fascist party, Falange. Finally, the venue becomes the set of the Canal Sur program, *El jardín de los poetas*. Crew members are shown covering up crumbling walls with garish decorations and placing studio equipment and disconcerting wax figures of iconic Generation of 1927 poets, including García Lorca sitting at a piano and Juan Ramón Jiménez standing by his legendary donkey, Platero.

All the historical layers pinned on the monastery invoke the classical conception of literature and culture as the soul of a nation, as the medium that reveals identity. In many ways, the historical sequence, assembled clip by clip, recalls the neat display at the Expo '92 Andalusian Pavilion, an arrow shooting from al-Andalus to the Generation of 1927, whose modernizing spirit was deflected by Francoism but revived in the post-dictatorial present (see chapter 4). Of course, the way Patino tells the tale is richly comic. In taking us behind the scenes of the fictional Canal Sur production, he stresses that what is wrapped up as fact is manipulated illusion. The producer says at one point, "This is television," by which he means that spectacle comes first, and anything that might disrupt it should be excluded, including the opinions of the young Andalusian poets invited as spectators, not participants, and a historian's revelations about García Lorca's assassination during the Civil War. To the unwelcome voices wishing to incorporate these elements into the telecast, the producer replies, "Whoever wants to read a book, should leave, buy it, and read it." If "it is not television," he concludes, "it won't be aired." This system of exclusion and inclusion responds mainly to crude commercialism. Marketing interests shape and control the set and stage, where the wax poets share the spotlight with young women in flamenco dresses, a live bull, and a large inflated bottle advertising the sponsor's brand of liquor. Cultural identity and history are pressed into the service of a banal exhibition of folkloric cheer meant to persuade viewers that in drinking a specific kind of wine, they are drinking the essence of Andalusia.

In subtle counterpoint to the no-nonsense producer, the disenchanted director, commenting on the production process in voice-over, hammers home the crucial point that television is another name for delusion. He scorns his work as a crafter of "fascinating stages that amplify myths, which amounts to amplifying nothingness." Later, he elaborates: "Isn't it a form of complicity to accept that everything that television touches will become a circus-like narrative that must please millions of spectators to recoup production costs through advertising?" His off-camera commentary drops the act and jolts viewers to a higher level of consciousness, urging us to face the empty allegory called "Andalusia."

The emptiness evoked by the director and the devastated walls towering over the flashy television set becomes apparent when, in a final act of poetic justice, the García Lorca wax puppet starts a fire that interrupts the live telecast and ignites a pile of fireworks meant to cap the spectacle. Fittingly, wax denotes the self-destructing yet illuminating properties of allegory. The explosion drives frenzied guests and crew members out of the monastery, which returns to peace once the fire is extinguished. The monastery's scorched ruins are at once the ground on which cultural history is founded, the setting for a grotesque show where history turns into a commodity, and the expression of their transience. In highlighting the emptiness and evanescence of historical meaning, Patino pushes us, not to gawping inaction, but to a lively consideration of crucial questions: What is Andalusia? Who defines it? For what purpose? Where and how is it manifest?

These questions, Patino suggests, should not summon identity but invite fascination. Fascination means both "sorcery, enchantment" and "irresistible attractive influence."[22] *Andalucía: Un siglo de fascinación* evokes the seductive, mesmerizing allure of a region that foreigners and locals alike have seen as an oriental dreamland but then strips it for parts and reassembles those parts as allegory. The familiar narrative retains its spellbinding appeal while exposing its artificiality. To achieve this effect, Patino flips back and forth between both senses of the word "fascination": between the counterfeit wisdom behind all charms and spells and the real attraction they produce. Like the sublime, fascination is a perilous borderline drawing us toward what will cripple us. In presenting Andalusia through the prism of fascination and allegory, Patino asks Canal Sur viewers to detach Andalusia from paralyzing identity paradigms while retaining a collective sense of self. Disavowing identity does not mean that you can be anyone anywhere, which is another way of saying that you are no one, nowhere.

Patino warns against parochialism but legitimates thinking about and from Andalusia. His allegorical rendering enchants without enthralling; it opens familiar myths in order to express southern difference, not as an anomaly or *hecho diferencial*, not as the unchanging stereotype of institutional decree and tourist brochure, but as a structure of feeling and thought that need not cohere in a fixed form of representation. Patino shows that Andalusians can appreciate and criticize, defend and mock, construct and deconstruct their common ground without sacrificing attachment. Through this operation, *Andalucía: Un siglo de fascinación* gives visual and narrative expression to my personal dilemma as someone skeptical about chest-thumping, flag-waving patriotism who yet feels Andalusian. The fascination the documentary evokes, a sublime feeling, is the driving force behind every page in this book.

NOTES

Introduction

1. Gala has expressed these views in print. See, for example, "Prólogo al Congreso de Cultura Andaluza," in *La identidad cultural de Andalucía: Aproximaciones, mixtificaciones, negacionismo y evidencias*, ed. Isidoro Moreno (Seville: Centro de Estudios Andaluces, 2008), 121–30.

2. Susan Martin-Márquez, *Disorientations: Spanish Colonialism in Africa and the Performance of Identity* (New Haven, Conn.: Yale University Press, 2008), 9.

3. Edward Said, *Orientalism* (New York: Vintage, 1979), 3.

4. Joan Ramon Resina, "Introduction: Iberian Modalities: The Logic of an Intercultural Field," in *Iberian Modalities: A Relational Approach to the Study of Culture in the Iberian Peninsula*, ed. Joan Ramon Resina (Liverpool, Eng.: Liverpool University Press, 2013), 2.

5. Ibid., 16.

6. Said, *Orientalism*, 20.

7. Immanuel Kant, *Observations on the Feeling of the Beautiful and the Sublime*, trans. John T. Goldthwait (Berkeley: University of California Press, 1960), 47.

8. Antonio Gramsci, *Selections from the Prison Notebooks*, ed. and trans. Quentin Hoare and Geoffrey Nowell Smith (London: Lawrence and Wishart, 1971), 324.

9. See, for instance, César Moreno Hidalgo, José Alvárez de la Cruz, and María del Rosario Ruiz Franco, eds., *Historia contemporánea de Andalucía* (Madrid: CSIC, 1995), a 199-page, 718-entry bibliography of journal articles published between 1975 and 1994.

10. "Orgullo andaluz," *ABC*, December 31, 1980, 2.

11. Margarita Capdepont, "El público de la Plaza Nueva a Alfonso Guerra: 'Que hable en andaluz,'" *ABC*, December 6, 1977, 15–16.

12. See Claudio Sánchez Albornoz, *España, un enigma histórico* (Buenos Aires: Editorial Sudamericana, 1953); and Serafín Fanjul, *Al-Andalus contra España: La forja del mito* (Madrid: Siglo Veintiuno, 2000) and *La quimera de al-Andalus* (Madrid: Siglo Veintiuno, 2004).

13. Luis Suárez Fernández, *Los Reyes Católicos: El tiempo de la Guerra de Granada* (Madrid: Rialp, 1989). On the Granada Venegas, see also David Coleman, *Creating Christian Granada: Society and Religious Culture in an Old-World Frontier City, 1492–1600* (Ithaca, N.Y.: Cornell University Press, 2003).

14. Juan Goytisolo, "Tierras del Sur," in *Obras completas* (Madrid: Aguilar, 1978), 2:1051–52.

15. Antonio Gómez Mendoza and Elena San Román, "Transportes y comunicaciones," in *Estadísticas históricas de España, siglos XIX–XX*, ed. Albert Carreras and Xavier Tafunell (Bilbao: Fundación BBVA, 2005), 532–58.

16. Xavier Tafunell, "Urbanización y vivienda," in *Estadísticas históricas*, 460.
17. Ibid., 484–85.
18. Martin Sherlock, *Letters from an English Traveler* (London: J. Nichols, 1780), 153.
19. George Gordon Byron, *Lord Byron: Selected Poems*, ed. Susan J. Wolfson and Peter J. Manning (London: Penguin, 1996), 74.
20. Victor Hugo, *Orientales et ballades* (Brussels: Louis Hauman, 1832), viii.
21. Stendhal [Marie-Henri Beyle], *Napoléon: Vie de Napoléon* (Geneva: Cercle du Bibliophile, 1970), 154.
22. Washington Irving, *The Alhambra* (New York: G. P. Putnam's Sons, 1861), 14.
23. Richard Ford, *A Hand-Book for Travellers in Spain, and Readers at Home* (Cambridge: Cambridge University Press, 2011), 1:119.
24. Julio Caro Baroja, *De etnología andaluza*, ed. Antonio Carreira (Malaga: Universidad de Málaga-Diputación Provincial de Málaga, 1993), 261.
25. On the affirmation of oriental and Andalusian stereotypes as Spain's rejection of northern European (particularly French) cultural supremacy in the eighteenth and nineteenth centuries, see Jesús Torrecilla, *Guerras literarias del XVIII español* (Salamanca: Universidad de Salamanca, 2008) and *España exótica: La formación de la imagen Española moderna* (Boulder, Colo.: Society of Spanish and Spanish-American Studies, 2004).
26. See Joaquín Álvarez Barrientos and Alberto Romero Ferrer, eds., *Costumbrismo andaluz* (Seville: Universidad de Sevilla, 1998).
27. Zeynep Çelik, *Displaying the Orient: Architecture of Islam at the Nineteenth-Century World's Fairs* (Berkeley: University of California Press, 1992), 69.
28. Kant, *Observations*, 98–99. On the differences between the beautiful and the sublime, see also Edmund Burke, *A Philosophical Enquiry into the Origin of Our Ideas of the Beautiful and the Sublime* (Oxford: Oxford University Press, 1998).
29. Immanuel Kant, *Anthropology from a Pragmatic Point of View*, ed. and trans. Robert B. Louden (Cambridge: Cambridge University Press, 2006), 218.
30. Théophile Gautier, *Travels in Spain*, trans. F.-C. de Sumichrast (Cambridge: Jenson Society, 1906), 213–15.
31. Edgar Quinet, *Mes vacances en Espagne* (Paris: Au Comptoir des Imprimeurs-Unis, 1846), 317.
32. See Uvedale Price, *An Essay on the Picturesque, as Compared with the Sublime and the Beautiful* (London: J. Robson, 1794).
33. Gautier, *Travels*, 215.
34. Jean-Luc Nancy, "The Sublime Offering," in *Of the Sublime: Presence in Question*, ed. Jean-François Courtine et al., trans. Jeffrey S. Librett (Albany: SUNY Press, 1993), 25.
35. Jean-François Lyotard, *The Postmodern Condition: A Report on Knowledge* (Minneapolis: University of Minnesota Press, 1982), 81.
36. Slavoj Žižek, *The Sublime Object of Ideology* (London: Verso, 1989), 206.
37. Luisa Elena Delgado, "Settled in Normal: Narratives of a Prozaic (Spanish) Nation," *Arizona Journal of Hispanic Cultural Studies* 7 (2003): 126.

38. Immanuel Kant, *Critique of the Power of Judgment*, ed. Paul Guyer, trans. Paul Guyer and Eric Matthews (Cambridge: Cambridge University Press, 2000), 141.

39. Raymond Carr, "Introduction," in *Spain: A History*, ed. Raymond Carr (Oxford: Oxford University Press, 2000), 1.

40. Delgado, "Settled in Normal," 128.

41. Mónica Burguera and Christopher Schmidt-Nowara, "Backwardness and Its Discontents," *Social History* 29, no. 3 (2004): 283.

42. Said, *Orientalism*, 1.

43. Ibid., 40.

44. Ford, *Hand-Book*, 1:ix.

45. Edward Said, "Prólogo a la nueva edición española," in *Orientalismo*, trans. María Luisa Fuentes (Barcelona: Debolsillo, 2003), 9–10.

46. On Italy and orientalism, see Franco Cassano, *Il pensiero meridiano* (Bari: Laterza, 1996); and Roberto Dainotto, "Orientalism, Mediterranean Style: The Limits of History at the Margins of Europe," in *Europe (In Theory)* (Durham, N.C.: Duke University Press, 2007), 172–217.

47. Charles de Secondat, Baron de Montesquieu, *The Spirit of the Laws*, ed. and trans. Anne M. Cohler, Basia Carolyn Miller, and Harold Samuel Stone (Cambridge: Cambridge University Press, 1989), 234.

48. Roberto M. Dainotto, "Does Europe Have a South? An Essay on Borders," *The Global South* 5, no. 1 (2011): 37. See also his *Europe (In Theory)*.

49. Ignacio Tofiño-Quesada, "Spanish Orientalism: Uses of the Past in Spain's Colonization in Africa," *Comparative Studies of South Asia, Africa and the Middle East* 23, no. 1–2 (2003): 143.

50. Joaquín Costa, "Los intereses de España en Marruecos," in *África a través del pensamiento español: De Isabel la Católica a Franco*, by Ángel Flores Morales (Madrid: CSIC, Instituto de Estudios Africanos, 1949), 160.

51. See Azucena Pedraz Marcos, *Quimeras de África: La Sociedad Española de Africanistas y Colonistas: El colonialismo español de finales del siglo XIX* (Madrid: Polifemo, 2000).

52. See Bernabé López García, *Orientalismo e ideología colonial en el arabismo español (1840–1917)* (Granada: Universidad de Granada, 2011).

53. Julián Ribera, *Music in Ancient Arabia and Spain* (New York: Da Capo, 1970), 9.

54. Francisco Javier Simonet, *El Siglo de Oro en la literatura arábigo-española: Discurso leído ante el claustro de la Universidad Central* (Granada: Imprenta de D. José María Zamora, 1867), 96.

55. Julián Ribera, *Disertaciones y opúsculos*, 2 vols. (Madrid: Imprenta de Estanislao Maestre, 1928), 1:26.

56. Miguel Asín Palacios, "¿Por qué lucharon a nuestro lado los musulmanes marroquíes?" in *Obras escogidas*, 2 vols. (Madrid: Editorial Maestre, 1948), 2:146–49.

57. Américo Castro, *España en su historia: Cristianos, moros y judíos* (Barcelona: Crítica, 1983), 14.

58. Américo Castro, *An Idea of History: Selected Essays of Américo Castro* (Columbus: Ohio State University Press, 1977), 112.

59. José Antonio González Alcantud, "Edward Said y el Orientalismo: Revisión crítica y perspectivas múltiples," in *Actas de la Jornada sobre "Orientalismo," ayer y hoy*, ed. Víctor Morales Lezcano (Madrid: Universidad Nacional de Educación a Distancia, 2006), 44. See also José Antonio González Alcantud, ed., *El orientalismo desde el sur* (Barcelona: Anthropos, 2006).

60. Barbara Fuchs, *Exotic Nation: Maurophilia and the Construction of Early Modern Spain* (Philadelphia: University of Pennsylvania Press, 2009), 7.

61. Lou Charnon-Deutsch, "Travels of the Imaginary Spanish Gypsy," in *Constructing Identity in Contemporary Spain: Theoretical Debates and Cultural Practice*, ed. Jo Labanyi (Oxford: Oxford University Press, 2002), 22–23. See also her *The Spanish Gypsy: The History of a European Obsession* (University Park: Pennsylvania State University Press, 2008).

62. Daniela Flesler, *The Return of the Moor: Spanish Responses to Contemporary Moroccan Immigration* (West Lafayette, Ind.: Purdue University Press, 2008); Tabea Alexa Linhard, *Jewish Spain: A Mediterranean Memory* (Stanford, Calif.: Stanford University Press, 2014).

63. Miguel de Unamuno, *Epistolario americano (1890–1936)*, ed. Laureano Robles (Salamanca: Universidad de Salamanca, 1996), 102.

64. Francisco Giner de los Ríos, "Paisaje," *La Lectura* 15, no. 1 (1915): 361–70.

65. Ernesto Giménez Caballero, *Memorias de un dictador* (Barcelona: Planeta, 1979), 58.

66. Antonio Espina, "Una tenida por el rito andaluz," *La Gaceta Literaria* 1, no. 7 (1927): 5.

67. "El Premio Fastenrath y la hora andaluza," *La Gaceta Literaria* 1, no. 8 (1927): 1.

68. Enric Prat de la Riba and Pere Muntanyola, *Compendi de la Doctrina Catalanista* (Sabadell: Imprenta de lo Catalanista, 1894), 88.

69. Sabino Arana, "Nuestros moros," in *La patria de los vascos*, ed. Antonio Elorza (San Sebastian: R. B. Ediciones, 1995), 155.

70. Melchor Fernández Almagro, "Los poetas de Málaga," *La Gaceta Literaria* 4, no. 86 (1930): 5.

71. Lluís Montanyà, "La jove poesía andaluza (*Perfíl del aire* de Luis Cernuda, *Caracteres* de José Bergamín)," *L'Amic de les Arts* 22 (1928): 165–66.

72. Federico García Lorca, "Estampa de Federico García Lorca," in *Obras completes,* 6 vols. (Barcelona: RBA-Instituto Cervantes, 2006), 3:355.

73. Aránzazu Ascunce Arenas, *Barcelona and Madrid: Social Networks of the Avant-Garde* (Lewisburg, Pa.: Bucknell University Press, 2012), 31.

74. José Martínez Ruíz "Azorín," "La Andalucía trágica," in *Los pueblos: Ensayos de vida provinciana* (Seville: Renacimiento, 1916), 167–205.

75. Constancio Bernaldo de Quirós, *Bandolerismo y delincuencia subversiva en la Baja Andalucía* (Seville: Renacimiento, 1992).

76. Juan Díaz del Moral, *Historia de las agitaciones campesinas andaluzas* (Madrid: Alianza, 1973), 25.

77. Alberto Egea Fernández-Montesinos, *García Lorca, Blas Infante y Antonio Gala: Un nacionalismo alternativo en la literatura andaluza* (Seville: Fundación Blas Infante, 2001).

78. Blas Infante, *Ideal Andaluz* (Seville: Imprenta de Joaquín L. Arévalo, 1915), 81.

79. Blas Infante, *La verdad sobre el complot de Tablada y el Estado Libre de Andalucía* (Granada: Aljibe, 1979), 63.

80. Martin-Márquez, *Disorientations*, 9.

81. Jane Schneider, ed., *Italy's "Southern Question": Orientalism in One Country* (Oxford: Berg, 1998); Nelson Moe, *The View from Vesuvius: Italian Culture and the Southern Question* (Berkeley: University of California Press, 2002).

82. García Lorca, "Estampa de Federico García Lorca."

83. Andrew E. G. Jonas, "Pro Scale: Further Reflections on the 'Scale Debate' in Human Geography," *Transactions of the Institute of British Geographers* 31, no. 3 (2006): 402.

84. Juan Goytisolo, "From *Count Julian* to *Makbara*: A Possible Orientalist Reading," in *Saracen Chronicles: A Selection of Literary Essays*, trans. Helen Lane (London: Quartet Books, 1992), 223.

Chapter 1

1. Lord Salisbury, "The Primrose League: Speech by Lord Salisbury," *The Times*, May 5, 1898, 7.

2. Antonio Cánovas del Castillo, *Apuntes para la historia de Marruecos* (Madrid: Librería General de Victoriano Suárez, 1914), 273.

3. Luis Bello, "Castillos de España: Conversación con un arabista," *El Sol*, February 13, 1924, 1.

4. Tofiño-Quesada, "Spanish Orientalism," 143.

5. Miguel Ángel Álvarez Ramos and Claudia Heide, "Gayangos and the World of Politics," in *Pascual de Gayangos: A Nineteenth-Century Spanish Arabist*, ed. Cristina Álvarez Millán and Claudia Heide (Edinburgh: Edinburgh University Press, 2008), 30–31.

6. Víctor Morales Lezcano, *España y el Norte de África: El Protectorado de Marruecos (1912–56)* (Madrid: UNED, 1986).

7. Álvarez Ramos and Heide, "Gayangos," 32–33.

8. See Aurora Rivière Gómez, *Orientalismo y nacionalismo español: Estudios árabes y hebreos en la Universidad de Madrid (1843–1868)* (Madrid: Editorial Dykinson, 2000); and López García, *Orientalismo*.

9. Francisco Javier Simonet, "La empresa de África," *La América* 3, no. 17 (November 8, 1859): 2.

10. Ibid., 3.

11. Rodolfo Gil Grimau, "Corrientes ideológicas internas en el africanismo español," in *Actas del Congreso Internacional el Estrecho de Gibraltar* (Madrid: UNED-Ayuntamiento de Ceuta, 1988), 3:277. The "colonial" current also appears in the 1920s as *hispanismo*. On *hispanismo*, see Frederick B. Pike, *Hispanismo, 1898–1936: Spanish Conservatives and Liberals and Their Relations with Spanish America* (London: University of Notre Dame Press, 1971). Pike defines *hispanismo* as an "unassailable faith in the existence of a transatlantic Hispanic family, community or *raza*" that sought to restore Spain's prestige in its American ex-colonies (1). On *hispanismo* and *africanismo*, see Rodolfo Gil Benumeya, "Ante el aumento y desarrollo de las intervenciones civiles: Africanismo e iberoamericanismo," *África* 52 (October 1932): 186–88.

12. Simonet, "La empresa," 2.

13. See María Jesús Viguera Molins, "Al-Andalus y su estudio," in *De civilización arabo-islámica*, ed. Francisco Vidal Castro (Jaen: Universidad de Jaén, 1995), 17–36; and Viguera Molins, "Al-Andalus y España: Sobre el esencialismo de los Beni Codera," in *Al-Andalus/España: Historiografías en contraste, Siglos XVII–XXI*, ed. Manuela Marín (Madrid: Casa de Velázquez, 2009), 67–81.

14. Ribera, *Music in Ancient Arabia and Spain*, 3.

15. José Manuel Sánchez Ron, ed., *Ciencia y sociedad en España: De la Ilustración a la Guerra Civil* (Madrid: El arquero/CSIC, 1988).

16. Irene González González, *Spanish Education in Morocco 1912–1956: Cultural Interactions in a Colonial Context* (Eastbourne, Eng.: Sussex Academic, 2015), 40.

17. Ribera, *Disertaciones*, 2:436. See González González, *Spanish Education*, 36–40.

18. Miguel Asín Palacios and Emilio García Gómez, "Nota preliminar," *Al-Andalus* 1 (1933): 1.

19. See José Hurtado Sánchez, Juan Ortiz Villalba, and Salvador Cruz Artacho, *Bética y el Regionalismo Andaluz: A propósito del centenario* (Seville: Centro de Estudios Andaluces, 2013).

20. Blas Infante, "El campesino andaluz," *Bética* 2, no. 5 (January 20, 1914): 3–5.

21. "Nuestro probable florecimiento," *Andalucía* 2, no. 9 (February 1917): 10.

22. Juan Antonio Lacomba, *Teoría y praxis del Andalucismo* (Malaga: Ágora, 1988), 21.

23. Blas Infante, "Crónica abreviada del movimiento regionalista," *Bética* 2, nos. 23–24 (December 31, 1914): 60.

24. Juan Antonio Lacomba, ed., *Cuatro textos políticos andaluces (1883–1933)* (Granada: Universidad de Granada, 1979), 43.

25. Manuel González de Molina Navarro and Eduardo Sevilla-Guzmán, "Movimiento jornalero y andalucismo histórico," in *Los nacionalismos en la España de la II República*, ed. Justo G. Beramendi and Ramón Máiz (Madrid: Siglo Veintiuno, 1991), 317.

26. Alejandro Guichot, "Del fondo de campos andaluces [1]," *Andalucía* 1, no. 4 (September 1916): 1–4; and "Del fondo de campos andaluces [2]," *Andalucía* 1, no. 5 (October 1916): 1–4.

27. Isidro de las Cagigas, "Notas sobre el regionalismo andaluz," *Andalucía* 2, no. 8 (January 1917): 6–8. On Andalusian anarchism, see Temma Kaplan, *Anarchists of Andalusia, 1868–1903* (Princeton, N.J.: Princeton University Press, 1977); and Jerome R. Mintz, *The Anarchists of Casas Viejas* (Bloomington: Indiana University Press, 1982).

28. Isidro de las Cagigas, "Apuntaciones para un estudio del regionalismo andaluz [1]," *Bética* 2, no. 16 (September 20, 1914): 4.

29. Isidro de las Cagigas, "Andalucismo: Apuntaciones sobre los elementos y características del tipo andaluz (pruebas psicológicas)," *Bética* 3, no. 40 (August 30, 1915): 37.

30. Alejandro Guichot, "Vida andaluza: Acerca del Ideal andaluz," *Bética* 1, no. 1 (November 20, 1913): 27. See Juan Antonio Lacomba, "Alejandro Guichot y el ideal andaluz," *Revista de Estudios Regionales* 5 (1980): 379–90.

31. Rafael Castejón, "Del Alma de Andalucía (Conclusión)," *Bética* 3, no. 38 (July 30, 1915): 6. See Juan Antonio Lacomba, "Rafael Castejón, Córdoba y Andalucía," *Revista de Estudios Regionales* 17 (1987): 231–63.

32. James Monroe, *Islam and the Arabs in Spanish Scholarship (Sixteenth Century to the Present)* (Leiden: Brill, 1970), 100.

33. Francisco Javier Simonet, *El Siglo de Oro en la literatura arábigo-española: Discurso leído ante el claustro de la Universidad Central* (Granada: Imprenta de D. José María Zamora, 1867), 96.

34. Ribera, *Disertaciones*, 1:26.

35. Infante, *Ideal*, 58–59.

36. Ibid., 83.

37. Ibid., 79.

38. Ibid., 46.

39. Ibid., 78.

40. Ibid.

41. Ellen Churchill Semple and Friedrich Ratzel, *Influences of Geographic Environment on the Basis of Ratzel's System of Antropo-Geography* (New York: Henry Holt, 1911), 209–28.

42. Said, *Orientalism*, 42–43.

43. Paul Topinard, *Anthropology* (London: Chapman and Hall, 1894).

44. Mariano Torres Ortiz, *Tartessos* (Madrid: Real Academia de la Historia, 2002), 236–37.

45. Plato, *Timaeus*, trans. Donald J. Zeyl (Indianapolis, Ind.: Hackett, 2000), 10.

46. Juan María Acosta Ferrero, *Elena Whishaw en Niebla, 75 años después* (Madrid: Cultiva Libros, 2012).

47. Infante, *Ideal*, 68.

48. Ibid., 63–64.

49. Manuel Gómez-Moreno, "Arquitectura Tartesia: La necrópoli de Antequera," *Boletín de la Real Academia de la Historia* 47 (1905): 99.

50. Manuel Gómez-Moreno, *Misceláneas: Historia, arte, arqueología* (Madrid: CSIC, 1949), 55.

51. Infante, *Ideal*, 63.

52. Ibid., 69.

53. G. W. F. Hegel, *Lectures on the Philosophy of World History: Introduction: Reason in History*, trans. H. B. Nisbet (Cambridge: Cambridge University Press, 1975), 197.

54. Blas Infante, *Andalucía: Teoría y fundamento político*, ed. Manuel Pimentel (Cordoba: Almuzara, 2008), 62.

55. Infante, *Ideal*, 77.

56. Ibid., 81.

57. Ibid., 80–82.

58. Tomás Mendigutía, "La historia de Andalucía," *Andalucía* 2, no. 16 (September 30, 2017): 4.

59. Carlos Colón Perales, *Sevilla: Ciudad de deseo (de Pierre Louÿs a Joseph Von Sternberg)* (Seville: El Ojo Andaluz, 1993), 36.

60. See Julio Caro Baroja, *Los moriscos del reino de Granada: Ensayo de historia social* (Madrid: Istmo, 1976); and Antonio Domínguez Ortiz and Bernard

Vincent, *Historia de los moriscos: Vida y tragedia de una minoría* (Madrid: Alianza, 1980).

61. Infante, *Ideal*, 134–35.

62. Ibid., 117.

63. Francesc Cambó, "Discurso pronunciado por Francisco Cambó en los Juegos Florales del Ateneo de Sevilla el 1 de mayo de 1913," in *El Ateneo de Sevilla y José María Izquierdo en el Andalucismo histórico,* by Enrique Barrero González (Sevilla: Algaida, 2009), 105–18.

64. "Don Francisco Cambó," *Bética* 2, no. 7 (February 20, 1914): 1.

65. Infante, *Verdad*, 63.

66. Vicente Galiana, "La lección de Cataluña: Apuntes," *Andalucía* 1, no. 5 (October 1916): 4.

67. Juan Sin Tierra, "El regionalismo en España," *Andalucía* 2, no. 9 (February 1917): 3.

68. Infante, *Verdad*, 68–69.

69. Ibid., 63–64.

70. Blas Infante, *Orígenes de lo flamenco y secreto del cante jondo*, ed. Manuel Barrios (Seville: Junta de Andalucía, 1980), 92.

71. Timothy Mitchell, *Flamenco Deep Song* (New Haven, Conn.: Yale University Press, 1994), 3.

72. For an annotated catalog of the holdings of Infante's library, see Miguel Cruz Giráldez, "La biblioteca," in *La casa de Blas Infante en Coria del Río* (Seville: Centro de Estudios Andaluces, 2004), 77–94.

73. See Mitchell, *Flamenco Deep Song*; and Gerhard Steingress, *Sobre flamenco y flamencología: Escritos escogidos 1988–1998* (Seville: Signatura, 1998); they discuss Infante's flamenco theories in detail but ignore Ribera's influence. Manuel Barrios, the editor of Infante's *Orígenes*, includes no references to Ribera in *Gitanos, moriscos y cante flamenco* (Seville: JRC, 1989), an elaboration of Infante's ideas.

74. Asín, "Introducción," in Ribera, *Disertaciones*, 1:c.

75. Ibid., 1:cx.

76. Ribera, *Disertaciones* 1:9.

77. Ribera, *Music in Ancient Arabia and Spain*, 227. See María Rosa Menocal, *The Arabic Role in Medieval Literary History: A Forgotten Heritage* (Philadelphia: University of Pennsylvania Press, 1987).

78. Ribera, *Music*, 7.

79. Infante, *Orígenes*, 12.

80. Ribera, *Music*, 142.

81. Ibid., 171.

82. Infante, *Orígenes*, 55.

83. Ibid., 34.

84. Ibid., 165.

85. See Miguel Ropero Nuñez, "Aproximación a la historia del flamenco: El problema histórico, cultural y etimológico," *Litoral* 238 (2004): 8–31.

86. Infante, *Orígenes*, 162.

87. Blas Infante, "Cartas Andalucistas," in *Antología de textos*, ed. Manuel Ruiz Lagos (Seville: Fundación Blas Infante, 1983), 277.

88. Mitchell, *Flamenco Deep Song*, 11.

89. Infante, *Orígenes*, 91.
90. Ibid., 88.
91. Cagigas, "Andalucismo," 89.
92. Ibid., 90.
93. Costa, "Intereses," 160.
94. Martin-Márquez, *Disorientations*, 59.
95. Isidro de las Cagigas, "Sobre Andalucía: Sus límites y su constitución," *Andalucía* 1, no. 4 (September 1916): 6.
96. Ibid., 5.
97. Federico Olóriz y Aguilera, *Distrubución geográfica del índice cefálico en España deducida del examen de 8.368 varones adultos* (Madrid: Imprenta del Memorial de Ingenieros, 1894), 229–30. On anthropology in Restoration Spain, see Joshua Goode, *Impurity of Blood: Defining Race in Spain, 1870–1930* (Baton Rouge: Louisiana State University Press, 2009).
98. Cagigas, "Sobre Andalucía," 6.
99. José Zurita y Calafat, "El problema de las alianzas," *Bética* 3, no. 29–30 (April 1915): 13.
100. Anne Christys, *Christians in Al-Andalus, 711–1000* (London: Routledge, 2013), 81. These views attained final form in *Los Mozárabes* (1947–48).
101. This conservative shift helped Cagigas to gain official recognition not only in Primo de Rivera's dictatorship but also in Franco Spain. His regionalist and republican past separated him from public office after the Civil War, although he was finally reinstated in 1950 and sent on a diplomatic mission to Libya, partly in recognition of years of research contributions to such Francoist venues as the Institute of African Studies and *África: Revista de Tropas Coloniales*, a journal that Franco himself edited from 1914 to 1929. For a detailed account of Cagigas's life and a complete annotated list of his publications, see Manuel Enrique Gutiérrez Camacho, *Vida y obra de Isidro de las Cagigas* (Seville: Fundación Blas Infante, 2006).
102. Humberto Cortacero Henares, "¿Andalucismo árabe, o arabismo español?" *África* 39 (March 1928): 67–68.
103. Ibid., 81–82.
104. See Gil Grimau, *Aproximación a una bibliografía española sobre el norte de África* (Madrid: Ministerio de Asuntos Exteriores, 1988), 365–72, for an extensive list of Gil Benumeya's main publications.
105. María Dolores López Enamorado, "La Mirada del otro: La vision del africanismo español (el Gil Benumeya de los años veinte)," in *Relaciones interétnicas y multiculturalidad en el Mediterráneo Occidental*, ed. Elías Zamora Acosta and Pedro Maya Álvarez (Melilla: V Centenario de Melilla, 1988), 261–78.
106. Benomar [Rodolfo Gil Torres], "El Andalucismo I," *África* 16 (April 1926): 83.
107. Infante, *Verdad*, 82.
108. Benomar [Rodolfo Gil Torres], "El Andalucismo II," *África* 17 (May 1926): 101.
109. Benomar [Rodolfo Gil Torres], "Andalucismo africano: La universidad árabe española," *África* 38 (February 1928): 34.
110. Enrique Iniesta Collaut-Valera, *Al-Andalus en Blas Infante* (Madrid: Editorial Darek-Nyumba, 1998), 12–13.

111. Rodolfo Gil Torres, *Marruecos andaluz* (Madrid: Vicesecretaria de Educación Popular, 1943), 201.

112. Ibid., 113.

113. See Eric Calderwood, "'In Andalucía, There Are No Foreigners': *Andalucismo* from Transperipheral Critique to Colonial Apology," *Journal of Spanish Cultural Studies* 15, no. 4 (2015): 399–417. Calderwood interprets Gil Benumeya's borrowings from Infante as a case of transmission from regionalism to Francoist colonial doctrine, arguing that "Infante's writings carried inscribed upon them the seeds of colonial domination" (409). This metaphor suggests that *andalucismo* is a single organism that develops inexorably from Infante's writings to Gil Benumeya's conservative version. I have chosen to use Derrida's "grafting" metaphor to highlight the alien elements Gil Benumeya inserted in the preexisting "host" to radically reframe and recodify it. Calderwood pays careful attention to Gil Benumeya's adaptation of Infante's ideas to Francoist foreign policy, but ignores his sweeping ideological editing. On "grafting," see Jacques Derrida, *Dissemination*, trans. Barbara Johnson (Chicago: University of Chicago Press, 1981), 39–41.

114. Benomar [Rodolfo Gil Torres], "El andalucismo I," 83.

115. Rodolfo Gil Torres, "Hacia una España mayor: Otra vez el andalucismo," *África* 38 (April 1929): 90.

116. Infante, *Verdad*, 82–83.

117. Rodolfo Gil Benumeya, "El Espíritu de la Mezquita: La baraka. I," *África* 42 (June 1928): 154.

118. Rodolfo Gil Benumeya, *Ni Oriente ni Occidente: El universo visto desde el Albayzín*, ed. José Antonio González Alcantud (Granada: Universidad de Granada, 1996), 8.

119. Gil Benumeya, "El Espíritu," 154. On the Left vs. Islam, see Amor Benomar [Rodolfo Gil Torres], "La abolición del Fez y el Bolcheviquismo," *África* 14 (February 1926): 38–40.

120. Enrique Iniesta Collaut-Valera, *Blas Infante: Toda su verdad, Volumen II 1919–1933* (Granada: Editorial Atrio), 232. On Andalusi-Moroccan musical ties, see Jonathan Holt Shannon, *Performing al-Andalus: Music and Nostalgia across the Mediterranean* (Bloomington: Indiana University Press, 2015), 84–118.

121. Gil Benumeya, "El Espíritu," 155.

122. Rodolfo Gil Benumeya, *Mediodía: Introducción a la historia andaluza* (Madrid: Compañía Ibero-Americana de Publicaciones, 1929), 9.

123. See Stanley G. Payne, *Fascism in Spain, 1923–1977* (Madison: University of Wisconsin Press, 1999). Payne writes that though "Franco never fully adopted the entire core fascist revolutionary ideology, there is no question that he identified his regime politically with the fascist powers and considered himself not merely an associate but virtually an ally of the Axis" (326). Payne describes the ideological frame of early Francoism as *fascismo frailuno*, "a hybrid fascism merged with rightism and religion" (473).

124. Benomar [Gil Torres], "Andalucismo africano," 34.

125. Tomás García Figueras, "Recuerdos de la campaña: Una opinión a favor del andalucismo árabe," *África* 4, no. 47 (November 1928): 283.

126. Marcelino Menéndez Pelayo, *Historia de los heterodoxos españoles* (Madrid: F. Maroto e Hijos, 1881), 3:834.

127. Ángel González Palencia, "Correspondencia entre Menéndez y Pelayo y Asín," *Al-Andalus* 12 (1947): 404.

128. Marcelino Menéndez Pelayo, "Prólogo," in *Algazel: Dogmática, moral, ascética,* by Miguel Asín Palacios (Zaragoza: Comas Hermanos, 1901), xv–xvi.

129. See *Huellas del Islam* (Madrid: Espasa-Calpe, 1941) for Asín's proposal of an evolutionary, "providential law" whereby "ideas, the most delicate product of human culture," could be transplanted from one time period or ethnic group to another (7).

130. Monroe, *Islam,* 174.

131. Rodolfo Gil Benumeya, "El Espíritu de la Mezquita: La Baraka, II," *África* 44 (August 1928): 208.

132. Gil Benumeya, "Ante el aumento," 186.

133. Asín Palacios, "¿Por qué lucharon?" 2:146–49.

134. Sebastian Balfour, *Deadly Embrace: Morocco and the Road to the Spanish Civil War* (Oxford: Oxford University Press, 2002), 280.

135. On the political and ideological uses of religion in the Spanish Protectorate, see Josep Lluís Mateo Dieste, *La "hermandad" hispano-marroquí: Política y religion bajo el protectorado español en Marruecos, 1912–1956* (Barcelona: Bellaterra, 2003), especially 221–74.

136. Pedro Laín Entralgo, *Descargo de conciencia (1930–1960)* (Barcelona: Barral, 1976), 285.

137. José María López Sánchez, *Heterodoxos españoles: El Centro de Estudios Históricos, 1910–1936* (Madrid: Marcial Pons-CSIC, 2006), 72–76.

138. Ángel González Palencia, "El Centro de Estudios Históricos," in *Una poderosa fuerza secreta: La Institución Libre de Enseñanza* (San Sebastián: Editorial Española, 1940), 195.

139. Quoted in Irene González González, "La 'hermandad hispano-árabe' en la política cultural del franquismo (1936–1956)," *Anales de Historia Contemporánea* 27 (2007): 185.

Chapter 2

1. José Ortega y Gasset, *Obras completas,* 10 vols. (Madrid: Taurus/Fundación Ortega y Gasset, 2004–2010), 4:159.

2. Ibid., 6:175.

3. Ibid., 6:179.

4. Ibid., 6:182.

5. Mary Vincent, *Spain 1833–2002: People and State* (Oxford: Oxford University Press, 2007), 47–48.

6. Ibid., 48.

7. Lou Charnon-Deutsch, *Fictions of the Feminine in the Nineteenth-Century Spanish Press* (University Park: Pennsylvania State University Press, 2000), 210.

8. Alfonso del Mar, "Paris y la Exposición: Impresiones a vuela pluma," *Hispania* 29 (1900): 138.

9. J. Francos Rodríguez, "La sombra de Raisuli," *África española* 30 (1915): 750.

10. Pío Baroja, "Tánger," in *Tánger, puerta de África: Antología de textos literarios hispánicos, 1860–1960,* ed. Abdellah Djbilou (Madrid: Cantarabia, 1989), 39–41. For demographic statistics about Spaniards in Tangier from the nineteenth

to the twenty-first century, see Bernabé López García, "Los españoles de Tánger," *Awraq* 5–6 (2012): 1–45.

11. Pío Baroja, *Divagaciones sobre la cultura* (Madrid: Caro Raggio, 1920), 122–23.

12. Eugenio Noel, *Diario íntimo: La novela de la vida de un hombre*, 2 vols. (Madrid: Taurus, 1962, 1968), 1:298. So strained were local tempers that the governor of Seville told Noel he could do nothing to "guarantee" his personal safety while in the city.

13. Noel, *Diario*, 2:76.

14. Eugenio Noel, *Señoritos, chulos, fenómenos, gitanos y flamencos* (Madrid: Renacimiento, 1916), 36.

15. Ibid., 20–21.

16. Ibid., 37.

17. See Vicente Cacho Viu, ed., *Els modernistes i el nacionalisme cultural (1881–1906)* (Barcelona: Edicions de la Magrana/Diputació de Barcelona, 1984).

18. Santiago Rusiñol, "Una 'juerga' trista," *Luz* 1, no. 1 (1897): 2.

19. Joan Maragall, "La independència de Catalunya," in *Els modernistes i el nacionalisme cultural (1881–1906)*, ed. Vicente Cacho Viu (Barcelona: Ediciones de la Magrana/Diputació de Barcelona, 1984), 171.

20. Pompeyo Gener, *Heregías: Estudios de crítica inductiva sobre asuntos españoles* (Barcelona: Luis Tasso Serra, 1887), 14.

21. Ibid., 15.

22. Pompeyo Gener, "Presentació," *Joventut: Periódich Catalanista* 1 (1900): 1.

23. On liberal historiography in the mid- to late nineteenth century, see Carolyn Boyd, *Historia Patria: Politics, History, and National Identity in Spain, 1875–1975* (Princeton, N.J.: Princeton University Press, 1997); and Inman Fox, *La invención de España* (Madrid: Cátedra, 1998), 35–54.

24. Rafael Altamira, *Historia de España y de la civilización española*, 4 vols. (Barcelona: Juan Gili, 1900–1911), 1:19. On Altamira's historiography, see Boyd, *Historia Patria*, 122–64; Armando Alberola Romá, ed., *Estudios sobre Rafael Altamira* (Alicante: Instituto de Estudios Juan Gil-Albert, 1987); and Pilar Altamira, *Diálogos con Rafael Altamira* (Murcia and Oviedo: Universidad de Murcia and Universidad de Oviedo, 2009).

25. Altamira, *Historia*, 2:238–39.

26. Rafael Altamira, *Mi viaje a América* (Madrid: Librería General de Victoriano Suárez, 1911), 42.

27. Quoted in José Manuel Lucía Megías, ed., *También los niños leen el Quijote* (Alcalá de Henares: Centro de Estudios Cervantinos, 2007), 40.

28. Azorín [José Martínez Ruiz], *La ruta de Don Quijote* (Madrid: Caro Raggio, 1919), 53.

29. Christopher Britt Arredondo, *Quixotism: The Imaginative Denial of Spain's Loss of Empire* (Albany: SUNY Press, 2005), 20.

30. Víctor Said Armesto, *La leyenda de Don Juan: Orígenes poéticos de la El burlador de Sevilla y El convidado de piedra* (Madrid: Sucesores de Hernando, 1908), 270–71.

31. Miguel de Unamuno, *Obras completas*, 9 vols, ed. Manuel García Blanco (Madrid: Escelicer, 1966–71), 3:327. On Unamuno and Don Juan, see María Eugenia Perojo-Arronte, "Byron and Unamuno's *Don Juan*," in *Aspects of*

Byron's Don Juan, ed. Peter Cochran (Newcastle upon Tyne, Eng.: Cambridge Scholars, 2013), 317–25.

32. Unamuno, *Obras*, 3:331.

33. See Payne, *Fascism*, 27. "For several years," Payne writes, "the Dictador himself would be a generally popular figure with many admirers. His bluff, informal manner and sly sense of humor were appreciated as he appeared frequently in public and made an effort to communicate directly with the citizenry."

34. Unamuno, *Obras*, 8:1139–40. On Unamuno's characterization of Primo de Rivera as Don Juan, see Bénédicte Vauthier, "Ironía, censura y retórica en el diario éxtimo del exilio," in *Miguel de Unamuno: Estudios sobre su obra*, ed. Ana Chaguaceda Toledano, 2 vols. (Salamanca: Universidad de Salamanca, 2005), 2:119–20.

35. On the Don Juan myth in the modern Spanish novel, see Ignacio Javier López, *Caballero de novela: Ensayo sobre el donjuanismo en la novela española moderna (1830–1930)* (Barcelona: Puvill, 1986).

36. Ramón Pérez de Ayala, *Las máscaras*, 2 vols. (Madrid: Saturnino Calleja, 1919), 2:266–68.

37. Ibid., 2:267.

38. Ibid., 2:269.

39. Ortega y Gasset, *Obras*, 6:199.

40. Ibid., 6:189.

41. Ibid., 6:190–91.

42. Ibid., 6:189.

43. Ibid., 3:445.

44. Ibid., 3:447.

45. Juan López-Morillas, *The Krausist Movement and Ideological Change in Spain, 1854–1874*, trans. Frances M. López-Morillas (Cambridge: Cambridge University Press, 1981).

46. Ibid., 365.

47. Francisco Giner de los Ríos, "Paisaje," *La Lectura* 15, no. 1 (1915): 367.

48. Carmen Pena López, "Presentación," in *Centro y periferia en la modernización de la pintura española (1880–1918)* (Madrid: Ministerio de Cultura, 1993), 21. See also Carmen Pena López, *El paisaje español del siglo XIX: Del naturalismo al impresionismo* (Madrid: Universidad Complutense, 1981); and Lily Litvak, *El tiempo de los trenes: El paisaje español y la literatura del realismo (1849–1918)* (Barcelona: Serbal, 1991).

49. Aureliano Beruete y Moret, *La pintura española en el siglo XIX: Elementos nacionales y extranjeros que han influido en ella* (Madrid: Blass, 1926), 131–32.

50. See Francisco Calvo Serraller, *La imagen romántica en España: Arte y arquitectura del siglo XIX* (Madrid: Alianza, 1995); and Antonio Reina Palazón, *La pintura costumbrista en Sevilla, 1830–1870* (Seville: Universidad de Sevilla, 1979).

51. José Álvarez Junco, *Spanish Identity in the Age of Nations* (Manchester, Eng.: Manchester University Press, 2011), 178.

52. Luis Méndez Rodríguez, *La imagen de Andalucía en el arte del siglo XIX* (Seville: Centro de Estudios Andaluces, 2008), 70–71.

53. See Edward J. Sullivan, "Mariano Fortuny y Marsal and Orientalism in Nineteenth-Century Spain," *Arts Magazine* 55, no. 8 (1981): 96–101.

54. Émile Verhaeren and Darío de Regoyos, *España Negra* (Zaragoza: Lecturas hispánicas, 2015), 31.

55. Enrique Lafuente Ferrari, "La pintura española y la Generación del 98," *Arbor* 36 (1948): 449–58. See also Carlos Cid Priego, ed., *Las artes españolas en la crisis del 98* (Oviedo: Universidad de Oviedo, 1996); and Gayana Jurkevich, *In Pursuit of the Natural Sign: Azorín and the Poetics of Ekphrasis* (Lewisburg, Pa.: Bucknell University Press, 1999).

56. Antonio Machado, *Poesías completas*, ed. Manuel Alvar (Madrid: Alianza, 2004), 172. See Xon de Ros, *The Poetry of Antonio Machado: Changing the Landscape* (Oxford: Oxford University Press, 2015).

57. Ortega y Gasset, *Obras*, 2:149.

58. Machado, *Poesías*, 214–15.

59. Richard Burgin, ed., *Jorge Luis Borges: Conversations* (Jackson: University of Mississippi Press, 1998), 69.

60. Pedro Salinas, "Antonio Machado," in *Obras completas*, ed. Andrés Soria Olmedo and Enric Bou (Madrid: Cátedra, 2007), 155–56.

61. See Inman Fox, especially "El estado y la cultura nacional: El Centro de Estudios Históricos y la obra de Menéndez Pidal," in Fox, *Invención*, 97–110.

62. Ramón Menéndez Pidal, *La España del Cid*, 2 vols. (Madrid: Editorial Plutarco, 1929), 1:iii.

63. Ibid., 2:699.

64. Tomás Navarro Tomás, *El acento castellano* (Madrid: Academia Española, 1935), 46.

65. Ibid., 30–31.

66. Said, *Orientalism*, 206.

67. Ortega y Gasset, *Obras*, 6:177–78.

68. Ibid., 6:179.

69. On the teaching of history during Primo de Rivera's dictatorship, see Boyd, *Historia*, 165–93.

70. Alejandro Quiroga, *Making Spaniards: Primo de Rivera and the Nationalization of the Masses, 1923–30* (New York: Palgrave Macmillan, 2007), 172.

71. José María Salaverría, *Sevilla y el andalucismo* (Barcelona: Gustavo Gili, 1929), 104.

72. Alfonso Braojos Garrido, *Alfonso XIII y la Exposición Iberoamericana de Sevilla* (Seville: Universidad de Sevilla, 1992).

73. Rockwell Gray, *The Imperative of Modernity: An Intellectual Biography of José Ortega y Gasset* (Berkeley: University of California Press, 1989), 186. See also Genoveva García Queipo de Llano, *Los intelectuales y la dictadura de Primo de Rivera* (Madrid: Alianza, 1988).

74. Jordi Gracia, *José Ortega y Gasset* (Madrid: Taurus, 2014), 401.

75. Ortega y Gasset, *Obras*, 6:177.

76. Ibid., 4:160.

77. In 1923 the first issue of Ortega y Gasset's journal, *Revista de Occidente*, included Schulten's essay "Tartessos, la más antigua ciudad de Occidente." A year later, Ortega edited the Spanish translation of Schulten's *Tartessos: Ein Beitrag zur ältesten Geschichte des Westens*. See Adolf Schulten, *Tartessos: Contribución a la historia más antigua de Occidente*, trans. Manuel García Morente (Sevilla:

Renacimiento, 2006). See also Leo Frobenius, "La cultura de la Atlántida," *Revista de Occidente* 1, no. 3 (1923): 298–318.

78. Ortega y Gasset, *Obras*, 3:765.

79. Ibid., 3:749.

80. Ibid., 3:506.

81. G. W. F. Hegel, *The Philosophy of History*, trans. J. Sibree (New York: Dover, 1956), 140.

82. Antonio-Enrique Pérez Luño, "Hegel y Ortega: Meditación sobre los presupuestos historiográficos de la filosofía del derecho," in *Meditaciones sobre Ortega y Gasset*, ed. José Luis Abellán et al. (Madrid: Tebar, 2005), 523–67.

83. Ortega y Gasset, *Obras*, 6:183.

84. Ibid., 3:506.

85. Post-Thebussem [Dionisio Pérez Gutiérrez], "La cocina andaluza, prez de España," *La Voz* [Madrid], May 6, 1927, 3.

86. Ortega y Gasset, *Obras*, 6:182.

87. Rogelio Buendía Abreu, "Vindicación de Andalucía," in *Actas del VI Congreso sobre el Andalucismo Histórico* (Seville: Fundación Blas Infante, 1993), 89.

88. Ibid., 91.

89. Rafael Alberti, *The Lost Grove*, trans. Gabriel Berns (Berkeley: University of California Press, 1976), 232. See also Dámaso Alonso, *Poetas españoles contemporáneos* (Madrid: Gredos, 1952); and Andrew Anderson, *El veintisiete en tela de juicio* (Madrid: Gredos, 2005). On Ortega y Gasset and the Generation of 1927, see Philip W. Silver, "La estética de Ortega y la generación de 1927," *Nueva Revista de Filología Hispánica* 20 (1971): 361–80; and Francie Cate-Arries, "Poetics and Philosophy: José Ortega y Gasset and the Generation of 1927," *Hispania* 71, no. 3 (1988): 503–11.

90. "Nuestras normas," *Mediodía* 1, no. 1 (1926): 2.

91. García Lorca, *Obras*, 3:421.

92. Juan Chabás, *Literatura española contemporánea, 1898–1950*, ed. Javier Pérez Bazo (Madrid: Verbum, 2001), 406.

93. Juan Ramón Jiménez, "Recuerdo de José Ortega y Gasset," in *La corriente infinita: Crítica y evocación*, ed. Francisco Garfias (Madrid: Aguilar, 1961), 156.

94. Juan Ramón Jiménez, *Antología poética*, ed. Francisco Javier Blasco (Madrid: Cátedra, 1987), 236. On Jiménez and Krausism, Giner de los Ríos, and Ortega y Gasset, see Richard Cardwell, "'The Universal Andalusian,' 'The Zealous Andalusian,' and the 'Andalusian Elegy,'" *Studies in Twentieth Century Literature* 7, no. 2 (1983): 201–24; and Cardwell, "Juan Ramón Jiménez y los intelectuales," *Hispanic Review* 53 (1985): 329–50.

95. Jiménez, "Recuerdo," 156.

96. Juan Ramón Jiménez, *Epistolario*, ed. Alfonso Alegre Heitzmann, 2 vols. (Madrid: Residencia de Estudiantes, 2006–12), 1:75. Jiménez was not alone in promoting "sad" Andalusia as a deep, depurated version of traditional folkloric images. Besides Sánchez Rodríguez, other Andalusian writers, including Nicolás María López and Juan Héctor, offered alternative literary visions of their region. For a discussion of *tristeza andaluza* and modernist aesthetics in Andalusia at the turn of the twentieth century, see Richard Cardwell, "La obra poética de José Sánchez Rodríguez en su contexto literario," in José Sánchez Rodríguez, *Alma andaluza (poesías completas)*, ed. Richard Cardwell (Granada: Universidad de

Granada, 1996), 15–89; Miguel Ángel García, *Melancolía vertebrada: La tristeza andaluza del modernismo a la vanguardia* (Barcelona: Anthropos, 2012); and Antonio Martín Infante, "Génesis de un tópico del modernismo español: 'La tristeza andaluza,' " *Nueva Revista de Filología Hispánica* 55, no. 2 (2007): 459–70.

97. Francisco Villaespesa, "Carta-Prólogo," in *Alma andaluza*, by José Sánchez Rodríguez (Madrid: Fernando Fé, 1903), 6–7.

98. On *alhambrismo* in literature and the arts, see Enrique Baltanás, *La materia de Andalucía: El ciclo andaluz de las letras de los siglos XIX y XX* (Seville: Fundación José Manuel Lara, 2003), 64–68.

99. Juan Ramón Jiménez, "Recuerdo del primer Villaespesa," in *Prosas críticas*, ed. Pilar Gómez Bedate (Madrid: Taurus, 1981), 70–82.

100. Ramón Gómez de la Serna, "Moguer (El pueblo pantomímico)," *Prometeo* 4, no. 33 (1911): 804.

101. Jiménez, *Epistolario*, 2:283.

102. Juan Ramón Jiménez, *Elejías andaluzas*, ed. Arturo del Villar (Barcelona: Bruguera, 1980), 67. Jiménez's fascination with the orient is also evident in his translation of the Indian writer Rabindranath Tagore. From 1917 to 1920 Jiménez and his wife, Zenobia Camprubí, translated about two dozen works by Tagore. See Graciela Palau de Nemes, *Vida y obra de Juan Ramón Jiménez* (Madrid: Gredos, 1974), 206–7. Jiménez once noted that the oriental settings of Tagore's writing often recalled his native Andalusia. See Jiménez, *Epistolario*, 2:73. On Tagore's influence on Jiménez's poetry, see R. Johnson, "Juan Ramón Jiménez, Rabindranath Tagore, and 'la poesía desnuda,' " *Modern Language Review* 60, no. 4 (1965): 534–46.

103. Antonio Blázquez, "El periplo de Himilco (siglo VI antes de la Era Cristiana)," *Boletín de la Real Sociedad Geográfica* 51 (1909): 325–92.

104. Jiménez, *Epistolario*, 2:348–49.

105. Juan Ramón Jiménez, "El Andaluz Universal: Autorretrato (para uso de reptiles de varia categoría)," in *Cuadernos de Juan Ramón Jiménez*, ed. Francisco Garfias (Madrid: Taurus, 1960), 122.

106. Gayle Rogers, "Jiménez, Modernism/o, and the Languages of Comparative Modernist Studies," *Comparative Literature* 66, no. 1 (2014): 129.

107. Ibid., 142–43.

108. Jiménez, "Recuerdo del primer Villaespesa," 78–81.

109. Francisco Javier Blasco Pascual, *La poética de Juan Ramón Jiménez: Desarrollo, contexto y sistema* (Salamanca: Universidad de Salamanca, 1981), 47.

110. Juan Ramón Jiménez, "Poesía abierta y poesía cerrada," in *Prosas críticas*, 192.

111. Ibid., 178.

112. Ibid., 180.

113. Juan Ramón Jiménez, *Diary of a Newlywed Poet*, ed. Michael P. Predmore, trans. Hugh A. Harter (Selingsgrove, Pa.: Susquehanna University Press, 2004), 402.

114. Jiménez, "Poesía abierta," 181.

115. Ibid., 195.

116. Juan Ramón Jiménez, "El romance, río de la lengua española," in *Prosas críticas*, 254–55.

117. On Tartessos-Tarshish, see Carolina López-Ruiz, "Tarshish and Tartessos Revisited: Textual Problems and Historical Implications," in *Colonial Encounters in Ancient Iberia: Phoenician, Greek, and Indigenous Relations*, ed. Michael Dietler and Carolina López-Ruiz (Chicago: University of Chicago Press, 2009), 255–80.

118. Jiménez, "Romance," 255.

119. Juan Guerrero Ruiz, *Juan Ramón Jiménez de viva voz* (Madrid: Ínsula, 1961), 435.

120. García Lorca, *Obras*, 4:104.

121. Ibid., 3:155.

122. Melchor Fernández Almagro, "Federico García Lorca: *Romancero Gitano*," *Revista de Occidente* 21, no. 63 (1928): 374–75.

123. García Lorca, *Obras*, 3:155.

124. Ibid., 2:255–59.

125. Sharon Handley, "Federico García Lorca and the 98 Generation: The *Andalucismo* Debate," *Anales de Literatura Española Contemporánea* 21, no. 1–2 (1996): 55.

126. García Lorca, *Obras*, 4:100.

127. Evidence of interaction between García Lorca and Ortega y Gasset is scant. The summer of 1920 found García Lorca wishing to leave Granada for Madrid to study "philosophy with Pepe Ortega"; see García Lorca, *Obras*, 4:51. A year later, he dedicated a copy of *Libro de Poemas* to "the master," and in 1929, he signed an open letter petitioning Ortega y Gasset to lead a new political party formed by liberal intellectuals; see García Lorca, *Obras*, 4:461–65.

128. Federico García Lorca, "Deep Song," in *In Search of Duende*, ed. and trans. Christopher Maurer (New York: New Directions, 1998), 1.

129. Ibid., 18.

130. Mitchell, *Flamenco Deep Song*, 165–66.

131. Christopher Maurer, *Federico García Lorca y su Arquitectura del Cante Jondo* (Granada: Comares, 2000), 93.

132. Carol Hess, *Manuel de Falla and Modernism in Spain, 1898–1936* (Chicago: University of Chicago Press, 2001). See also Nelson Orringer, *Lorca in Tune with Falla: Literary and Musical Interludes* (Toronto: University of Toronto Press, 2014).

133. García Lorca, "Deep Song," 1–2.

134. Gaspar de Nava Álvarez de Noroña, ed. and trans., *Poesías asiáticas puestas en verso castellano* (Paris: Imprenta de Julio Didot Mayor, 1883), v.

135. García Lorca, "Deep Song," 18.

136. Ibid., 4–5.

137. Ibid., 25.

138. Ian Gibson, *Federico García Lorca: A Life* (New York: Random House, 1989), 84–85.

139. García Lorca, "Deep Song," 10–11.

140. Ortega y Gasset, *Obras*, 3:853.

141. García Lorca, "Deep Song," 14.

142. Ortega y Gasset, *Obras*, 4:94.

143. García Lorca, *Obras*, 1:307–9.

144. García Lorca, "Deep Song," 8.

145. Lynn Garafola, *Diaghilev's Ballets Russes* (Oxford: Oxford University Press, 1989), viii.

146. Ortega y Gasset, *Obras*, 2:444.

147. Ibid., 2:372.

148. Manuel de Falla, "Introducción a la nueva música," *Revista musical hispanoamericana* (December 1916): 5.

149. Maurer, *Federico García Lorca*, 217.

150. Ibid., 222.

151. García Lorca, "Deep Song," 9.

152. Ibid., 8.

153. Hess, *Manuel de Falla*, 87–129.

154. Ibid., 175.

155. "Los bailes rusos y el arte español," *La Correspondencia de España*, October 8, 1916, 4.

156. On Stravinsky and Falla, see Hess, *Manuel de Falla*, 161–98.

157. Adolfo Salazar, *Música y músicos de hoy* (Madrid: Mundo Latino, 1929), 147.

158. Ibid., 134–38.

159. Federico García Lorca, "Play and Theory of the Duende," in *In Search of Duende*, ed. and trans. Maurer, 49.

160. Ibid., 55.

161. Ibid., 53.

162. Ibid., 62.

163. Ibid., 53.

164. Luis Cernuda, *Prosa completa*, ed. Derek Harris and Luis Maristany (Barcelona: Barrall, 1975), 906.

165. See poems such as "Quisiera estar solo en el sur," "A un muchacho andaluz," and "El andaluz," among others in Luis Cernuda, *Poesía completa*, ed. Derek Harris and Luis Maristany (Madrid: Siruela, 2002). On Cernuda and Andalusia, see Juan Alfredo Bellón Cabazán, "La Andalucía de Luis Cernuda: Apuntes y divagaciones sobre los mitos edénicos y demás paraísos naturales y artificiales," *Letras del Sur* 3–4 (1978): 32–36; Luis García Montero, "Andalucía como imagen literaria," in *Literaturas regionales en España: Historia y crítica*, ed. José-Carlos Mainer (Zaragoza: Institución Fernando el Católico, 1994), 101–15; and Luis García Montero, "Luis Cernuda y Andalucía," in *Nostalgia de una patria imposible: Estudios sobre la obra de Luis Cernuda*, ed. Juan Matas Caballero et al. (Madrid: Akal, 2005), 47–61.

166. Cernuda, *Prosa*, 1282–96.

167. Ibid., 1282.

168. Ibid., 1288.

169. Ibid., 1295.

170. García Montero ("Luis Cernuda y Andalucia," 54) notes affinities between Ortega's "Teoría de Andalucía" and "Divagación sobre la Andalucía romántica," but does not discuss Cernuda's subtle yet pervasive criticism of the philosopher's view of the south.

171. Dorothy M. Figueira, *The Exotic: A Decadent Quest* (Albany: SUNY Press, 1994), 2.

172. Cernuda, *Prosa*, 1301.

173. Ibid., 1285. On Cernuda and Romanticism, see Philip W. Silver, *Ruin and Restitution: Reinterpreting Romanticism in Spain* (Nashville, Tenn.: Vanderbilt University Press, 1997), 99–121.

174. Cernuda, *Prosa*, 1228. According to the Dictionary of the Spanish Academy, *norte* means, among other things, both the compass point directly opposite to the south as well as "guide, reference point."

Chapter 3

1. Isidro Gomá y Tomás, *Pastorales de la Guerra de España* (Madrid: Rialp, 1955), 59.

2. For a complete analysis of Soviet and Communist intervention in Spain from the early twentieth century to the end of the Civil War, see Stanley Payne, *The Spanish Civil War, the Soviet Union, and Communism* (New Haven, Conn.: Yale University Press, 2008).

3. Gerald H. Meaker, *The Revolutionary Left in Spain, 1914–1923* (Stanford, Calif.: Stanford University Press, 1974), 126.

4. Francisco Sánchez Ruano, *Islam y Guerra Civil Española: Moros con Franco y con la República* (Madrid: La Esfera de los Libros, 2004).

5. Balfour, *Deadly Embrace*, 272–73. According to Balfour, the fundamental motive for "the successful recruitment of thousands of Moroccans into the ranks of the rebel army was economic."

6. Dolores Ibarruri, "la Pasionaria," as quoted in Goytisolo, "From *Count Julian* to *Makbara*," in *Saracen Chronicles*, 221.

7. Raymond Carr, *Modern Spain, 1875–1980* (Oxford: Oxford University Press, 1980), 164.

8. Manuel Vázquez Montalbán, *Crónica sentimental de España* (Barcelona: Lumen, 1971), 26.

9. On the duality of visual and literary representations of the Spanish gypsy, see Lou Charnon-Deutsch, "Travels of the Imaginary Spanish Gypsy," in *Constructing Identity in Contemporary Spain*, ed. Jo Labanyi (Oxford: Oxford University Press, 2002), 22–40.

10. Ibid., 23.

11. On *gitanismo*, see Torrecilla, *España exótica*, 52–71.

12. Sebastián Herrero, "La gitana," in *Los españoles pintados por sí mismos* (Madrid: Gaspar y Roig Editores, 1851), 121.

13. See Eva Woods, "From Rags to Riches: The Ideology of Stardom in Folkloric Musical Comedy of the Late 1930s and 1950s," in *Spanish Popular Cinema*, ed. Antonio Lázaro Reboll and Andrew Willis (Manchester, Eng.: Manchester University Press, 2004), 40–59.

14. Quoted in Román Gubern, *El cine sonoro en la II República, 1929–1936* (Barcelona: Lumen, 1977), 127.

15. See Julio Pérez Perucha, "Narración de un aciago destino (1896–1930)," in *Historia del cine español*, ed. Román Gubern et al. (Madrid: Cátedra, 2009), 19–121.

16. On the social component of musicals produced during the Second Republic, see Jo Labanyi, "Miscegenation, Nation Formation, and Cross-Racial Identifications in the Early Francoist Folkloric Film Musical," in *Hybridity and Its Discontents*, ed. Avtar Brah and Annie Coombes (London: Routledge, 2005), 56–71.

17. Sander L. Gilman, *Difference and Pathology: Stereotypes of Sexuality, Race, and Madness* (Ithaca, N.Y.: Cornell University Press, 1985), 30.

18. José F. Colmeiro, "Rehispanicizing Carmen: Cultural Representations in Spanish Cinema," in *Carmen: From Silent Film to MTV*, ed. Chris Perriam and Ann Davies (Amsterdam: Rodopi, 2005), 94. See also Alberto González Troyano, *La desventura de Carmen: Una divagación sobre Andalucía* (Madrid: Espasa Calpe, 1990); Carlos Serrano, *El nacimiento de Carmen: Símbolos, mitos y nación* (Madrid: Taurus, 1999); and José F. Colmeiro, "Exorcising Exoticism: *Carmen* and the Construction of Oriental Spain," *Comparative Literature* 54, no. 2 (2002), 127–44.

19. Vázquez Montalbán, *Crónica sentimental*, 23.

20. Eva Woods Peiró, *White Gypsies: Race and Stardom in Spanish Musicals* (Minneapolis: University of Minnesota Press, 2012), 207. On the *españolada* as counter-myth, see Kathleen M. Vernon, "Culture and Cinema to 1975," in *The Cambridge Companion to Modern Spanish Culture*, ed. David T. Gies (Cambridge: Cambridge University Press, 1999), 254.

21. Manuel Vázquez Montalbán, ed., *Cancionero general del franquismo, 1939–1975* (Barcelona: Crítica, 2000), 65.

22. José Romero Marchent, "Cinema nacional comentarios al margen: Imperio Argentina y el cinema español," *Radiocinema: Revista cinematográfica nacional* 21 (1939).

23. Enrique Selva Roca de Togores, ed., *Arte y Estado* (Madrid: Biblioteca Nueva, 2009), 209.

24. Antonio Román, "Lo que vi en *Carmen la de Triana*," *Radiocinema* 21 (1939).

25. "Pathé Cinema: 'Carmen la de Triana,' " *ABC* [Seville], November 12, 1938, 18.

26. Florián Rey, "Españoladas," *Vértice: Revista nacional de Falange Española Tradicionalista y de la J.O.N.S.* 71 (February 1944): 46.

27. See María Jesús Ruiz Muñoz and Inmaculada Sánchez Alarcón, *La imagen de la mujer andaluza en el cine español* (Seville: Centro de Estudios Andaluces, 2008), 52–53.

28. On *coplas* as a coping mechanism for women in postwar Spain, see Carmen Martín Gaite, *Usos amorosos de la postguerra española* (Barcelona: Anagrama, 2007).

29. Tico Medina, *Lola, en carne viva: Memorias de Lola Flores* (Madrid: Ediciones Temas de Hoy, 1990), 25.

30. Peiró, *White Gypsies*, 24.

31. See Daniel Pineda Novo, *Las Folklóricas* (Seville: Editorial Castillejo, 1990).

32. Medina, *Lola, en carne viva*, 346.

33. Royal Decree 2396/1998, quoted in José Daniel Barquero and Luis Fernando Fernández Sánchez, *Los secretos del protocolo, las relaciones públicas y la publicidad* (Valladolid: Lex Nova, 2007), 60.

34. On Francoist uses of *Hispanidad*, see María A. Escudero, "Hispanist Democratic Thought versus Hispanist Thought of the Franco Era: A Comparative Analysis," in *Bridging the Atlantic: Toward a Reassessment of Iberian and Latin American Cultural Ties*, ed. Marina Pérez de Mendiola (Albany: SUNY Press,

1996), 169–86. See also Lorenzo Delgado Gómez-Escalonilla, *Imperio de papel: Acción cultural y política exterior durante el primer franquismo* (Madrid: CSIC, 1992).

35. See Paco Ignacio Taibo I, *Un cine para un imperio: Historia de las películas franquistas* (Mexico City: Conaculta, 2000).

36. See Raúl Morodo, *Los orígenes ideológicos del franquismo: Acción Española* (Madrid: Alianza, 1985).

37. José María Pemán, "Revisión del Descartes escolar," in *Meditación Española* (Madrid: Afrodisio Aguado, 1963), 404–16.

38. Hipólito Escolar Sobrino, *La cultura durante la Guerra Civil* (Madrid: Alhambra, 1987), 201.

39. On Pemán's private views about Franco and the regime, see Javier Tussell and Gonzalo Álvarez Chillida, *Pemán: Un trayecto intelectual desde la extrema derecha hasta la democracia* (Madrid: Planeta, 1998).

40. José María Pemán, "Meditación para franceses," in *Meditación Española*, 15.

41. Pemán, *Meditación Española*, 27–32.

42. "Estoicismo y economía," *ABC*, September 9, 1959, 3.

43. José María Pemán, *Obras completas*, 7 vols. (Madrid: Escelicer, 1947–65), 5:486–89.

44. Ibid., 4:145.

45. José María Pemán, "Llanto por el mar profanado," *Ellas* 13 (August 11, 1932): 2.

46. Pemán, *Obras*, 1:990.

47. Florentino Pérez-Embid, "Pequeña teoría de Andalucía," in *Paisajes de la tierra y el alma* (Madrid: Rialp, 1963), 20.

48. Ibid., 24.

49. Rafael Alberti, *Antología comentada (Poesía)*, ed. María Asunción Mateo (Madrid: Ediciones de la Torre, 1990), 125.

50. World Bank, *The Economic Development of Spain* (Baltimore, Md.: Johns Hopkins University Press, 1963).

51. Quoted in Martín Gaite, *Usos amorosos*, 29.

52. Vázquez Montalbán, *Crónica sentimental*, 187.

53. Quoted in Sasha D. Pack, *Tourism and Dictatorship: Europe's Peaceful Invasion of Franco's Spain* (New York: Palgrave Macmillan, 2006), 145.

54. Vázquez Montalbán, *Crónica sentimental*, 192.

55. Justin Crumbaugh, *Destination Dictatorship: The Spectacle of Spain's Tourist Boom and the Reinvention of Difference* (Albany: SUNY Press, 2009), 83–84.

56. Casimiro Torreiro, "¿Una dictadura liberal? (1962–1969)," in *Historia del cine español*, ed. Román Gubern et al. (Madrid: Cátedra, 2009), 302–3.

57. "Nuestra carta para usted: La moral y los medios difusores," *Tele/Radio* 192 (1961): 13.

58. José María Pemán, "Capitalismo," *Gaceta Ilustrada* 606 (May 1968).

59. José María de Llanos, "No a Pemán, campeón del capitalismo," *El Ciervo* 17, no. 172 (1968): 11.

60. José María Pemán, "El Séneca y los turistas," in *Meditación Española*, 219.

61. José María Pemán, *Andalucía* (Barcelona: Destino, 1958), 7.

62. Ibid., 85.
63. Ibid., 165.
64. Ibid., 85.
65. Ibid., 405.
66. Ibid., 475.
67. Manuel Delgado Cabeza, "La globalización de la cultura andaluza: Evolución y vigencia de la 'cuestión agraria' en Andalucía," in *La cuestión agraria en la historia de Andalucía: Nuevas perspectivas*, ed. Manuel González de Molina (Seville: Centro de Estudios Andaluces, 2014), 99.
68. Antonio Cazorla Sánchez, *Fear and Progress: Ordinary Lives in Franco's Spain* (Oxford: Wiley Blackwell, 2010), 73.
69. Ibid., 124.
70. Juan Goytisolo, *The Countryside of Níjar and La Chanca*, trans. Luigi Luccarelli (Plainfield, Ind.: Alembic, 1987), 125.
71. Pemán, *Andalucía*, 384–85.
72. José María Pemán, "Sociología andaluza," in *Meditación Española*, 57–62.
73. José María Pemán, "Prólogo," in *Meditación Española*, 16.
74. José María Pemán, "El Séneca y el trabajo," in *Meditación Española*, 206–10.
75. José María Maravall, *La política de la transición* (Madrid: Taurus, 1981), 27.
76. See Joe Foweraker, *Making Democracy in Spain: Grass-Roots Struggle in the South, 1955–1975* (Cambridge: Cambridge University Press, 1989).
77. José María Pemán, "El Séneca y los juguetes," in *Meditación Española*, 173–76.
78. Pedro Laín Entralgo, "La Andalucía de Pemán," in *En torno a Pemán* (Cadiz: Excma. Diputación Provincial de Cádiz, 1974), 182.
79. Ibid., 192.
80. Ibid., 193.
81. Ibid., 194.
82. Ibid., 193.
83. Richard Gunter, "Spain: The Very Model of Elite Settlement," in *Elites and Democratic Consolidation in Latin America and Southern Europe*, ed. John Higley and Richard Gunter (Cambridge: Cambridge University Press, 1992), 41.
84. Manuel Vázquez Montalban, "Pemán y 'el Séneca,' una tragedia liberal," *Triunfo* 494, no. 26 (1971): 19–23.
85. Stuart Hall, "Notes on Deconstructing 'the Popular,'" in *People's History and Socialist Theory*, ed. Raphael Samuel (London: Routledge and Kegan Paul, 1981), 239.
86. On the magazine's history, see Alicia Alted and Paul Aubert, eds., *Triunfo en su época* (Madrid: Casa de Velázquez, 1995).
87. Joaquín Romero Murube, "Sevilla," *Triunfo* 18, no. 47 (1963): 62.
88. Alfonso Carlos Comín, "Andalucía: Sus hombres, sus tierras, su presente y su futuro," *Triunfo* 22, no. 265 (1967): 26–35, 56–57; "Andalucía II: La diáspora," *Triunfo* 22, no. 266 (1967): 26–35, 56–57; "Andalucía III: Los otros andaluces," *Triunfo* 22, no. 267 (1967): 18–23, 60–61; "Andalucía IV: La industria del sur," *Triunfo* 22, no. 268 (1967): 36–41, 61. See also Alfonso Carlos Comín, *España del Sur* (Madrid: Tecnos, 1966).

89. The poet Juan Gil-Albert quickly responded to Comín with an impassioned defense of Ortega's "Teoría de Andalucía." In his view, economic approaches to Andalusia are incompatible with an appreciation of its culture. Like Comín, he was locked in an either-or impasse that other *Triunfo* contributors sought to overcome. See Gil-Albert, "A propósito del arte, de Ortega y Gasset y otras cuestiones patrias," in *Los días están contados* (Barcelona: Tusquets, 1974), 55–86.

90. Comín, "Andalucía: Sus hombres, sus tierras, su presente y su futuro," 28.

91. Comín, "Andalucía IV," 37.

92. Comín, "Andalucía III," 22.

93. Comín, "Andalucía: Sus hombres, sus tierras, su presente y su futuro," 29.

94. Karl Marx, *The Communist Manifesto*, ed. Frederic L. Bender (New York: Norton, 1988), 72.

95. Ibid., 73.

96. Antonio Gramsci, "Observations on Folklore," in *Selections from Cultural Writings*, ed. David Forgacs and Geoffrey Nowell-Smith, trans. William Boelhower (Cambridge, Mass.: Harvard University Press, 1985), 189.

97. Ibid., 190.

98. Francisco Almazán Marcos, "El cante del pueblo I," *Triunfo* 24, no. 384 (1969): 17.

99. Francisco Almazán Marcos, "El cante del pueblo en Granada," *Triunfo* 24, no. 392 (1969): 12.

100. Francisco Almazán Marcos, "50 años de nacional flamenquismo," *Triunfo* 27, no. 510 (1972): 33.

101. Ibid., 32.

102. José Luis Ortiz Nuevo, "El pensamiento político del cante flamenco," *Triunfo* 28, no. 584 (1973): 64.

103. José Menese quoted in Ortiz Nuevo, "El pensamiento," 63.

104. Almazán Marcos, "El cante del pueblo I," 16.

105. Antonio Ramos Espejo, "*Triunfo* de carambola," in *Triunfo: Una revista abierta al sur*, ed. José Romero Portillo (Seville: Centro de Estudios Andaluces, 2012), 61.

106. Antonio Ramos Espejo, "La Chanca," *Triunfo* 35, no. 8 (1981): 27.

107. Carmen Sotomayor, *Una lectura orientalista de Juan Goytisolo* (Madrid: Fundamentos, 1990), 41–59.

108. Juan Goytisolo, "Volver al sur," in *España y sus ejidos* (Madrid: Hijos de Muley Rubio, 2003), 75.

109. Juan Goytisolo, *Forbidden Territory and Realms of Strife*, trans. Peter Bush (London: Verso, 2003), 207.

110. Luce López-Baralt, "Toward a 'Mudéjar' Reading of Juan Goytisolo's *Makbara*," in *Islam in Spanish Literature: From the Middle Ages to the Present*, trans. Andrew Hurley (Leiden: Brill, 1992), 259–300.

111. Goytisolo, "From *Count Julian* to *Makbara*," in *Saracen Chronicles*, 216.

112. Goytisolo, *Forbidden Territory*, 208.

113. Ibid., 236.

114. Antonio Ramos Espejo, "Blas Infante en la polémica de la nacionalidad andaluza," *Triunfo* 33, no. 864 (1979): 22–24.

115. Antonio Burgos, *Andalucía, ¿tercer mundo?* (Barcelona: Círculo de Lectores, 1972), 182.

116. José Aumente, "¿Una alternativa 'andaluza' a la democracia y el socialismo? 'El poder andaluz'?" *Triunfo* 31, no. 710 (1976): 32–33. See also Aumente, *La cuestión nacional andaluza y los intereses de clase* (Madrid: Mañana, 1979).

117. Blas Infante, quoted in Enrique Iniesta Coullaut-Valera, *Blas Infante: Toda su verdad, Vol. 2: 1919–1933* (Granada: Editorial Atrio, 2003), 216.

118. Infante, quoted in Ramos Espejo, "Con los descendientes de Al-Motamid," *Triunfo* 33, no. 911 (1980): 38.

119. Infante, quoted in Iniesta Coullaut-Valera, *Blas Infante*, 224.

120. Antonio Ramos Espejo, "Boabdil cabalga de nuevo," *Triunfo* 34, no. 2 (1980): 81.

121. Samuel P. Huntington, *The Third Wave: Democratization in the Late Twentieth Century* (Norman: University of Oklahoma Press, 1992).

122. Antonio Burgos, "¿Otra nueva colonización? Andalucía votará partido, no región," *Triunfo* 32, no. 747 (1977): 44–45.

Chapter 4

1. *Asimetría y cohesión en el estado autonómico* (Madrid: Instituto Nacional de Administración Pública, 1997), 18–21.

2. Xavier Rubert de Ventós, *De la modernidad: Ensayo de filosofía crítica* (Barcelona: Península, 1980), 209.

3. Roland Barthes, *Mythologies*, trans. Annette Lavers (New York: Hill and Wang, 1972), 109.

4. Ibid., 143.

5. Ley orgánica 6/1981, de 30 de diciembre, de Estatuto de Autonomía para Andalucía, *Boletín Oficial de la Junta de Andalucía*, 22.

6. *Estatuto de Autonomía para Andalucía* (Seville: Junta de Andalucía, 2007), 5.

7. Carlos Castilla del Pino, "Andalucía no existe," *La Ilustración Regional* 4 (1974): 14–15.

8. José María de los Santos, *Sociología de la transición andaluza* (Malaga: Ágora, 1990), 66.

9. Eurostat, "Unemployment Statistics at Regional Level" (2016), http://ec.europa.eu/eurostat/statistics-explained/index.php/Unemployment_statistics_at_regional_level.

10. Alfred P. Montero, *Shifting States in Global Markets: Subnational Industrial Policy in Contemporary Brazil and Spain* (University Park: Pennsylvania State University Press, 2002), 175.

11. Jorge Luis Borges, "Translators of *The Thousand and One Nights*," in *Selected Non-Fictions*, ed. Eliot Weinberger, trans. Ester Allen, Suzanne Jill Levine, and Eliot Weinberger (London: Penguin, 1999), 1:110.

12. See, for instance, José Acosta Sánchez, *Historia y cultura del pueblo andaluz* (Barcelona: Anagrama, 1979); José Manuel Cuenca Toribio, *Andalucía: Una introducción histórica* (Cordoba: Monte de Piedad y Caja de Ahorros, 1979); José Antonio Lacomba, ed., *Historia de Andalucía*, 8 vols. (Barcelona: Planeta, 1980–81); and Manuel Moreno Alonso, *Historia general de Andalucía* (Seville: Argantonio, 1981).

13. Isidoro Moreno, "Antropología del andaluz," in *Gran Enciclopedia de Andalucía*, ed. José María Javierre and Manuel Ángel Vázquez Medel (Seville: Promociones Culturales Andaluzas, 1979), 1:216.

14. Blas Infante, *La verdad*, 63.

15. Claudio Sánchez Albornoz, *De la Andalucía Islámica a la de hoy* (Madrid: Rialp, 1983), 11.

16. Serafín Fanjul, "¿Andalucía árabe?" *El País,* August 11, 1984, reprinted as "Antiprólogo" in *Al-Andalus contra España: La forja del mito* (Madrid: Siglo Veintiuno, 2000), xxi–xxii.

17. See Antonio Narbona, Rafael Cano, and Ramón Morillo, *El español hablado en Andalucía* (Seville: Fundación José Manuel Lara, 2003).

18. Juan Alberto Fernández Bañuls and José María Pérez Orozco, *El Correo de Andalucía,* October 7, 1979, 16.

19. "El Correo en blanco y verde: El castellano y el andaluz," *El Correo de Andalucía,* January 13, 1980, 5.

20. *El legado andalusí: Una propuesta plástica* (Granada: Fundación Caja de Granada, 1995).

21. Eric Calderwood, "The Invention of al-Andalus: Discovering the Past and Creating the Present in Granada's Islamic Tourism Sites," *The Journal of North African Studies* 19, no. 1 (2014): 41.

22. *Itinerario cultural de Almorávides y Almohades* (Granada: Junta de Andalucía, 1999).

23. Mikaela Rogozen-Soltar, "Al-Andalus in Andalusia: Negotiating Moorish History and Regional Identity in Southern Spain," *Anthropological Quarterly* 80, no. 3 (2007): 869.

24. Daniela Flesler, *The Return of the Moor: Spanish Responses to Contemporary Moroccan Immigration* (West Lafayette, Ind.: Purdue University Press, 2008), 9.

25. Juan Goytisolo, "De la migración a la inmigración," in *España y sus ejidos*, 51.

26. Partha Chatterjee, *Nationalist World and the Colonial World: A Derivative Discourse* (Minneapolis: University of Minnesota Press, 1986), 2.

27. Barthes, *Mythologies*, 143.

28. On regional television during the transition, see Richard Maxwell, *The Spectacle of Democracy: Spanish Television, Nationalism, and Political Transition* (Minneapolis: University of Minnesota Press, 1995).

29. Antonio Muñoz Molina, *La huerta del Edén: Escritos y diatribas sobre Andalucía* (Madrid: Ollero y Ramos, 1996), 148.

30. Barthes, *Mythologies*, 117–21.

31. Juan Luis Manfredi, "RTVA: Por una programación en Andalucía," *ABC* [Seville], February 2, 1996, 76.

32. On how formulaic patterns preestablish the "attitudinal pattern of the spectator before he is presented with any specific content," see Theodor W. Adorno, "How to Look at Television," in *The Culture Industry: Selected Essays on Mass Culture* (London: Routledge, 1991), 158–77.

33. Pierre Bourdieu, *On Television*, trans. Priscilla Parkhurst (New York: New, 1998), 21.

34. Ron Lembo, *Thinking Through Television* (Cambridge: Cambridge University Press, 2000), 99.

35. Ibid., 108–13.

36. Guy Debord, *The Society of the Spectacle*, trans. Donald Nicholson-Smith (New York: Zone Books, 1995), 12.

37. UNESCO (United Nations Educational, Scientific, and Cultural Organization), "Alhambra, Generalife and Albayzín, Granada," *World Heritage List* (2016), http://whc.unesco.org/en/list/314.

38. Jane Feuer, "The Concept of Live Television: Ontology as Ideology," in *Regarding Television: Critical Approaches*, ed. E. Ann Kaplan (Los Angeles: American Film Institute, 1983), 20.

39. Tony Bennett, *The Birth of the Museum: History, Theory, Politics* (London: Routledge, 1995), 210.

40. Quoted in María A. Escudero, "Hispanist Democratic Thought versus Hispanist Thought of the Franco Era," in *Bridging the Atlantic*, ed. Marina Pérez de Mendiola, (Albany: SUNY Press, 1996), 199.

41. Bennett, *The Birth of the Museum*, 210.

42. Antonio Caballero, quoted in Marina Pérez de Mendiola, "The Universal Exposition Seville 1992: Presence and Absence, Remembrance and Forgetting," in *Bridging the Atlantic*, 198–99.

43. On the symbolic relation between Spain and Spanish America at the Expo, see Pérez de Mendiola, *Bridging the Atlantic*.

44. King Juan Carlos I, quoted in Escudero, "Hispanist," in *Bridging the Atlantic*, 177.

45. Junta de Andalucía, "Avance de la programación de contenidos y actividades del Pabellón de Andalucía en Expo '92," box 9601, Archivo General de Andalucía, 9.

46. Zeynep Çelik, *Displaying the Orient: Architecture of Islam at the Nineteenth-Century World's Fairs* (Berkeley: University of California Press, 1992), 51–93.

47. Roger Benjamin, *Orientalist Aesthetics: Art, Colonialism, and French North Africa, 1880–1930* (Berkeley: University of California Press, 2003), 118–22.

48. Richard Maddox, *The Best of All Possible Islands: Seville's Universal Exposition, the New Spain, and the New Europe* (Albany: SUNY Press, 2004), 77.

49. Umberto Eco, "A Theory of Expositions," in *Travels in Hyperreality*, trans. William Weaver (London: Harcourt Brace, 1986), 299.

50. "Performative," *Oxford English Dictionary*, 2nd ed., 20 vols. (Oxford: Oxford University Press, 1989).

51. María José Bueno Fidel, *Arquictectura y nacionalismo: Pabellones españoles en las exposiciones universales del siglo diecinueve* (Malaga: Universidad de Málaga/Colegio de Arquitectos, 1987).

52. Neal M. Rosendorf, *Franco Sells Spain to America: Hollywood, Tourism, and Public Relations as Postwar Spanish Soft Power* (New York: Palgrave Macmillan, 2014), 199; see also chapter 6, "The Spanish Pavilion at the 1964–65 New York World's Fair: Franco Spain's $7 Million US Outreach *Summa*."

53. Junta de Andalucía, "Avance," 3.

54. Ibid., 7.

55. Ibid.

56. Juan Zozoya, "The Fortifications of al-Andalus," in *Al-Andalus: The Art of Islamic Spain*, ed. Jerrilynn D. Dodds (New York: Metropolitan Museum of Art, 1992), 63–73.

57. *Guia oficial Expo '92* (Seville: Sociedad Estatal para la Exposición Universal, 1992), 142.

58. Creaciones Elba, "Informe del anteproyecto 'La memoria productiva,'" box 9690, Archivo General de Andalucía, 5.

59. Fredric Jameson, *Postmodernism; or, the Cultural Logic of Late Capitalism* (Durham, N.C.: Duke University Press, 1991), 21.

60. Junta de Andalucía, "Avance," 3.

61. Lev Manovich, *The Language of New Media* (Cambridge, Mass.: MIT Press, 2001), 129.

62. Manuel Castells and Peter Hall, eds., *Andalucía: Innovación tecnológica y desarrollo económico* (Madrid: Espasa Calpe, 1992), 1:232.

63. Stéphane Mallarmé, *Oeuvres complètes*, ed. Henri Mondor and G. Jean Aubry (Paris: Gallimard, 1945), 378.

64. Javier Hernández Ramírez, *La imagen de Andalucía en el turismo* (Seville: Centro de Estudios Andaluces, 2008), 117.

65. *Estatuto de Autonomía*, 1.

66. Ibid.

67. Eugenia Afinoguénova, "Andalucía: Una *Comunidad turística* sin andaluces," in *La retórica del sur: Representaciones y discursos sobre Andalucía en el período democrático*, ed. Antonio Gómez L. Quiñones and José M. del Pino (Seville: Alfar, 2015), 254.

68. Michael T. Newton, *Institutions of Modern Spain: A Political and Economic Guide* (Cambridge: Cambridge University Press, 1997), 129–30.

69. Hernández Ramírez, *La imagen*, 116.

70. Ibid., 114.

71. Bennett, *The Birth of the Museum*, 129.

72. For a sample of graded activities and worksheets, see the museum's official website, http://maa.centrodeestudiosandaluces.es/index.php?mod=plan-didactico.

73. Bico Bermúdez, "Inmersión en el universo de Blas Infante: El proyecto museográfico de la Casa de la Alegría," in *La Casa de Blas Infante: El legado* (Seville: Centro de Estudios Andaluces, 2010), 54.

74. Ibid., 59.

75. In June 2016, the judge investigating the so-called "ERE" (Expediente de Regulación de Empleo, or Employment Regulation Order) scandal charged Chaves and Griñán with administrative misconduct and embezzlement of public funds for illegal severance pay. The trial is scheduled to begin in December 2017. For details on this case, see Javier Martín-Arroyo, "Chaves y Griñán, procesados por el 'caso ERE' a 25 días de las elecciones." El País (1 June 2016); http://politica.elpais.com/politica/2016/05/30/actualidad/1464638380_111019.html.

76. Blas Infante, "Las insignias de Andalucía," *Andalucía* 173 (December 31, 1919).

77. Selma Reuben Holo, *Beyond the Prado: Museums and Identity in Democratic Spain* (Washington: Smithsonian Institution Press, 1999), 12.

Afterword

1. Oscar Wilde, "The Critic as Artist Part I," in *The Major Works*, ed. Isobel Murray (Oxford: Oxford University Press, 1989), 256.

2. Hayden White, *Metahistory: The Historical Imagination in Nineteenth-Century Europe* (Baltimore, Md.: Johns Hopkins University Press, 1975), ix.

3. Said, *Orientalism*, 177.
4. Karl Marx and Friedrich Engels, *On Religion* (New York: Dover, 2008), 42.
5. Isidoro Moreno, "La identidad andaluza en el marco del Estado español, la Unión Europea y la globalización," in *La identidad cultural de Andalucía: Aproximaciones, mixtificaciones, negacionismo y evidencias*, ed. Isidoro Moreno (Seville: Centro de Estudios Andaluces, 2008), 252.
6. Ibid., 259–61.
7. Monserrat Guibernau, *The Identity of Nations* (Cambridge: Polity, 2007), 10.
8. Frank R. Ankersmit, *Sublime Historical Experience* (Stanford, Calif.: Stanford University Press, 2005), xv.
9. Ibid., 9.
10. Ibid., 14.
11. *Andalucía: Un siglo de fascinación*, directed by Basilio Martín Patino (1996; Madrid: Suevia, 2004), DVD.
12. Michael Hardt and Antonio Negri, *Empire* (Cambridge, Mass.: Harvard University Press, 2000), 23–24.
13. Ibid., 25.
14. Muñoz Molina, *La huerta del Edén*, 148.
15. See Fernando González, "Basilio Martin Patino: Pensar la historia," *Film-Historia* 7, no. 2 (1997): 141–60; and Rafael Utrera Macias, ed., *Andalucía: Un siglo de fascinación: Homenaje a Basilio Martín Patino* (Sanlúcar de Barrameda: Pedro Romero-Eihceroa, 2006).
16. Marshall McLuhan, *Understanding Media: The Extensions of Man* (New York: McGraw-Hill, 1964).
17. Walter Benjamin, *The Origin of German Tragic Drama*, trans. John Osborne (London: Verso, 1998), 177–78.
18. Lyotard, *The Postmodern Condition*, 81.
19. Žižek, *The Sublime Object*, 206.
20. Benjamin, *Origin of German Tragic Drama*, 233.
21. See Óscar Cornago Bernal, "La puesta en escena de la autenticidad: *Andalucía, un siglo de fascinación*, de Basilio Martín Patino, y el 'materialismo histórico' en Walter Benjamin," *ARBOR: Ciencia, Pensamiento y Cultura* 187, no. 748 (2011): 223–36. Cornago connects Benjamin's views on history and Patino's audiovisual techniques, but does not explore the treatment of Andalusian identity in the documentary.
22. "Fascination," *Oxford English Dictionary*, 2nd ed., 20 vols. (Oxford: Oxford University Press, 1989).

BIBLIOGRAPHY

Archives

Archivo de la Institución Libre de Enseñanza (Madrid)
Archivo General de Andalucía (Seville)
Biblioteca Nacional de España (Madrid)
Biblioteca Virtual de Arabistas y Africanistas Españoles, Ministerio de Ciencia e Innovación (Madrid)
Fondo Digital "Revistas de la Edad de Plata," Residencia de Estudiantes (Madrid)
Fondo Documental Blas Infante (Coria del Río, Seville)
Hemeroteca Digital, Biblioteca Nacional de España (Madrid)
Hemeroteca Municipal (Seville)

Newspapers and Periodicals

ABC
Acción Española
África Española: Revista de colonización
África: Revista de tropas coloniales
Al-Andalus
Andalucía
Awraq
Bética
Boletín de la Institución Libre de Enseñanza
Boletín Oficial de la Junta de Andalucía
Cambio 16
Cuadernos para el diálogo
Destino
El Ciervo
El Correo de Andalucía
Ellas
El País
El Sol
España
Europa en África
Gaceta Ilustrada
Hispania
Ideal
Joventut: Periódich Catalanista
La América
La Correspondencia de España
La Gaceta Literaria

La Ilustración Regional
La Lectura
L'Amic de les Arts
La Voz
Litoral
Luz
Mediodía
Prometeo
Radiocinema: Revista cinematográfica nacional
Revista de Estudios Andaluces
Revista de Estudios Regionales
Revista de Occidente
Revista Hispano-Africana
Revista musical hispanoamericana
Sur
Tele/Radio
Triunfo
Vértice

Articles and Books

Acosta Ferrero, Juan María. *Elena Whishaw en Niebla, 75 años después*. Madrid: Cultiva, 2012.

Acosta Sánchez, José. *Historia y cultura del pueblo andaluz*. Barcelona: Anagrama, 1979.

Adorno, Theodor W. *The Culture Industry: Selected Essays on Mass Culture*. London: Routledge, 1991.

Alberola Romá, Armando, ed. *Estudios sobre Rafael Altamira*. Alicante: Instituto de Estudios Juan Gil-Albert, 1987.

Alberti, Rafael. *Antología comentada (Poesía)*. Ed. María Asunción Mateo. Madrid: Ediciones de la Torre, 1990.

———. *The Lost Grove*. Trans. Gabriel Berns. Berkeley: University of California Press, 1976.

Alonso, Dámaso. *Poetas españoles contemporáneos*. Madrid: Gredos, 1952.

Altamira, Pilar. *Diálogos con Rafael Altamira*. Murcia and Oviedo: Universidad de Murcia and Universidad de Oviedo, 2009.

Altamira, Rafael. *Historia de España y de la civilización española*. 4 vols. Barcelona: Juan Gili, 1900–1911.

———. *Mi viaje a América*. Madrid: Librería General de Victoriano Suárez, 1911.

Alted, Alicia, and Paul Aubert, eds. *Triunfo en su época*. Madrid: Casa de Velázquez, 1995.

Álvarez Barrientos, Joaquín, and Alberto Romero Ferrer, eds. *Costumbrismo andaluz*. Seville: Universidad de Sevilla, 1998.

Álvarez Chillida, Gonzalo. *José María Pemán: Pensamiento y trayectoria de un monárquico (1897–1941)*. Cadiz: Universidad de Cádiz, 1996.

Álvarez Junco, José. *Spanish Identity in the Age of Nations*. Manchester, Eng.: Manchester University Press, 2011.

Álvarez Millán, Cristina, and Claudia Heide, eds. *Pascual de Gayangos: A Nineteenth-Century Spanish Arabist*. Edinburgh: Edinburgh University Press, 2008.

Anderson, Andrew. *El veintisiete en tela de juicio*. Madrid: Gredos, 2005.
Ankersmit, Frank R. *Sublime Historical Experience*. Stanford, Calif.: Stanford University Press, 2005.
Arana, Sabino. "Nuestros moros." In *La patria de los vascos*, ed. Antonio Elorza, 155–56. San Sebastián: R. R. Ediciones, 1995.
Ascunce Arenas, Aránzazu. *Barcelona and Madrid: Social Networks of the Avant-Garde*. Lewisburg, Pa.: Bucknell University Press, 2012.
Asimetría y cohesión en el estado autonómico. Madrid: Instituto Nacional de Administración Pública, 1997.
Asín Palacios, Miguel. *Algazel: Dogmática, moral, ascética*. Zaragoza: Comas Hermanos, 1901.
———. *El Islam cristianizado*. Madrid: Plutarco, 1931.
———. *Huellas del Islam*. Madrid: Espasa-Calpe, 1941.
———. "Introducción." In *Disertaciones y opúsculos*, by Julián Ribera, xv–cxvi.
———. "¿Por qué lucharon a nuestro lado los musulmanes marroquíes?" In *Obras escogidas*, 2 vols., 2:125–52. Madrid: Editorial Maestre, 1948.
Aumente, José. *La cuestión nacional andaluza y los intereses de clase*. Madrid: Mañana, 1979.
Azorín [José Martínez Ruiz]. *La ruta de Don Quijote*. Madrid: Caro Raggio, 1919.
———. *Los pueblos: Ensayos de vida provinciana*. Seville: Renacimiento, 1916.
Balfour, Sebastian. *Deadly Embrace: Morocco and the Road to the Spanish Civil War*. Oxford: Oxford University Press, 2002.
Baltanás, Enrique. *La materia de Andalucía: El ciclo andaluz de las letras de los siglos XIX y XX*. Seville: Fundación José Manuel Lara, 2003.
Baroja, Pío. *Divagaciones sobre la cultura*. Madrid: Caro Raggio, 1920.
Barquero, José Daniel, and Luis Fernando Fernández Sánchez. *Los secretos del protocolo, las relaciones públicas y la publicidad*. Valladolid: Lex Nova, 2007.
Barrero González, Enrique. *El Ateneo de Sevilla y José María Izquierdo en el Andalucismo histórico*. Seville: Algaida, 2009.
Barrios, Manuel. *Gitanos, moriscos y cante flamenco*. Seville: JRC, 1989.
Barthes, Roland. *Mythologies*. Trans. Annette Lavers. New York: Hill and Wang, 1972.
Bécker González, Jerónimo. *Historia de las relaciones exteriores de España durante el siglo XIX*. 3 vols. Madrid: Jaime Ratés, 1924–27.
Bellón Cabazán, Juan Alfredo. "La Andalucía de Luis Cernuda: Apuntes y divagaciones sobre los mitos edénicos y demás paraísos naturales y artificiales." *Letras del Sur* 3–4 (1978): 32–36.
Benjamin, Roger. *Orientalist Aesthetics: Art, Colonialism, and French North Africa, 1880–1930*. Berkeley: University of California Press, 2003.
Benjamin, Walter. *The Origin of German Tragic Drama*. Trans. John Osborne. London: Verso, 1998.
Bennett, Tony. *The Birth of the Museum: History, Theory, Politics*. London: Routledge, 1995.
Beramendia, Justo G., and Ramón Máiz, eds. *Los nacionalismos en la España de la II República*. Madrid: Siglo Veintiuno, 1991.
Bernaldo de Quirós, Constancio. *Bandolerismo y delincuencia subversiva en la Baja Andalucía*. Seville: Renacimiento, 1992.

Beruete y Moret, Aureliano. *La pintura española en el siglo XIX: Elementos nacionales y extranjeros que han influido en ella*. Madrid: Blass, 1926.

Blasco Pascual, Francisco Javier. *La poética de Juan Ramón Jiménez: Desarrollo, contexto y sistema*. Salamanca: Universidad de Salamanca, 1981.

Blázquez, Antonio. "El periplo de Himilco (siglo VI antes de la Era Cristiana)." *Boletín de la Real Sociedad Geográfica* 51 (1909): 325–92.

Borges, Jorge Luis. *Selected Non-Fictions*. Ed. Eliot Weinberger. Trans. Ester Allen, Suzanne Jill Levine, and Eliot Weinberger. Vol. 1. London: Penguin, 1999.

Bourdieu, Pierre. *On Television*. Trans. Priscilla Parkhurst. New York: New, 1998.

Boyd, Carolyn. *Historia Patria: Politics, History, and National Identity in Spain, 1875–1975*. Princeton, N.J.: Princeton University Press, 1997.

Brah, Avtar, and Annie Coombes, eds. *Hybridity and Its Discontents*. London: Routledge, 2005.

Braojos Garrido, Alfonso. *Alfonso XIII y la Exposición Iberoamericana de Sevilla*. Seville: Universidad de Sevilla, 1992.

Britt Arredondo, Christopher. *Quixotism: The Imaginative Denial of Spain's Loss of Empire*. Albany: SUNY Press, 2005.

Buendía Abreu, Rogelio. "Vindicación de Andalucía." *Actas del VI Congreso sobre el Andalucismo Histórico*, 89–93. Seville: Fundación Blas Infante, 1993.

Bueno Fidel, María José. *Arquictectura y nacionalismo: Pabellones españoles en las exposiciones universales del siglo diecinueve*. Malaga: Universidad de Málaga/Colegio de Arquitectos, 1987.

Burgin, Richard, ed. *Jorge Luis Borges: Conversations*. Jackson: University of Mississippi Press, 1998.

Burgos, Antonio. *Andalucía, ¿tercer mundo?* Barcelona: Círculo de Lectores, 1972.

Burguera, Mónica, and Christopher Schmidt-Nowara. "Backwardness and Its Discontents." *Social History* 29, no. 3 (2004): 279–83.

Burke, Edmund. *A Philosophical Enquiry into the Origin of Our Ideas of the Beautiful and the Sublime*. Oxford: Oxford University Press, 1998.

Byron, George G. *Lord Byron: Selected Poems*. Ed. Susan J. Wolfson and Peter J. Manning. London: Penguin, 1996.

Cacho Viu, Vicente, ed. *Els modernistes i el nacionalisme cultural (1881–1906)*. Barcelona: Edicions de la Magrana/Diputació de Barcelona, 1984.

Cadalso, José. *Cartas marruecas: Noches lúgubres*. Ed. Joaquín Arce. Madrid: Cátedra, 1978.

Cagigas, Isidro de las. *Los mozárabes*. Madrid: CSIC, Instituto de Estudios Africanos, 1947.

———. *Los mudéjares*. 2 vols. Madrid: CSIC, Instituto de Estudios Africanos, 1948–49.

Calderwood, Eric. "'In Andalucía, There Are No Foreigners': *Andalucismo* from Transperipheral Critique to Colonial Apology." *Journal of Spanish Cultural Studies* 15, no. 4 (2015): 399–417.

———. "The Invention of al-Andalus: Discovering the Past and Creating the Present in Granada's Islamic Tourism Sites." *The Journal of North African Studies* 19, no. 1 (2014): 27–55.

Calvo Serraller, Francisco. *La imagen romántica en España: Arte y arquitectura del siglo XIX*. Madrid: Alianza, 1995.

Cano Ballesta, Juan. *La poesía española entre pureza y revolución (1920–1936)*. Mexico, DF: Siglo Veintiuno, 1996.
Cánovas del Castillo, Antonio. *Apuntes para la historia de Marruecos*. Madrid: Librería General de Victoriano Suárez, 1914.
Cardwell, Richard A. "Juan Ramón Jiménez y los intelectuales." *Hispanic Review* 53 (1985): 329–50.
———. "La obra poética de José Sánchez Rodríguez en su contexto literario." In *Alma andaluza (poesías completas)*, by José Sánchez Rodríguez, ed. Richard Cardwell, 15–89. Granada: Universidad de Granada, 1996.
———. "'The Universal Andalusian,' 'The Zealous Andalusian,' and the 'Andalusian Elegy.'" *Studies in Twentieth Century Literature* 7, no. 2 (1983): 201–24.
Caro Baroja, Julio. *De etnología andaluza*. Ed. Antonio Carreira. Malaga: Universidad de Málaga-Diputación Provincial de Málaga, 1993.
———. *Los moriscos del reino de Granada*. Madrid: Istmo, 1976.
Carr, Raymond. *Modern Spain, 1875–1980*. Oxford: Oxford University Press, 1980.
———, ed. *Spain: A History*. Oxford: Oxford University Press, 2000.
Carreras, Albert, and Xavier Tafunell, eds. *Estadísticas históricas de España, siglos XIX–XX*. Bilbao: Fundación BBVA, 2005.
Cassano, Franco. *Il pensiero meridiano*. Bari: Laterza, 1996.
Castells, Manuel, and Peter Hall, eds. *Andalucía: Innovación tecnológica y desarrollo económico*. 2 vols. Madrid: Espasa Calpe, 1992.
Castro, Américo. *España en su historia: Cristianos, moros y judíos*. Barcelona: Crítica, 1983.
———. *An Idea of History: Selected Essays of Américo Castro*. Columbus: Ohio State University Press, 1977.
Cate-Arries, Francie. "Poetics and Philosophy: José Ortega y Gasset and the Generation of 1927." *Hispania* 71, no. 3 (1988): 503–11.
Cazorla Sánchez, Antonio. *Fear and Progress: Ordinary Lives in Franco's Spain*. Oxford: Wiley Blackwell, 2010.
Çelik, Zeynep. *Displaying the Orient: Architecture of Islam at the Nineteenth-Century World's Fairs*. Berkeley: University of California Press, 1992.
Centro y periferia en la modernización de la pintura española (1880–1918). Madrid: Ministerio de Cultura, 1993.
Cernuda, Luis. *Poesía completa*. Ed. Derek Harris and Luis Maristany. Madrid: Siruela, 2002.
———. *Prosa completa*. Ed. Derek Harris and Luis Maristany. Barcelona: Barral, 1975.
Chabás, Juan. *Literatura española contemporánea, 1898–1950*. Ed. Javier Pérez Bazo. Madrid: Verbum, 2001.
Charnon-Deutsch, Lou. *Fictions of the Feminine in the Nineteenth-Century Spanish Press*. University Park: Pennsylvania State University Press, 2000.
———. *The Spanish Gypsy: The History of a European Obsession*. University Park: Pennsylvania State University Press, 2008.
Chatterjee, Partha. *Nationalist World and the Colonial World: A Derivative Discourse*. Minneapolis: University of Minnesota Press, 1986.
Christys, Anne. *Christians in Al-Andalus, 711–1000*. London: Routledge, 2013.

Churchill Semple, Ellen, and Friedrich Ratzel, *Influences of Geographic Environment on the Basis of Ratzel's System of Antropo-Geography*. New York: Henry Holt, 1911.

Cid Priego, Carlos, ed. *Las artes españolas en la crisis del 98*. Oviedo: Universidad de Oviedo, 1996.

Coleman, David. *Creating Christian Granada: Society and Religious Culture in an Old-World Frontier City, 1492–1600*. Ithaca, N.Y.: Cornell University Press, 2003.

Colmeiro, José F. "Exorcising Exoticism: *Carmen* and the Construction of Oriental Spain." *Comparative Literature* 54, no. 2 (2002): 127–44.

Comín, Alfonso C. *España del Sur*. Madrid: Tecnos, 1966.

Cornago Bernal, Óscar. "La puesta en escena de la autenticidad: *Andalucía, un siglo de fascinación*, de Basilio Martín Patino, y el 'materialismo histórico' en Walter Benjamin." *Arbor* 187 (2011): 223–36.

Cortines Torres, Jacobo. "Las patrias de Don Juan." In *Sevilla y la literatura*, ed. Rogelio Reyes Cano, Mercedes de los Reyes Peña, and Klaus Wagner, 215–30. Seville: Universidad de Sevilla, 2001.

Courtine, Jean-François, et al., eds. *Of the Sublime: Presence in Question*. Albany: SUNY Press, 1993.

Crespo, Ángel. *Juan Ramón Jiménez y la pintura*. Salamanca: Universidad de Salamanca, 1999.

Crumbaugh, Justin. *Destination Dictatorship: The Spectacle of Spain's Tourist Boom and the Reinvention of Difference*. Albany: SUNY Press, 2009.

Cuenca Toribio, José Manuel. *Andalucía: Una introducción histórica*. Cordoba: Monte de Piedad y Caja de Ahorros, 1979.

Dainotto, Roberto M. "Does Europe Have a South? An Essay on Borders." *The Global South* 5, no. 1 (2011): 37–50.

———. *Europe (In Theory)*. Durham, N.C.: Duke University Press, 2007.

Darío, Rubén. "La tristeza andaluza." In *Tierras solares*, 69–80. Madrid: Leonardo Williams, 1904.

Debord, Guy. *The Society of the Spectacle*. Trans. Donald Nicholson-Smith. New York: Zone Books, 1995.

Delgado, Luisa Elena. "Settled in Normal: Narratives of a Prozaic (Spanish) Nation." *Arizona Journal of Hispanic Cultural Studies* 7 (2003): 119–34.

Delgado Gómez-Escalonilla, Lorenzo. *Imperio de papel: Acción cultural y política exterior durante el primer franquismo*. Madrid: CSIC, 1992.

De los Santos, José María. *Sociología de la transición andaluza*. Malaga: Ágora, 1990.

De Nava Álvarez de Noroña, Gaspar, ed. and trans. *Poesías asiáticas puestas en verso castellano*. Paris: Imprenta de Julio Didot Mayor, 1883.

De Ros, Xon. *The Poetry of Antonio Machado: Changing the Landscape*. Oxford: Oxford University Press, 2015.

Derrida, Jacques. *Dissemination*. Trans. Barbara Johnson. Chicago: University of Chicago Press, 1981.

Díaz del Moral, Juan. *Historia de las agitaciones campesinas andaluzas*. Madrid: Alianza, 1973.

Djbilou, Abdellah, ed. *Tánger, puerta de África: Antología de textos literarios hispánicos, 1860–1960*. Madrid: Cantarabia, 1989.

Dodds, Jerrilynn D., ed. *Al-Andalus: The Art of Islamic Spain*. New York: Metropolitan Museum of Art, 1992.
Domínguez Ortiz, Antonio, and Bernard Vincent. *Historia de los moriscos: Vida y tragedia de una minoría*. Madrid: Alianza, 1980.
Eco, Umberto. *Travels in Hyperreality*. Trans. William Weaver. London: Harcourt Brace, 1986.
Egea Fernández-Montesinos, Alberto, ed. *García Lorca, Blas Infante y Antonio Gala: Un nacionalismo alternativo en la literatura andaluza*. Seville: Fundación Blas Infante, 2001.
———. *La casa de Blas Infante en Coria del Río*. Seville: Junta de Andalucía, 2007.
El legado andalusí: Una propuesta plástica. Granada: Fundación Caja de Granada, 1995.
En torno a Pemán. Cadiz: Excelentísima Diputación Provincial de Cádiz, 1974.
Escolar Sobrino, Hipólito. *La cultura durante la Guerra Civil*. Madrid: Alhambra, 1987.
Estatuto de Autonomía para Andalucía. Seville: Junta de Andalucía, 2007.
Estébanez Calderón, Serafín. *Escenas Andaluzas*. Ed. Alberto González Troyano. Madrid: Cátedra, 1985.
———. *Manual del oficial de Marruecos*. Madrid: Ignacio Boix, 1844.
Falla, Manuel de. *Escritos sobre música y músicos*. Ed. Federico Sopeña Ibañez. Madrid: Espasa-Calpe, 1988.
Fanjul, Serafín. *Al-Andalus contra España: La forja del mito*. Madrid: Siglo Veintiuno, 2000.
———. *La quimera de al-Andalus*. Madrid: Siglo Veintiuno, 2004.
Figueira, Dorothy M. *The Exotic: A Decadent Quest*. Albany: SUNY Press, 1994.
Flesler, Daniela. *The Return of the Moor: Spanish Responses to Contemporary Moroccan Immigration*. West Lafayette, Ind.: Purdue University Press, 2008.
Flores Morales, Ángel. *África a través del pensamiento español: De Isabel la Católica a Franco*. Madrid: CSIC, Instituto de Estudios Africanos, 1949.
Ford, Richard. *A Hand-Book for Travellers in Spain, and Readers at Home*. 2 vols. Cambridge: Cambridge University Press, 2011.
Foweraker, Joe. *Making Democracy in Spain: Grass-Roots Struggle in the South, 1955–1975*. Cambridge: Cambridge University Press, 1989.
Fox, Inman. *La invención de España*. Madrid: Cátedra, 1998.
Fuchs, Barbara. *Exotic Nation: Maurophilia and the Construction of Early Modern Spain*. Philadelphia: University of Pennsylvania Press, 2009.
Fusi, Juan Pablo, and Jordi Palafox. *España 1808–1996: El desafío de la modernidad*. Madrid: Espasa Calpe, 1997.
Gaos, Vicente, ed. *Antología del Grupo Poético del 27*. Madrid: Cátedra, 1975.
Garafola, Lynn. *Diaghilev's Ballets Russes*. Oxford: Oxford University Press, 1989.
García, Miguel Ángel. "El andalucismo nórdico de Luis Cernuda." *Bulletin Hispanique* 113, no. 2 (2011): 611–32.
———. *Melancolía vertebrada: La tristeza andaluza del modernismo a la vanguardia*. Barcelona: Anthropos, 2012.
García Gómez, Emilio. *Tres discursos y dos prólogos recientes*. Madrid: Orbis, 1979.

García Lorca, Federico. *In Search of Duende*. Ed. and trans. Christopher Maurer. New York: New Directions, 1998.

———. *Obras completas*. 6 vols. Barcelona: RBA-Instituto Cervantes, 2005–6.

García Montero, Luis. "Andalucía como imagen literaria." In *Literaturas regionales en España: Historia y crítica*, ed. José-Carlos Mainer, 101–15. Zaragoza: Institución Fernando el Católico, 1994.

———. "Luis Cernuda y Andalucía." In *Nostalgia de una patria imposible: Estudios sobre la obra de Luis Cernuda*, ed. Juan Matas Caballero et al., 47–61. Madrid: Akal, 2005.

García Queipo de Llano, Genoveva. *Los intelectuales y la dictadura de Primo de Rivera*. Madrid: Alianza, 1988.

Gautier, Théophile. *Travels in Spain*. Trans. F.-C. de Sumichrast. Cambridge: Jenson Society, 1906.

Gener, Pompeyo. *Heregías: Estudios de crítica inductiva sobre asuntos españoles*. Barcelona: Luis Tasso Serra, 1887.

Gibson, Ian. *Federico García Lorca: A Life*. New York: Random House, 1989.

Gies, David T. *The Cambridge Companion to Modern Spanish Culture*. Cambridge: Cambridge University Press, 1999.

Gil-Albert, Juan. "A propósito del Arte, de Ortega y Gasset y otras cuestiones patrias." In *Los días están contados*, 55–86. Barcelona: Tusquets, 1974.

Gil Grimau, Rodolfo. *Aproximación a una bibliografía española sobre el norte de África*. Madrid: Ministerio de Asuntos Exteriores, 1988.

———. "Corrientes ideológicas internas en el africanismo español." In *Actas del Congreso Internacional el Estrecho de Gibraltar*, 3:277–85. Madrid: UNED-Ayuntamiento de Ceuta, 1988.

Gilman, Sander L. *Difference and Pathology: Stereotypes of Sexuality, Race, and Madness*. Ithaca, N.Y.: Cornell University Press, 1985.

Gil Torres, Rodolfo. *Marruecos andaluz*. Madrid: Vicesecretaria de Educación Popular, 1943.

———. *Mediodía: Introducción a la historia andaluza*. Madrid: Compañía Ibero-Americana de Publicaciones, 1929.

———. *Ni Oriente ni Occidente: El universo visto desde el Albayzín*. Ed. José Antonio González Alcantud. Granada: Universidad de Granada, 1996.

Giménez Caballero, Ernesto. *Arte y Estado*. Ed. Enrique Selva Roca de Togores. Madrid: Biblioteca Nueva, 2009.

———. *Memorias de un dictador*. Barcelona: Planeta, 1979.

Gomá y Tomás, Isidro. *Pastorales de la Guerra de España*. Madrid: Rialp, 1955.

Gómez L. Quiñones, Antonio, and José M. del Pino, eds. *La retórica del sur: Representaciones y discursos sobre Andalucía en el período democrático*. Seville: Alfar, 2015.

Gómez-Moreno, Manuel. "Arquitectura Tartesia: La necrópoli de Antequera." *Boletín de la Real Academia de la Historia* 47 (1905): 81–132.

———. *Misceláneas: Historia, arte, arqueología*. Madrid: CSIC, 1949.

González, Fernando. "Basilio Martin Patino: Pensar la historia." *Film-Historia* 7, no. 2 (1997): 141–60

González Alcantud, José Antonio, ed. *El orientalismo desde el sur*. Barcelona: Anthropos, 2006.

González de Molina, Manuel, ed. *La cuestión agraria en la historia de Andalucía: Nuevas perspectivas*. Seville: Centro de Estudios Andaluces, 2014.
González González, Irene. "La 'hermandad hispano-árabe' en la política cultural del franquismo (1936–1956)." *Anales de Historia Contemporánea* 27 (2007): 183–97.
———. *Spanish Education in Morocco 1912–1956: Cultural Interactions in a Colonial Context*. Eastbourne, Eng.: Sussex Academic, 2015.
González Troyano, Alberto. *La desventura de Carmen: Una divagación sobre Andalucía*. Madrid: Espasa Calpe, 1990.
Goode, Joshua. *Impurity of Blood: Defining Race in Spain, 1870–1930*. Baton Rouge: Louisiana State University Press, 2009.
Goytisolo, Juan. *The Countryside of Níjar and La Chanca*. Trans. Luigi Luccarelli. Plainfield, Ind.: Alembic, 1987.
———. *España y sus ejidos*. Madrid: Hijos de Muley Rubio, 2003.
———. *Forbidden Territory and Realms of Strife*. Trans. Peter Bush. London: Verso, 2003.
———. *Saracen Chronicles: A Selection of Literary Essays*. Trans. Helen Lane. London: Quartet Books, 1992.
———. "Tierras del Sur." In *Obras completes: Relatos y ensayos,* vol. 2: 1036–56. Madrid: Aguilar, 1978.
Gracia, Jordi. *José Ortega y Gasset*. Madrid: Taurus, 2014.
Gramsci, Antonio. *Selections from Cultural Writings*. Ed. David Forgacs and Geoffrey Nowell-Smith. Trans. William Boelhower. Cambridge, Mass.: Harvard University Press, 1985.
———. *Selections from the Prison Notebooks*, ed. and trans. Quentin Hoare and Geoffrey Nowell Smith. London: Lawrence and Wishart, 1971.
Gray, Rockwell. *The Imperative of Modernity: An Intellectual Biography of José Ortega y Gasset*. Berkeley: University of California Press, 1989.
Gubern, Román. *El cine sonoro en la II República, 1929–1936*. Barcelona: Lumen, 1977.
Gubern, Román, et al., eds. *Historia del cine español*. Madrid: Cátedra, 2009.
Guerrero Ruiz, Juan. *Juan Ramón Jiménez de viva voz*. Madrid: Ínsula, 1961.
Guía oficial Expo '92. Seville: Sociedad Estatal para la Exposición Universal, 1992.
Guibernau, Monserrat. *The Identity of Nations*. Cambridge: Polity, 2007.
Gutiérrez Camacho, Manuel Enrique. *Vida y obra de Isidro de las Cagigas*. Seville: Fundación Blas Infante, 2006.
Handley, Sharon. "Federico García Lorca and the 98 Generation: The *Andalucismo* Debate." *Anales de Literatura Española Contemporánea* 21, no. 1–2 (1996): 41–58.
Hardt, Michael, and Antonio Negri. *Empire*. Cambridge, Mass.: Harvard University Press, 2000.
Hegel, G. W. F. *Lectures on the Philosophy of World History: Introduction: Reason in History*. Trans. H. B. Nisbet. Cambridge: Cambridge University Press, 1975.
———. *The Philosophy of History*. Trans. J. Sibree. New York: Dover, 1956.
Hernández Ramírez, Javier. *La imagen de Andalucía en el turismo*. Seville: Centro de Estudios Andaluces, 2008.

Hess, Carol. *Manuel de Falla and Modernism in Spain, 1898–1936*. Chicago: University of Chicago Press, 2001.
Higley, John, and Richard Gunter, eds. *Elites and Democratic Consolidation in Latin America and Southern Europe*. Cambridge: Cambridge University Press, 1992.
Hugo, Victor. *Orientales et ballades*. Brussels: Louis Hauman, 1832.
Huntington, Samuel P. *The Third Wave: Democratization in the Late Twentieth Century*. Norman: University of Oklahoma Press, 1992.
Hurtado Sánchez, José, Juan Ortiz Villalba, and Salvador Cruz Artacho. *Bética y el Regionalismo Andaluz: A propósito del centenario*. Seville: Centro de Estudios Andaluces, 2013.
Infante, Blas. *Andalucía: Teoría y fundamento político*. Ed. Manuel Pimentel. Cordoba: Almuzara, 2008.
———. *Antología de textos*. Ed. Manuel Ruiz Lagos. Seville: Fundación Blas Infante, 1983.
———. *Ideal Andaluz*. Seville: Imprenta de Joaquín L. Arévalo, 1915.
———. *La verdad sobre el complot de Tablada y el Estado libre de Andalucía*. Granada: Aljibe, 1979.
———. *Orígenes de lo flamenco y secreto del cante jondo*. Ed. Manuel Barrios. Seville: Junta de Andalucía, 1980.
Iniesta Collaut-Valera, Enrique. *Al-Andalus en Blas Infante*. Madrid: Editorial Darek-Nyumba, 1998.
———. *Blas Infante: Toda su verdad, Vol. 2: 1919–1933*. Granada: Editorial Atrio, 2003.
Irving, Washington. *The Alhambra*. New York: G. P. Putnam's Sons, 1861.
Jameson, Frederic. *Postmodernism; or, the Cultural Logic of Late Capitalism*. Durham, N.C.: Duke University Press, 1991.
Javierre, José María, and Manuel Ángel Vázquez Medel, eds. *Gran Enciclopedia de Andalucía*. 10 vols. Seville: Promociones Culturales Andaluzas, 1979.
Jonas, Andrew E. G. "Pro Scale: Further Reflections on the 'Scale Debate' in Human Geography." *Transactions of the Institute of British Geographers* 31, no. 3 (2006): 399–406.
Jiménez, Juan Ramon. *Antología poética*. Ed. Francisco Javier Blasco. Madrid: Cátedra, 1987.
———. *Cuadernos de Juan Ramón Jiménez*. Ed. Francisco Garfias. Madrid: Taurus, 1960.
———. *Diary of a Newlywed Poet*. Ed. Michael P. Predmore. Trans. Hugh A. Harter. Selingsgrove, Pa.: Susquehanna University Press, 2004.
———. *Elejías andaluzas*. Ed. Arturo del Villar. Barcelona: Bruguera, 1980.
———. *Epistolario*. 2 vols. Ed. Alfonso Alegre Heitzmann. Madrid: Residencia de Estudiantes, 2006–12.
———. *La corriente infinita: Crítica y evocación*. Ed. Francisco Garfias. Madrid: Aguilar, 1961.
———. *Prosas críticas*. Ed. Pilar Gómez Bedate. Madrid: Taurus, 1981.
Johnson, R. "Juan Ramón Jiménez, Rabindranath Tagore, and 'la poesía desnuda.'" *Modern Language Review* 60, no. 4 (1965): 534–46.
Jurkevich, Gayana. *In Pursuit of the Natural Sign: Azorín and the Poetics of Ekphrasis*. Lewisburg, Pa.: Bucknell University Press, 1999.

Kant, Immanuel. *Anthropology from a Pragmatic Point of View*. Ed. and trans. Robert B. Louden. Cambridge: Cambridge University Press, 2006.

———. *Observations on the Feeling of the Beautiful and the Sublime*. Trans. John T. Goldthwait. Berkeley: University of California Press, 1960.

Kaplan, E. Ann, ed. *Regarding Television: Critical Approaches*. Los Angeles: American Film Institute, 1983.

Kaplan, Temma. *Anarchists of Andalusia, 1868–1903*. Princeton, N.J.: Princeton University Press, 1977.

Labanyi, Jo, ed. *Constructing Identity in Contemporary Spain*. Oxford: Oxford University Press, 2002.

La Casa de Blas Infante: El legado. Seville: Centro de Estudios Andaluces, 2010.

Lacomba, José Antonio, ed. *Historia de Andalucía*. 8 vols. Barcelona: Planeta, 1980–81.

———. *Teoría y praxis del Andalucismo*. Malaga: Ágora, 1988.

Lafuente Ferrari, Enrique. "La pintura española y la Generación del 98." *Arbor* 36 (1948): 449–58.

Laín Entralgo, Pedro. *Descargo de conciencia (1930–1960)*. Barcelona: Barral, 1976.

Lázaro Reboll, Antonio, and Andrew Willis, eds. *Spanish Popular Cinema*. Manchester, Eng.: Manchester University Press, 2004.

Lembo, Ron. *Thinking Through Television*. Cambridge: Cambridge University Press, 2000.

Linhard, Tabea Alexa. *Jewish Spain: A Mediterranean Memory*. Stanford, Calif.: Stanford University Press, 2014.

Litvak, Lily. *El tiempo de los trenes: El paisaje español y la literatura del realismo (1849–1918)*. Barcelona: Serbal, 1991.

López, Ignacio Javier. *Caballero de novela: Ensayo sobre el donjuanismo en la novela española moderna (1830–1930)*. Barcelona: Puvill, 1986.

López-Baralt, Luce. *Islam in Spanish Literature: From the Middle Ages to the Present*. Trans. Andrew Hurley. Leiden: Brill, 1992.

López Enamorado, María Dolores. "La Mirada del otro: La vision del africanismo español (el Gil Benumeya de los años veinte)." In *Relaciones interétnicas y multiculturalidad en el Mediterráneo Occidental*, ed. Elías Zamora Acosta and Pedro Maya Álvarez, 261–78. Melilla: V Centenario de Melilla, 1988.

López García, Bernabé. *Orientalismo e ideología colonial en el arabismo español (1840–1917)*. Granada: Universidad de Granada, 2011.

López-Morillas, Juan. *The Krausist Movement and Ideological Change in Spain, 1854–1874*. Trans. Frances M. López-Morillas. Cambridge: Cambridge University Press, 1981.

López-Ruiz, Carolina. "Tarshish and Tartessos Revisited: Textual Problems and Historical Implications." In *Colonial Encounters in Ancient Iberia: Phoenician, Greek, and Indigenous Relations*, ed. Michael Dietler and Carolina López-Ruiz, 255–80. Chicago: University of Chicago Press, 2009.

López Sánchez, José María. *Heterodoxos españoles: El Centro de Estudios Históricos, 1910–1936*. Madrid: Marcial Pons-CSIC, 2006.

Los españoles pintados por sí mismos. Madrid: Gaspar y Roig Editores, 1851.

Lucía Megías, José Manuel, ed. *También los niños leen el Quijote*. Alcalá de Henares: Centro de Estudios Cervantinos, 2007.

Lyotard, Jean-François. *The Postmodern Condition: A Report on Knowledge*. Minneapolis: University of Minnesota Press, 1982.

Machado, Antonio. *Poesías completas*. Ed. Manuel Alvar. Madrid: Alianza, 2004.

Madariaga, Rosa María de. *Los moros que trajo Franco: La intervención de las tropas coloniales en la guerra civil española*. Barcelona: Martínez Roca, 2012.

Maddox, Richard. *The Best of All Possible Islands: Seville's Universal Exposition, the New Spain, and the New Europe*. Albany: SUNY Press, 2004.

Mainer, José-Carlos. "La invención estética de las periferias." In *Centro y periferia en la modernización de la pintura española (1880–1918)*, 26–33. Madrid: Ministerio de Cultura, 1993.

Manovich, Lev. *The Language of New Media*. Cambridge, Mass.: MIT Press, 2001.

Maragall, Joan. "La independència de Catalunya." In *Els modernistes i el nacionalisme cultural (1881–1906)*, ed. Vicente Cacho Viu, 169–71. Barcelona: Edicions de la Magrana/Diputació de Barcelona, 1984.

Maravall, José María. *La política de la transición*. Madrid: Taurus, 1981.

Marín, Manuela ed. *Al-Andalus-España: Historiografías en contraste, siglos XVII–XXI*. Madrid: Casa de Velázquez, 2009.

Martín Gaite, Carmen. *Usos amorosos de la postguerra española*. Barcelona: Anagrama, 2007.

Martín Infante, Antonio. "Génesis de un tópico del modernismo español: 'La tristeza andaluza.'" *Nueva Revista de Filología Hispánica* 55, no. 2 (2007): 459–70.

Martin-Márquez, Susan. *Disorientations: Spanish Colonialism in Africa and the Performance of Identity*. New Haven, Conn.: Yale University Press, 2008.

Marx, Karl. *The Communist Manifesto*. Ed. Frederic L. Bender. New York: Norton, 1988.

Mateo Dieste, Josep Lluís. *La "hermandad" hispano-marroquí: Política y religión bajo el protectorado español en Marruecos, 1912-1956*. Barcelona: Bellaterra, 2003.

Maurer, Christopher. *Federico García Lorca y su Arquitectura del Cante Jondo*. Granada: Comares, 2000.

Maxwell, Richard. *The Spectacle of Democracy: Spanish Television, Nationalism, and Political Transition*. Minneapolis: University of Minnesota Press, 1995.

McLuhan, Marshall. *Understanding Media: The Extensions of Man*. New York: McGraw-Hill, 1964.

Meaker, Gerald H. *The Revolutionary Left in Spain, 1914–1923*. Stanford, Calif.: Stanford University Press, 1974.

Medina, Tico. *Lola, en carne viva: Memorias de Lola Flores*. Madrid: Ediciones Temas de Hoy, 1990.

Méndez Rodríguez, Luis. *La imagen de Andalucía en el arte del siglo XIX*. Seville: Centro de Estudios Andaluces, 2008.

Menéndez Pelayo, Marcelino. *Historia de los heterodoxos españoles*. 3 vols. Madrid: F. Maroto e Hijos, 1881.

———. "Prólogo." In *Algazel: Dogmática, moral, ascética*, by Miguel Asín Palacios, vii–xxxix. Zaragoza: Comas Hermanos, 1901.

Menéndez Pidal, Ramón. *España, eslabón entre la Cristiandad y el Islam*. Madrid: Espasa-Calpe, 1956.

———. *La España del Cid*. 2 vols. Madrid: Editorial Plutarco, 1929.
———. *The Spaniards in Their History*. Trans. Walter Starkie. London: Hollis and Carter, 1950.
Menocal, María Rosa. *The Arabic Role in Medieval Literary History: A Forgotten Heritage*. Philadelphia: University of Pennsylvania Press, 1987.
Mérimée, Prosper. *Carmen and Other Stories*. Trans. Nicholas Jotcham. Oxford: Oxford University Press, 1989.
Mintz, Jerome. *The Anarchists of Casas Viejas*. Bloomington: Indiana University Press, 1982.
Moe, Nelson. *The View from Vesuvius: Italian Culture and the Southern Question*. Berkeley: University of California Press, 2002.
Monroe, James. *Islam and the Arabs in Spanish Scholarship (Sixteenth Century to the Present)*. Leiden: Brill, 1970.
Montero, Alfred P. *Shifting States in Global Markets: Subnational Industrial Policy in Contemporary Brazil and Spain*. University Park: Pennsylvania State University Press, 2002.
Morales Lezcano, Víctor. *España y el Norte de África: El Protectorado de Marruecos (1912–56)*. Madrid: UNED, 1986.
Moreno, Isidoro, ed. *La identidad cultural de Andalucía: Aproximaciones, mixtificaciones, negacionismo y evidencias*. Seville: Centro de Estudios Andaluces, 2008.
Moreno Alonso, Manuel. *Historia general de Andalucía*. Seville: Argantonio, 1981.
Moreno Hidalgo, César, José Alvárez de la Cruz, and María del Rosario Ruiz Franco, eds. *Historia contemporánea de Andalucía*. Madrid: CSIC, 1995.
Morodo, Raúl. *Los orígenes ideológicos del franquismo: Acción Española*. Madrid: Alianza, 1985.
Muñoz Molina, Antonio. *La huerta del Edén: Escritos y diatribas sobre Andalucía*. Madrid: Ollero y Ramos, 1996.
Narbona, Antonio, Rafael Cano, and Ramón Morillo. *El español hablado en Andalucía*. Seville: Fundación José Manuel Lara, 2003.
Navarro Tomás, Tomás. *El acento castellano*. Madrid: Academia Española, 1935.
Newton, Michael T. *Institutions of Modern Spain: A Political and Economic Guide*. Cambridge: Cambridge University Press, 1997.
Noel, Eugenio. *Diario íntimo: La novela de la vida de un hombre*. 2 vols. Madrid: Taurus, 1962–68.
———. *Señoritos, chulos, fenómenos, gitanos y flamencos*. Madrid: Renacimiento, 1916.
Olóriz y Aguilera, Federico. *Distrubución geográfica del índice cefálico en España deducida del examen de 8.368 varones adultos*. Madrid: Imprenta del Memorial de Ingenieros, 1894.
Orringer, Nelson. *Lorca in Tune with Falla: Literary and Musical Interludes*. Toronto: University of Toronto Press, 2014.
Ortega y Gasset, José. *Obras completas*. 10 vols. Madrid: Taurus/Fundación Ortega y Gasset, 2004–10.
Pack, Sasha D. *Tourism and Dictatorship: Europe's Peaceful Invasion of Franco's Spain*. New York: Palgrave Macmillan, 2006.
Palau de Nemes, Graciela. *Vida y obra de Juan Ramón Jiménez*. Madrid: Gredos, 1974.

Payne, Stanley G. *Fascism in Spain, 1923–1977*. Madison: University of Wisconsin Press, 1999.

———. *The Spanish Civil War, the Soviet Union, and Communism*. New Haven, Conn.: Yale University Press, 2008.

Pedraz Marcos, Azucena. *Quimeras de África: La Sociedad Española de Africanistas y Colonistas: El colonialismo español de finales del siglo XIX*. Madrid: Polifemo, 2000.

Pemán, José María. *Andalucía*. Barcelona: Destino, 1958.

———. *Meditación Española*. Madrid: Afrodisio Aguado, 1963.

———. *Obras completas*. 7 vols. Madrid: Escelicer, 1947–65.

Pena López, Carmen. *El paisaje español del siglo XIX: Del naturalismo al impresionismo*. Madrid: Universidad Complutense, 1981.

Pérez de Ayala, Ramón. *Las máscaras*. 2 vols. Madrid: Saturnino Calleja, 1919.

Pérez de Mendiola, Marina, ed. *Bridging the Atlantic: Toward a Reassessment of Iberian and Latin American Cultural Ties*. Albany: SUNY Press, 1996.

Pérez-Embid, Florentino. "Pequeña teoría de Andalucía." In *Paisajes de la tierra y el alma*, 15–25. Madrid: Rialp, 1963.

Pérez Luño, Antonio-Enrique. "Hegel y Ortega: Meditación sobre los presupuestos historiográficos de la filosofía del derecho." In *Meditaciones sobre Ortega y Gasset*, ed. José Luis Abellán et al., 523–67. Madrid: Editorial Tebar, 2005.

Perojo-Arronte, María Eugenia. "Byron and Unamuno's *Don Juan*." In *Aspects of Byron's Don Juan*, ed. Peter Cochran, 317–25. Newcastle upon Tyne, Eng.: Cambridge Scholars, 2013.

Perriam, Chris, and Ann Davies, eds. *Carmen: From Silent Film to MTV*. Amsterdam: Rodopi, 2005.

Pike, Frederick B. *Hispanismo, 1898–1936: Spanish Conservatives and Liberals and Their Relations with Spanish America*. London: University of Notre Dame Press, 1971.

Pineda Novo, Daniel. *Las Folklóricas*. Seville: Editorial Castillejo, 1990.

Plato. *Timaeus*. Trans. Donald J. Zeyl. Indianapolis, Ind.: Hackett, 2000.

Prat de la Riba, Enric, and Pere Muntanyola. *Compendi de la Doctrina Catalanista*. Sabadell: Imprenta de lo Catalanista, 1894.

Price, Uvedale. *An Essay on the Picturesque, as Compared with the Sublime and the Beautiful*. London: J. Robson, 1794.

Quinet, Edgar. *Mes vacances en Espagne*. Paris: Au Comptoir des Imprimeurs-Unis, 1846.

Quiroga, Alejandro. *Making Spaniards: Primo de Rivera and the Nationalization of the Masses, 1923–30*. New York: Palgrave Macmillan, 2007.

Ramon Resina, Joan. *Iberian Modalities: A Relational Approach to the Study of Culture in the Iberian Peninsula*. Liverpool: Liverpool University Press, 2013.

Reina Palazón, Antonio. *La pintura costumbrista en Sevilla, 1830–1870*. Seville: Universidad de Sevilla, 1979.

Reuben Holo, Selma. *Beyond the Prado: Museums and Identity in Democratic Spain*. Washington: Smithsonian Institution Press, 1999.

Ribera y Tarragó, Julián. *Disertaciones y opúsculos*. 2 vols. Madrid: Imprenta de Estanislao Maestre, 1928.

———. *Music in Ancient Arabia and Spain*. New York: Da Capo, 1970.

Rivière Gómez, Aurora. *Orientalismo y nacionalismo español: Estudios árabes y hebreos en la Universidad de Madrid (1843–1868)*. Madrid: Editorial Dykinson, 2000.

Rogers, Gayle. "Jiménez, Modernism/o, and the Languages of Comparative Modernist Studies." *Comparative Literature* 66, no. 1 (2014): 127–47.

Rogozen-Soltar, Mikaela. "Al-Andalus in Andalusia: Negotiating Moorish History and Regional Identity in Southern Spain." *Anthropological Quarterly* 80, no. 3 (2007): 863–86.

Romero Portillo, José, ed. *Triunfo: Una revista abierta al sur*. Seville: Centro de Estudios Andaluces, 2012.

Rosendorf, Neal M. *Franco Sells Spain to America: Hollywood, Tourism, and Public Relations as Postwar Spanish Soft Power*. New York: Palgrave Macmillan, 2014.

Rubert de Ventós, Xavier. *De la modernidad: Ensayo de filosofía crítica*. Barcelona: Península, 1980.

Ruiz Muñoz, María Jesús, and Inmaculada Sánchez Alarcón. *La imagen de la mujer andaluza en el cine español*. Seville: Centro de Estudios Andaluces, 2008.

Said, Edward W. *Orientalism*. New York: Vintage, 1979.

———. "Prólogo a la nueva edición española." In *Orientalismo*, trans. María Luisa Fuentes, 9–10. Barcelona: Debolsillo, 2003.

Said Armesto, Víctor. *La leyenda de Don Juan: Orígenes poéticos de la El burlador de Sevilla y El convidado de piedra*. Madrid: Sucesores de Hernando, 1908.

Salaverría, José María. *Sevilla y el andalucismo*. Barcelona: Gustavo Gili, 1929.

Salazar, Adolfo. *Música y músicos de hoy*. Madrid: Mundo Latino, 1929.

Salinas, Pedro. "Antonio Machado." In *Obras completas*, ed. Enric Bou and Andrés Soria Olmedo, vol. 2: 155–57. Madrid: Cátedra, 2007.

Samuel, Raphael. *People's History and Socialist Theory*. London: Routledge and Kegan Paul, 1981.

Sánchez Albornoz, Claudio. *De la Andalucía Islámica a la de hoy*. Madrid: Rialp, 1983.

———. *España, un enigma histórico*. Buenos Aires: Editorial Sudamericana, 1953.

Sánchez Rodríguez, José. *Alma andaluza*. Madrid: Fernando Fé, 1903.

Sánchez Ron, José Manuel, ed. *Ciencia y sociedad en España: De la Ilustración a la Guerra Civil*. Madrid: El Arquero/CSIC, 1988.

Sánchez Ruano, Francisco. *Islam y guerra civil española: Moros con Franco y con la República*. Madrid: La Esfera de los Libros, 2004.

Schneider, Jane, ed. *Italy's "Southern Question": Orientalism in One Country*. Oxford: Berg, 1998.

Schulten, Adolf. *Tartessos: Contribución a la historia más antigua de Occidente*. Trans. Manuel García Morente. Seville: Renacimiento, 2006.

Secondat, Charles de, Baron de Montesquieu. *The Spirit of the Laws*. Ed. and trans. Anne M. Cohler, Basia Carolyn Miller, and Harold Samuel Stone. Cambridge: Cambridge University Press, 1989.

Serrano, Carlos. *El nacimiento de Carmen: Símbolos, mitos y nación*. Madrid: Taurus, 1999.

Sevilla Guzmán, Eduardo. *Aproximación sociológica al andalucismo histórico*. Cordoba: Ayuntamiento de Córdoba, 1990.

Shannon, Jonathan Holt. *Performing al-Andalus: Music and Nostalgia across the Mediterranean*. Bloomington: Indiana University Press, 2015.

Sherlock, Martin. *Letters from an English Traveler*. London: J. Nichols, 1780.

Silver, Philip W. "La estética de Ortega y la generación de 1927." *Nueva Revista de Filología Hispánica* 20 (1971): 361–80.

———. *Ruin and Restitution: Reinterpreting Romanticism in Spain*. Nashville, Tenn.: Vanderbilt University Press, 1997.

Simonet, Francisco Javier. *El Siglo de Oro en la literatura arábigo-española: Discurso leído ante el claustro de la Universidad Central*. Granada: Imprenta de D. José María Zamora, 1867.

———. *Historia de los mozárabes de España*. 2 vols. Madrid: Real Academia de la Historia, 1897.

Sotomayor, Carmen. *Una lectura orientalista de Juan Goytisolo*. Madrid: Fundamentos, 1990.

Steingress, Gerhard. *Sobre flamenco y flamencología: Escritos escogidos 1988–1998*. Seville: Signatura, 1998.

Stendhal [Marie-Henri Beyle]. *Napoléon: Vie de Napoléon*. Geneva: Cercle du Bibliophile, 1970.

Suárez Fernández, Luis. *Los Reyes Católicos: El tiempo de la Guerra de Granada*. Madrid: Rialp, 1989.

Sullivan, Edward J. "Mariano Fortuny y Marsal and Orientalism in Nineteenth-Century Spain." *Arts Magazine* 55, no. 8 (1981): 96–101.

Taibo I, Paco Ignacio. *Un cine para un imperio: Historia de las películas franquistas*. Mexico City: Conaculta, 2000.

Tofiño-Quesada, Ignacio. "Spanish Orientalism: Uses of the Past in Spain's Colonization in Africa." *Comparative Studies of South Asia, Africa and the Middle East* 23, no. 1–2 (2003): 141–48.

Topinard, Paul. *Anthropology*. London: Chapman and Hall, 1894.

Torrecilla, Jesús. *España Exótica: La formación de la imagen española moderna*. Boulder, Colo.: Society of Spanish and Spanish-American Studies, 2004.

———. *Guerras literarias del XVIII español*. Salamanca: Universidad de Salamanca, 2008.

Torres Ortiz, Mariano. *Tartessos*. Madrid: Real Academia de la Historia, 2002.

Tusell, Javier. *España, una angustia nacional*. Madrid: Espasa, 1999.

Tusell, Javier, and Gonzalo Álvarez Chillida. *Pemán: Un trayecto intelectual desde la extrema derecha hasta la democracia*. Madrid: Planeta, 1998.

Unamuno, Miguel de. *Epistolario americano (1890–1936)*. Ed. Laureano Robles. Salamanca: Universidad de Salamanca, 1996.

———. *Obras completas*. Ed. Manuel García Blanco. 9 vols. Madrid: Escelicer, 1966–71.

Una poderosa fuerza secreta: La Institución Libre de Enseñanza. San Sebastián: Editorial Española, 1940.

Utrera Macias, Rafael, ed. *Andalucia: Un siglo de fascinación: Homenaje a Basilio Martín Patino*. Sanlúcar de Barrameda: Pedro Romero-Eihceroa, 2006.

Vauthier, Bénédicte. "Ironía, censura y retórica en el diario éxtimo del exilio." In *Miguel de Unamuno: Estudios sobre su obra*, ed. Ana Chaguaceda Toledano, vol. 2: 113–27. Salamanca: Universidad de Salamanca, 2005.

Vázquez Montalbán, Manuel, ed. *Cancionero general del franquismo, 1939–1975*. Barcelona: Crítica, 2000.

———. *Crónica sentimental de España*. Barcelona: Lumen, 1971.

Viguera Molins, María Jesús. "Al-Andalus y su estudio." In *De civilización arabo-islámica*, ed. Francisco Vidal Castro, 17–36. Jaen: Universidad de Jaén, 1995.

Villaespesa, Francisco. "Carta-Prólogo." In *Alma andaluza*, by José Sánchez Rodríguez, 5–9. Madrid: Fernando Fé, 1903.

Washabaugh, William. *Flamenco and National Identity in Spain*. Burlington, Vt.: Ashgate, 2012.

White, Hayden. *Metahistory: The Historical Imagination in Nineteenth-Century Europe*. Baltimore, Md.: Johns Hopkins University Press, 1975.

Wilde, Oscar. *The Major Works*. Ed. Isobel Murray. Oxford: Oxford University Press, 1989.

Woods Peiró, Eva. *White Gypsies: Race and Stardom in Spanish Musicals*. Minneapolis: University of Minnesota Press, 2012.

World Bank. *The Economic Development of Spain*. Baltimore, Md.: Johns Hopkins University Press, 1963.

Žižek, Slavoj. *The Sublime Object of Ideology*. London: Verso, 1989.

FILMOGRAPHY

Andalucía: Un siglo de fascinación (dir. Basilio Martín Patino, 1996)
¡Bienvenido Mister Marshall! (dir. Luis García Berlanga, 1951)
Carmen la de Triana (dir. Florián Rey, 1938)
Cristobal Colón de oficio descubridor (dir. Mariano Ozores, 1981)
Currito de la cruz (dir. Alejandro Pérez Lugín, 1925)
El barbero de Sevilla (dir. Benito Perojo, 1938)
El sueño de Andalucía (dir. Luis Lucia, 1951)
Juana la Loca, de vez en cuando (dir. José Ramón Larraz, 1983)
La blanca paloma (dir. Claudio de la Torre, 1942)
La canción de Aixa (dir. Florián Rey, 1939)
La Faraona (dir. René Cardona, 1956)
La gitana y el charro (dir. Gilberto Martínez Solares, 1964)
La verbena de la Paloma (dir. José Buchs, 1921)
Lola la piconera (dir. Luis Lucia, 1951)
Macarena (dir. Antonio Guzmán Merino, 1944)
Mariquilla terremoto (dir. Benito Perojo, 1938)
Morena Clara (dir. Florián Rey, 1936)
Morena Clara (dir. Luis Lucia, 1954)
¡Pasaremos! (dir. Fernando Gutiérrez Mantilla, 1936)
Suspiros de España (dir. Benito Perojo, 1939)
Un beso en el puerto (dir. Ramón Torrado, 1966)

INDEX